BERLIOZ REMEMBERED

Michael Rose was born in 1926. After three years of eminently forgettable military service, he read Modern Languages at Oxford and subsequently studied composition for two years with Bernard Stevens. In 1954 he produced, with Hanns Hammelmann, the first of a series of radio programmes – *Birth of an Opera* – which continued intermittently until 1976. From 1961 to 1981 he lived in Italy, where he arranged scripts and music for television documentaries and provided articles and advice for *The New Grove*. He wrote the music entries for the new *Oxford Companion to English Literature,* and with John Amis compiled an anthology – *Words and Music* – published by Faber in 1989. More recently he was general editor of the Everyman–EMI Music Companions, and provided a commentary for Erich Auerbach's magnificent photographs in *Images of Music.*

BERLIOZ REMEMBERED

MICHAEL ROSE

faber and faber

First published in 2001
by Faber and Faber Limited
3 Queen Square London WC1N 3AU
Published in the United States by Faber and Faber Inc.
an affiliate of Farrar, Straus and Giroux, New York

Photoset by Agnesi Text, Hadleigh, Suffolk
Printed in England by Clays Ltd, St Ives plc

A CIP record for this book is available from the British Library

ISBN 0–571–17863–4

2 4 6 8 10 9 7 5 3 1

CONTENTS

LIST OF ILLUSTRATIONS

TO BETH

INTRODUCTION

'Berlioz?' said Vaughan Williams to me in 1951. 'Holst and I always thought he was a dull fellow.' He had asked about the composers we young people were interested in these days, and his reaction to my reply seemed extraordinary. Dull? Berlioz? Anything else – but surely not *dull*.

I love and admire Vaughan Williams, but I suppose I should not have been surprised. Ever since I became interested in Berlioz (fired by the writings of Cecil Gray and W. J. Turner), it had been clear that he was not a figure who recommended himself naturally to the older generation of British musicians. Gray and Turner were enthusiasts, often as impetuous as their subject himself, but they were exceptions: J. H. Elliot, who wrote the standard biography in Dent's *Master Musicians*, presented the more generally accepted view in the last paragraph of his book: 'We come back to the old problem: was Berlioz a great composer or an adventurer in music? He was both. He was a great genius and he wrote great music – but his work is littered with the crude, the humdrum and the grotesque . . . Berlioz's best is wonderful: his worst is appalling – and the twain, with the degrees between them, are inextricably confused together.'

This was in 1937. Sixty-four years on, it seems curious, to say the least, that a writer with such views should have been seen as an impartial authority, but he was by no means alone. Cecil Forsyth, whose book on orchestration was for years the bible of orchestral students, found *Harold in Italy* 'monumentally dull', and added that 'one hearing . . . is [usually] quite enough to put the listener off the viola for the rest of his life'. Of the famous passage for flutes and trombones in the *Hostias* of the *Requiem*, he comments: 'It probably sounds very nasty' (to which Gordon Jacob, who quoted the remark in his own book on orchestral technique sixteen years later, adds: 'The present writer has heard the passage. It does!'). At best, Forsyth sees Berlioz as a quixotic madman, and a similar patronizing condescension lies behind the endless tiltings of Sir Donald Tovey, professor of music at the University of Edinburgh, whose six volumes of essays in musical analysis were required reading for the intelligent musical public. 'Boiling oil awaits me for my irreverent treatment of Berlioz in the fourth volume of these Essays', wrote Tovey. Very possibly – and it was perhaps strange to omit Berlioz entirely from his article on 'Instrumentation' in the fourteenth edition of the *Encyclopedia Britannica*. But at least Tovey was aware that the debate was not closed. 'We must be careful!' he warns in a footnote: 'You never know where you are with Berlioz. Towards the end of March 1935 Dr Erik Chisholm produced the whole of both parts of *Les Troyens* in Glasgow, and revealed it as one of the most gigantic and convincing masterpieces of music-drama.' Curious to compare this with Elliot's comment on the final scene of the work: 'But to accept the whole immense opera because of these flashes of genius, and in spite of pages of monotonous, uninspired and mortally fatiguing music, is another matter altogether . . .'

Dullness again. The fact is that the generation that formed the backbone of the British musical establishment in the twenties and thirties was essentially brought up in the great German tradition from Bach to Brahms, and was accustomed to a richness of emotional expression and a received view of structure which lay worlds away from the French classical tradition to which Berlioz was heir. Beethoven and Wagner were still the dominating figures, and the few French composers to find favour were those who sheltered under the German symphonic blanket (like César Franck or Saint-Saëns), or who sneaked in via the opera house (Gounod, Bizet, perhaps Massenet), or who could be safely categorized as 'modern' (Debussy, Ravel). Berlioz's brand of French Romanticism, with its basically classical foundation and disciplined emotional rhetoric, found little sympathy. The orchestral virtuosity was grudgingly acknowledged; for the rest, 'programme music' was a safe pigeon-hole if you wanted to be kind, 'eccentric' or 'extravagant' if you wanted to be less so.

One reason for the misjudgement of Berlioz by English musicians was the quality, and even more the style, of the average performance. London had been the scene for some of Berlioz's greatest successes as a conductor, but the brilliance of his own example was no proof against the musical traditions of London after his death. *The Damnation of Faust*, for instance, received fairly regular outings largely because it was seen as a candidate for the great British oratorio tradition – a monumental misunderstanding which did the real Berlioz few favours, as Bernard Shaw pointed out after a performance by the Royal Choral Society in 1893:

> Berlioz' Faust is a particularly stiff subject for Albert Hall treatment. To comb that wild composer's hair, stuff him into a frock-coat and tall hat, stick a hymn-book in his hand, and obtain reverent applause for his ribald burlesque of an Amen chorus as if it were a genuine Handelian solemnity, is really a remarkable feat, and one which few conductors except Sir Joseph Barnby could achieve. Instead of the brimstonish orgy in Auerbach's cellar we have a *soirée* of the Young Men's Christian Association; the drunken blackguardism of Brander is replaced by the decorous conviviality of a respectable young bank clerk . . .; the whiskered pandoors and the fierce hussars on the banks of the Danube become a Volunteer corps on the banks of the Serpentine; and all Brixton votes Berlioz a great composer . . . This does not mean that Berlioz has converted Brixton: it means that Brixton has converted Berlioz . . .

After Berlioz's death, nobody else for many years had the same understanding of his orchestral intentions, and the expressive meanings of the more unusual of them were missed or simply written off as clever 'effects'. There is no composer more difficult to judge from the score alone; it is absolutely necessary to *hear* this music, and in the absence of adequate performances (or, in many cases, of any performances at all) legends about it grew up based on a very sketchy idea of what it actually sounded like. It was not until conductors like Harty and Beecham took him up that audiences in this country began to get a proper sense of the Berlioz idiom, and Monteux and Munch did much the same in France and later in the USA.

But the definitive revaluation came only after the Second World War, when Jacques Barzun published his ground-breaking two-volume *Berlioz and the Romantic Century* and, in the English-speaking countries at least, the production of *Les Troyens* at Covent

Garden in 1957 magnificently vindicated Tovey's judgement and provided a crucial stimulus to the Berlioz revival. A new generation of conductors, chief among them the young Colin Davis, took a fresh look at the man and the music and based performances on a new and unprejudiced study of the scores (which were at last being issued in a genuinely complete edition). As a result, the illusion of a series of huge and unpractical works for enormous forces built on some impossibly romantic 'programme' and riddled with quirky tricks of instrumentation began to be broken down and the range of that notorious orchestral virtuosity to be seen for what it really is. Certainly Berlioz's mind was often filled with huge and ambitious projects, and certainly a few big works did get written – none bigger in Berlioz's time – but the *Requiem*, the *Te Deum*, the *Symphonie funèbre et triomphale* and a couple of public cantatas make up a relatively small part of his output, and even then, though the full sonority can be overwhelming, many of the most memorable effects are produced by carefully restraining the forces involved. At the other end of the scale are works like *Les nuits d'été* and the orchestral songs, *L'enfance du Christ*, *Béatrice et Bénédict*, the love music and Queen Mab scherzo in *Roméo et Juliette* and innumerable passages in *La damnation de Faust*, *Les Troyens* and elsewhere. What we have realized in the last fifty years is the extraordinary precision, indeed economy, with which this prodigy of the orchestra can handle the complex instrument that he understands so well.

He still has his detractors, and one thing that emerges from the evidence in this book is the extent to which, from the very beginning, a lack of musical training was seen as the reason for the so-called 'weaknesses' in Berlioz's style. That this should have been the view of observers brought up in the structured tradition of German music is possibly understandable, but the same attitude in France looks more like reluctance to move out of the rut of musical fashion and listen to something new on its own terms. Today, after a century in which virtually every rule and recognized assumption in music has been turned on its head, we are perhaps better placed to see the 'weaknesses' not as weaknesses but as personal characteristics, and to regard the absence of orthodox training as an accident which lifted obstructions from the path of a powerful instinct for music and a natural aptitude for assimilation, and allowed Berlioz

to write as he wanted to rather than as he should. In fact to see that
the lack of conventional instruction had its positive aspect in liber-
ating the 'originality' which no one denies in Berlioz.

But what is original is unexpected, and what is unexpected is
unsettling. Berlioz does not always make for easy listening; there is
no reassuring familiarity of style to fall back on, no regular melodic
cadence in the German or Italian manner, no cushion of warm
harmony – a point which Constant Lambert identified long ago in
a witty comparison with the rich harmonic idiom of that other
great orchestrator, Richard Strauss: 'Strauss merely jumps up and
down on a spring mattress, whereas Berlioz leaps from trapeze to
trapeze above the heads of the spectators'. And for all the brilliance
of the presentation, there is a private quality to this musical personality which does not give up its secrets easily. Here, curiously, is
a figure popularly regarded as the archetype of the Romantic artist,
yet with a temperamental aversion to sensuality, and what almost
seems an inability to luxuriate in emotion. As David Cairns has
said, this is not 'consoling music. Its nerves are exposed . . . You
cannot wallow in it.' Compare Berlioz's Romeo with Tchaikovsky's,
or Tristan and Isolde with Berlioz's Dido and Aeneas. 'There's a
rock in my path,' he wrote towards the end of his life in a letter
about *Les Troyens*; 'the feelings to be expressed move me too
deeply. That's no good. You have to try and do coolly things that
are fiery.' Was this an attitude that might, perhaps, have seemed
'dull' to a generation brought up with the emotional thunder of
Wagner in its ears?

Perhaps in the end Berlioz was not so much a dull fellow as a
secretive chap. At any rate, the memories collected in this book do
more to support this view than to confirm the flamboyant image of
musical legend. And it has to be said that the legend was one for
which Berlioz himself was partly to blame. His own Memoirs,
unquestionably one of the best reads in musical literature, quickly
earned a reputation for unreliability; 'that masterly work (? of fiction)'
Stanford called it, and if later research has shown that this is an
unfair judgement, it is still true that Berlioz finds it hard to resist a
good story and that, though on the whole he doesn't invent, he
writes colourfully, exaggerates with conviction, and has a memory
no more (and no less) accurate than most people's memories
towards the end of a busy life. His is a view of himself that

skates over much that is most private and most characteristic, and encourages a romantic portrait that readers have sometimes tended to accept, or not accept, rather too literally.

The writers gathered together here can lay no claim to better memories than Berlioz, and several of them labour under the disadvantage of having put their recollections on paper after the publication of the Memoirs. The important offerings of Hiller, Legouvé and others contain material that almost certainly comes from that source, consciously or unconsciously. I have therefore had to pick and choose carefully, avoiding anything that seemed to have a published origin by the composer himself (unless in a very different form), but feeling it fair to include personal information that – as in the case of Hiller, for example – obviously came from daily conversations over a substantial period. I have not been put off by inaccuracies of detail, and nor should the reader be. This book is entitled *Berlioz Remembered*, and what people remember is after all not always precisely what happened. Several of those quoted here were writing after an interval of many years, Hiller and Legouvé after half a century; they were not particularly concerned with historical exactitude and maybe had no records by them as they wrote. So when Pontmartin, at sixty-eight, recalls going to see a Shakespeare play at the age of sixteen, or Legouvé, at nearly eighty, describes Berlioz interrupting a performance at the Théâtre Italien fifty years earlier, no one need be surprised if the details are shaky. What matters is the impression and sense of authenticity that remains – and in both cases, this is vivid and convincing. (I have of course identified any errors that can be checked against historical fact.)

Letters are another matter. As I have taken the epithet 'Remembered' to include 'Described by those who knew him', I have been able to call on contemporary evidence in the form of correspondence by friends and colleagues, as well as newspaper articles and reviews. With the last category I have had to be careful: critical reactions to Berlioz would make a volume in themselves (*Berlioz Dismembered*, perhaps?) but this is a book about Berlioz the man, not the music, and I have tried to limit press material to descriptions of personal public appearances and, of course, to conducting. But Berlioz was easily a prey to self pity, particularly in later years: it is not one of his most attractive characteristics, and I felt it only reasonable to give some idea of the critical hostility to which he was so frequently exposed, and which was to a great extent its cause. I have done this principally in the sections headed 'The critic among critics' and 'The composer among critics'. By the same token, for a man very much involved in the intellectual society and musical politics of his time, some idea of the cultural world in which Berlioz moved seemed essential – hence the occasional description of a concert audience, or a soirée, or even the furniture in his apartment.

As to the arrangement of the book, a chronological structure looked like being the best way to organize material dealing with such widely differing aspects and periods of the composer's life, though the problems of arranging non-chronological material in a chronological sequence has necessitated a certain amount of editorial in-filling, and in one or two places I have introduced pauses in the narrative to deal with individual subjects – criticism, composition, conducting, etc. – which would otherwise have become dispersed through the text and lost their cumulative effect. I have tried to keep my own contributions to a minimum, but some linking commentary was necessary to provide continuity and a sense of direction. However readers should beware of regarding the overall result as a full account of Berlioz's life. Taken in that way it can only appear lopsided and incomplete. The contents and subject matter depend entirely on the memories and impressions left by contemporaries: where these don't exist they can't be invented, and gaps and evasions are inevitable. Nor do the opinions expressed necessarily accord with our view today – but that is no reason to censor them. Berlioz was not always seen as the giant of the French nineteenth century that we now recognize him to be, and this fact is a natural ingredient of the book.

Translations from French or German are my own, except in a very few cases where practical considerations have made access to the originals difficult. In such cases, and in translations from Russian, the translators have been indicated and I offer them my thanks. I have left occasional phrases in French: in the case of texts originally in English or German I have simply retained such phrases where they were used by the original authors, in order to produce particular effects which I have not wanted to spoil; when they occur in my own translations from French texts it is generally because the phrase in question seemed to me too idiomatic to go effectively into English, and was anyhow not difficult to get the gist of – though I know this is a point on which opinions may differ.

My enjoyment in writing this book has been greatly increased, and the labour lightened, by the help of many friends. First, I think, must come Richard Macnutt, who has encouraged me from the start, placed his unrivalled collection of Berlioz material at my disposal, and read the text with the eagle eye of critic, friend and Berlioz scholar. I have incorporated most of his excellent suggestions in the final text. David Cairns, who was at work on his own magnificent volumes on Berlioz during most of the period that I was writing this, nevertheless found the time to answer innumerable questions with characteristic enthusiasm and generosity. I owe an enormous debt of gratitude to Tom Hemsley, who read through all my German translations in detail, advised me on the subtler points of idiomatic German and saved me from more than one linguistic pitfall; I am grateful too for a number of helpful suggestions in German interpretation from Timothy McFarland and, in French, from Clémence Jacquinet. I am also deeply indebted to Gunther Braam for giving me the benefit of his expertise in the field of Berlioz iconography and to Pauline Del Mar for compiling the index. At Faber my thanks go to Belinda Matthews, most patient and least intimidating of editors, and to Kate Ward, for what I hope (at the time of writing) will be her sympathetic attitude to my corrections in proof.

But most of all I have to thank my long-suffering partner, Beth Wilson, who must have found Berlioz and me an exasperating pair; she has had to put up with us for a lot longer than she can possibly have expected when I first took him on, and I dedicate this book gratefully to her.

M. R.

CHRONOLOGY

1800		[*18 March* Birth of Harriet Smithson at Ennis, County Clare, Ireland]
1803		*11 December* Birth of Louis-Hector Berlioz at La Côte-Saint-André, first child of Dr Louis Berlioz and his wife Joséphine Marmion

Haydn 71; Gossec 69; Paisiello 63; Grétry 62; Lesueur 43; Cherubini 43; Méhul 40; Reicha 33; Beethoven 32; Spontini 29; Boieldieu 27; Auber 21; Paganini 21; Spohr 19; Weber 17; Meyerbeer 12; Rossini 11; Schubert 6; Donizetti 6; Halevy 4; Bellini 2
Beethoven: composition of the *Eroica*
Adolphe Adam born

1804		Glinka born
		Napoleon crowned Emperor
1805	aged 1	Beethoven: *Fidelio* (Vienna)
		Battles of Austerlitz, Trafalgar
1806	aged 2	*17 February* Birth of Nanci Berlioz (sister)
		Napoleon in Berlin
1807	aged 3	Birth of Louise Berlioz (sister)
		Spontini: *La Vestale* (Paris)
1808	aged 4	Beethoven: Symphonies 5, 6 (Vienna)
		Goethe: *Faust*, Part I, published
		French armies in Rome, Madrid

1809 aged 5   Haydn dies
                  Mendelssohn, Tennyson, Darwin born

1810 aged 6   Chopin, Schumann, de Musset born
                  Rossini's first opera performed

1811 aged 7   Liszt, Ambroise Thomas, Gautier born
                  Beethoven: *Emperor* Concerto (Vienna)

1812 aged 8   Dickens born
                  Napoleon in Russia; retreat from Moscow

1813 aged 9   Grétry dies
                  Wagner, Verdi born
                  Beethoven: 7th Symphony (Vienna)
                  Rossini: *Tancredi, L'Italiana in Algeri*
                  French defeated at Leipzig, Vitoria

1814 aged 10   *April* La Côte-Saint-André occupied for ten
                  weeks by Austrian troops
                  8 May Birth of Adèle Berlioz (sister)
                  [Birth of Marie Martin, later Recio]

                  Allies in Paris, Napoleon banished to Elba,
                  Congress of Vienna

1815 aged 11   Death of Louise Berlioz, aged 8

                  Battle of Waterloo, Napoleon banished to St Helena,
                  Louis XVIII restored to the throne

1816 aged 12   Learns the flageolet and later the flute
                  Meets Estelle Dubeuf and falls desperately in love
                  for the first time

                  Paisiello dies
                  Charlotte Brontë born
                  Rossini: *Il Barbiere de Siviglia* (Rome)

1817 aged 13   Takes lessons from a local music master and joins
                  in domestic music making
                  First attempts at composition

Méhul, Jane Austen die
Rossini: *Cenerentola* (Rome)

1818 aged 14 Composes two quintets for flute and strings

Gounod, Turgenev born

1819 aged 15 Begins guitar lessons. Offers songs and other
works to Paris publishers; one song accepted

Offenbach born
Spontini: *Olimpie* (Paris)
Géricault: *Le radeau de la Méduse*

1820 aged 16 Birth of Prosper Berlioz (brother)

Lamartine: *Méditations poétiques*

1821 aged 17 *March* Passes *baccalauréat* at Grenoble
End of October Leaves for Paris and enrols in the
School of Medicine
First visits to the Opéra (Salieri: *Les Danaïdes*;
Gluck: *Iphigénie en Tauride*)

Napoleon dies at St Helena
Keats dies
Baudelaire, Flaubert born
Weber: *Der Freischütz* (Berlin)

1822 aged 18 Reluctantly continues medical studies. Frequents
the library of the Conservatoire de Musique
Publishes several songs at his own expense
October Visit to La Côte
December Meets Jean-François Lesueur, shows
him his first substantial work – a cantata, *Le
cheval arabe*. Begins elementary harmony lessons
with one of Lesueur's pupils

Shelley dies
Franck born
Beethoven: last two piano sonatas
Hugo: first poems published
Delacroix: first painting exhibited

1823 aged 19 *January* Becomes a pupil of Lesueur
                March Summoned to La Côte by his father, who
                eventually and unwillingly accepts his determina-
                tion to continue studying music. Compositions
                include an opera and an oratorio (lost)
                    Lalo, Ernest Reyer born
                    Rossini: *Semiramide* (Venice)
                    Weber: *Euryanthe* (Vienna)

1824 aged 20 12 *January* Passes *baccalauréat-ès-science
                physiques* at the Institute, then effectively
                abandons medicine
                Messe solennelle commissioned for the church
                of St Roch
                June/July Third visit to La Côte ends in emotion-
                al scenes
                Hears *Der Freischütz* for the first time
                Mass completed and unsuccessfully rehearsed

                    Géricault, Byron die
                    Bruckner, Smetana born
                    Accession of Charles X
                    Beethoven: *Missa solemnis*, 9th Symphony (Vienna)
                    Liszt's Paris début (aged 12)
                    Rossini takes up residence in Paris

1825 aged 21 More parental conflicts
                10 July The *Mass* performed with success
                August–October Fourth visit to La Côte
                Composes *Scène héroïque*

                    Salieri dies
                    Johann Strauss born
                    Boieldieu: *La dame blanche* (Paris)

1826 aged 22 Starts work on the opera *Les francs-juges*
                Enters for the Prix de Rome but is eliminated at
                the preliminary exam. Enrols at the Conservatoire
                in the classes of Lesueur and Reicha
                November Signs on as a member of the chorus at
                the Théâtre des Nouveautés

Weber: *Oberon* (London)
Weber dies
Beethoven: last three string quartets (Vienna)
De Vigny: *Poèmes antiques et modernes*; *Cinq-Mars*
Hugo: *Odes et ballades*

1827 aged 23 Composes *Waverley* overture
July Passes preliminary exam for the Prix de
Rome and sets test cantata, *La mort d'Orphée*,
which is declared unperformable
September Revelation of Shakespeare. Sees
Hamlet and *Romeo and Juliet* at the Odéon, with
Harriet Smithson as Ophelia and Juliet. Falls
instantly in love with Harriet

Beethoven dies
Schubert: *Winterreise*; last piano trios (Vienna)
Mendelssohn: *Midsummer Night's Dream* overture
(Berlin)
Delacroix: *La mort de Sardanapale*
Liszt returns to Paris

1828 aged 24 *March/April* Hears Beethoven's 3rd and 5th
symphonies at the Conservatoire Concerts
26 May Gives first orchestral concert
July Enters for Prix de Rome again, sets cantata
Herminie but wins only second prize
September At La Côte. Reads Goethe's *Faust* and
composes *Huit scènes de Faust*
Meets Ferdinand Hiller

Schubert, Goya die
Tolstoy born
Auber: *La muette de Portici* (Paris)
Rossini: *Le comte Ory* (Paris)

1829 aged 25 *Huit scènes de Faust* published as Op. 1, *Le ballet
des ombres* as Op. 2
March Harriet Smithson leaves Paris
Hears Beethoven's 6th and 7th symphonies,
Fidelio, string quartets Opp. 131 and 135

July Third failure at the Prix de Rome with the
cantata *Cléopâtre*
November Gives second orchestral concert
Composes *Neuf mélodies*

> Gossec dies
> Rossini: *Guillaume Tell* (Paris)
> Chopin: Variations on *Là ci darem la mano* (Vienna)
> Hugo: *Les Orientales*

1830 aged 26 *March–April* Composes *Symphonie fantastique*
Meets Camille Moke, becomes her lover and later
agrees to marry her
May Abortive rehearsal of the *Fantastique*
July Fourth attempt at the Prix de Rome with the
cantata *Sardanapale* achieves first prize
Composes overture on *The Tempest*
December Meets Liszt. Third concert, including
first performance of the *Symphonie fantastique*

> Hugo: *Hernani* (Paris)
> Auber: *Fra Diavolo* (Paris)
> Donizetti: *Anna Bolena* (Milan)
> July Revolution: abdication of Charles X; accession
> of Louis-Philippe, the bourgeois monarch
> Stendhal: *Le rouge et le noir*
> Lamartine: *Harmonies poétiques et religieuses*

1831 aged 27 *January* After a month at La Côte-Saint-André
travels to Rome via Marseille and Florence
Arrives at the Villa Medici, early March. Meets
Mendelssohn. Finding no letters from Camille,
sets out again for Paris, but in Florence receives
news of her engagement to Pleyel. Continues to
France bent on vengeance, but stops in Nice
Sketches two overtures, *Le roi Lear* and *Rob
Roy*
Returns to Rome. Composes *Le retour à la vie*
(later called *Lélio*) as a sequel to the *Symphonie
fantastique*. Visits Tivoli, Naples, Pompeii, and
Subiaco in the Abruzzi

Meyerbeer: *Robert le diable* (Paris)
Bellini: *La sonnambula* and *Norma* (Milan)
Hugo: *Marion de Lorme*; *Notre-Dame de Paris*
Balzac: *La peau de chagrin*
Delacroix: *Liberty leading the people*
Paganini's first appearance in Paris
Chopin arrives in Paris

1832 aged 28 Last visit to Subiaco, composes *La captive*
Returns to France via Terni, Spoleto, Perugia,
Florence, Milan. After five months at La Côte
returns to Paris (7 November) and immediately
plans concert for 9 December to include the
revised version of the *Fantastique* and *Le retour
à la vie*. Harriet Smithson (recently returned to
Paris) is present at the performance, and is introduced to Berlioz a few days later

Goethe dies
Manet born
Hérold: *Le Pré aux clercs* (Paris)
Donizetti: *Elisir d'amore* (Milan)
Hugo: *Le roi s'amuse* (Paris)

1833 aged 29 Stormy courtship and marriage (3 October) to
Harriet. Organizes five public concerts, including
two benefits for Harriet, in a pattern that will
become a feature of Parisian musicial life for the
next nine years
August Project for a dramatic oratorio, *Le
dernier jour du monde*, rejected by the Opéra
Composes *Le jeune pâtre breton*. Becomes regular
music critic for *Le Rénovateur*

Brahms born
Auber: *Gustav III* (Paris)
Cherubini: *Ali Baba* (Paris)
Bellini: *Beatrice di Tenda* (Venice)
Chopin: 12 *Etudes*, Op. 10 (dedicated to Liszt)
Mendelssohn: *Italian Symphony*
Balzac: *Eugénie Grandet*

1834 aged 30 *January* Paganini commissions a work for viola
and orchestra, finished as *Harold en Italie* in June,
though not to Paganini's expectations
April Berlioz and Harriet settle in Montmartre,
where their son Louis is born, 14 August
Libretto of *Benvenuto Cellini* turned down by the
Opéra-comique. Composes *Sara la baigneuse*
November–December Gives four concerts, with
first performances of *Harold en Italie*, *Sara*, etc.
Contributes his first article to the *Journal des débats*

> Boieldieu dies
> Borodin born
> Adam: *Le chalet* (Paris)
> Wagner: completes first opera, *Die Feen*
> Schumann: founds *Neue Zeitschrift für Musik*
> (Leipzig)

1835 aged 31 *January* Becomes music critic of the *Journal des
débats*
April–May Gives two concerts with Liszt (who
leaves Paris in July), and four later in the year
(at the last of which he begins conducting his
own concerts himself). Works on a *Fête musicale
funèbre*, later to provide material for the
Symphonie funèbre et triomphale (1840), but
now resulting only in the cantata *Le cinq mai*
Libretto of *Benvenuto Cellini* accepted by the Opéra

> Bellini dies
> Saint-Saëns, Cui born
> Bellini: *I puritani* (Paris)
> Halévy: *La juive* (Paris)
> Donizetti: *Lucia di Lammermoor* (Naples)
> De Vigny: *Chatterton*
> Balzac: *Le père Goriot*

1836 aged 32 *Spring–summer* After some hesitation, settles
down to compose *Benvenuto Cellini*
December Gives two concerts. Harriet makes her
last stage appearance

Reicha dies
Delibes born
Meyerbeer: *Les Huguenots* (Paris)
Glinka: *A Life for the Tsar* (St Petersburg)

1837 aged 33 Completes *Benvenuto Cellini*, early April
March Receives commission for the *Requiem*
Completes the work by the end of June, but the
performance in July is cancelled and eventually
takes place in December, conducted by Habeneck

Lesueur, Hummel die
Balakirev born
Schumann: *Carnaval*
William IV dies; accession of Queen Victoria

1838 aged 34 *18 February* Death of Berlioz's mother
May Rehearsals of *Benvenuto Cellini* at the
Opéra meet with hostility from the artists
Performance, 10 September, a failure
November, December Two concerts. Paganini
hears *Harold en Italie* for the first time and makes
Berlioz a gift of 20,000 francs

Bizet born
Chopin goes to Majorca with George Sand
Donizetti arrives in Paris

1839 aged 35 *January* Begins work on *Roméo et Juliette* (dedi-
cated to Paganini). Completes it in September and
gives three performances in November and
December
December Meets Wagner
Relations with Harriet deteriorating

Musorgsky, Cézanne born
Verdi: *Oberto* (Milan)
Wagner arrives in Paris
Stendhal: *La chartreuse de Parme*

1840 aged 36 *Early June* Receives commission for a work to
commemorate the martyrs of the July Revolution
Symphonie funèbre et triomphale composed in six
weeks and performed in the open air, 28 July
Two (indoor) performances follow
August–September At La Côte-Saint-André
November 'Festival de M. Berlioz' at the Opéra

> Paganini dies
> Tchaikovsky, Daudet, Monet, Rodin born
> Donizetti: *La fille du régiment* (Paris)
> Hugo: *Les rayons et les ombres*

1841 aged 37 Completes *Les nuits d'été* (six songs with piano
accompaniment, published September)
May Composes recitatives and orchestrates
L'invitation à la valse for performances of *Der
Freischütz* at the Opéra
Begins opera, *La nonne sanglante* (never finished)
Begins an affair with Marie Recio

> Chabrier, Dvořák born
> Schumann: 1st Symphony (Leipzig)

1842 aged 38 Four concerts in Paris, but little composition
September First foreign concert tour, to Brussels,
accompanied by Marie Recio
December Second tour (again with Marie), to
Brussels, Frankfurt and Stuttgart

> Cherubini dies
> Massenet, Sullivan born
> Verdi: *Nabucco* (Milan)
> Wagner: *Rienzi* (Dresden)
> Glinka: *Ruslan and Lyudmilla* (St Petersburg)

1843 aged 39 Tour continues to Mannheim, Frankfurt again,
Weimar, Leipzig (first triumph in Germany),
Dresden (meets Wagner and sees *Rienzi* and *Der
fliegende Holländer*), Leipzig again (his only
meeting with Schumann), Brunswick, Hamburg,
Berlin, Hanover and Darmstadt

4 *June* Returns to Paris. Composes *Carnaval romain* overture. Completes *Grand traité d'instrumentation et d'orchestration modernes*

Grieg, Henry James born
Wagner: *Der fliegende Holländer* (Dresden)
Donizetti: *Don Pasquale* (Paris)
Mendelssohn: *Midsummer Night's Dream* music (Potsdam)

1844 aged 40 Three concerts, and composes *Hymne à la France* for a fourth at the Festival de l'Industrie (August)
Publishes *Voyage musical en Allemagne et en Italie*
Holiday in Nice, where he composes the overture *La tour de Nice* (later re-titled *Le corsaire*)
October Harriet's progressive alcoholism leads to a final separation
November Composes *Marche funèbre pour la dernière scène d'Hamlet*

Rimsky-Korsakov, Verlaine born
Verdi: *Ernani* (Venice)
David: *Le désert* (Paris)
Turner: *Rain, Steam and Speed* (London)
Marx and Engels meet in Paris

1845 aged 41 *January–April* Four concerts at the Cirque Olympique
June–July Concerts in Marseilles and Lyons
August Attends the unveiling of the Beethoven statue in Bonn
Begins work on *La damnation de Faust*
Composes *Le chasseur danois* and *Zaïde*
October Leaves with Marie for Vienna (three concerts)

Fauré, Widor born
Wagner: *Tannhäuser* (Dresden)
Mendelssohn: Violin Concerto (Leipzig)

1846 aged 42 Two more concerts in Vienna, then Prague, back to Vienna, Pest (where his arrangement of the

Rákóczy March has a spectacular success), Breslau
and Prague again. Works at *La damnation de
Faust* throughout the tour. Returns to Paris (May)
Chant des chemins de fer, for the inauguration of
the Chemin de Fer du Nord, written in three days
and performed in Lille (June)
La damnation de Faust completed; first performance
(6 December) a failure

> Mendelssohn: *Elijah* (Birmingham)
> Balzac: *La cousine Bette*
> Lear: *Book of Nonsense*

1847　aged 43　*February–May* Concert tour to St Petersburg and
Moscow – without Marie, who joins him in Berlin
on the return journey. Back in Paris in July
September Visits La Côte-Saint-André with Louis
Finally gives up *La nonne sanglante*
November Leaves for London to conduct Jullien's
opera season at Drury Lane Theatre

> Mendelssohn dies
> Verdi: *Macbeth* (Florence)
> Charlotte Brontë: *Jane Eyre*
> Emily Brontë: *Wuthering Heights*

1848　aged 44　Jullien's opera season fails
February Revolution in Paris. Berlioz stays on in
London until July. Two successful concerts of his
own works; begins assembling the *Mémoires*
28 July Berlioz's father dies; visit to La Côte
October Big concert at Versailles
November Harriet suffers her first stroke, causing
partial paralysis and permanently impaired speech
Begins composing a *Te Deum*. Early signs of the
intestinal disorder which plagues his later years

> Donizetti dies
> Duparc, Gauguin born
> Louis-Philippe abdicates; Second Republic proclaimed
> Rebellion in Austria, North Italy, Rome
> Louis Napoleon elected president of France

1849 aged 45 *January* At work on the *Te Deum* (completed
              October, but no performance in prospect)
              February Harriet has a second stroke, followed
              by three more in summer and autumn
              Begins assembling *Tristia* and *Vox populi* for
              publication

>   Chopin dies
>   Meyerbeer: *Le prophète* (Paris)
>   Verdi: *Luisa Miller* (Naples)
>   Revolt in Dresden; Wagner forced to flee

1850 aged 46 *February* Takes a leading role in launching the
              Société philharmonique de Paris and conducts
              its first seven concerts (to December). Succeeds
              to the post of head librarian at the
              Conservatoire
              May Berlioz's sister, Nanci, dies of cancer
              September Composes *Adieu des bergers à la
              sainte famille* as an albumleaf, and includes it in
              two concerts of the *Société philharmonique* as the
              work of 'Pierre Ducré'. Later composes two more
              movements to complete *La fuite en Égypte*

>   Balzac, Wordsworth die
>   Schumann: *Genoveva* (Leipzig)
>   Wagner: *Lohengrin* (Weimar)
>   *Bach-Gesellschaft* founded, to publish complete
>   works of J. S. Bach (Leipzig)
>   Turgenev: *A month in the country*

1851 aged 47 *January–April* Conducts the last four concerts of
              the *Société philharmonique*, which closes
              May–July Second visit to London, as a member
              of the jury for musical instruments at the Great
              Exhibition. Completes final version of *Tristia*

>   Spontini, Turner die
>   Verdi: *Rigoletto* (Venice)
>   Coup d'état; dissolution of the National Assembly,
>   plebiscite in France

1852 aged 48 *March–June* Third visit to London. Conducts the first six concerts of the New Philharmonic Society, including two performances of Beethoven's 9th Symphony that seal his English reputation as the world's greatest conductor
March Benvenuto Cellini revived in Weimar, Liszt conducting. The score drastically revised for two further performances in November in Berlioz's presence
Publication of *Les soirées de l'orchestre*

> Schumann: *Manfred* (Leipzig)
> Dumas: *La dame aux camélias* (Paris)
> Gautier: *Emaux et camées*
> Dickens: *Bleak House*
> Louis Napoleon becomes Emperor as Napoleon III

1853 aged 49 *May–July* Fourth visit to London. *Benvenuto Cellini* at Covent Garden is viciously attacked by an Italian claque and withdrawn after one performance
August Festival concert at Baden-Baden, two concerts in Frankfurt, home via Munich
October Liszt and Wagner in Paris
October–December Concert tour to Brunswick, Hanover, Bremen, Leipzig (first performance of *La fuite en Égypte*)

> Verdi: *Il trovatore* (Rome), *La traviata* (Venice)
> Wagner completes text of *Der Ring des Nibelungen*
> Liszt composes Sonata in B minor
> Schumann: 4th symphony (Düsseldorf)

1854 aged 50 *January* Composes *L'arrivé à Saïs* as a sequel to *La fuite en Égypte*
3 March Harriet dies, aged 53
April Concert tour to Hanover, Brunswick, Dresden, home via Weimar
July Adds *Le songe d'Hérode* as a prologue to *La fuite en Égypte* and completes *L'enfance du Christ*

Composes cantata *L'impériale*. Completes the first
draft of the *Mémoires*
19 October Marries Marie Recio
December First performances of *L'enfance du
Christ*, a great success

> Janáček, Rimbaud, Wilde born
> Meyerbeer: *L'étoile du nord* (Paris)
> Wagner completes *Das Rheingold*
> Liszt composes *Faust Symphony*
> Schumann goes into an asylum for the insane
> French involvement in the Crimean War begins

1855 aged 51 *February* Concerts in Weimar; first tentative
suggestion to Liszt and the Princess Sayn-
Wittgenstein of a work based on the *Aeneid* of
Virgil. Home via Gotha
March Three concerts in Brussels
30 April First performance of the *Te Deum* at
St.-Eustache
June–July Fifth visit to London. Conducts two
concerts of the New Philharmonic Society, meets
Wagner again
Writes *Le chef d'orchestre* as the pendant to a
new edition of the *Traité d'instrumentation*
Serves on the jury of the Exposition Universelle
and conducts (November) the three concluding
concerts at the Palais de l'Industrie, including the
first performance of *L'impériale*

> Chausson born
> Verdi: *Les vêpres siciliennes* (Paris)
> Delacroix: first of the *Lion hunts*
> Tennyson: *Maud*
> First Exposition Universelle in Paris

1856 aged 52 *February* Visits Gotha and Weimar, and is urged
by Liszt and the Princess to write his opera on the
Aeneid
Back in Paris, completes the orchestral version of
Les nuits d'été, and in April begins the libretto
of *Les Troyens*

Mid-June Writes music as well as words for the
love duet in Act IV. 26 June: completes the libretto
21 June Elected to the Institut de France on the
death of Adolphe Adam
July–August Visits Plombières, concert Baden-Baden
October Moves into 4, rue de Calais
Bouts of intestinal trouble more severe

> Schumann, Adam, Heine die
> Freud, Bernard Shaw born
> Wagner completes *Die Walküre*
> Liszt completes *Dante Symphony*
> Hugo: *Les contemplations*
> Paris peace congress ends Crimean War

1857　aged 53　*February* Act I of *Les Troyens* finished. Reads the
libretto to various audiences. 8 April: Act IV
finished; returns to Act II
July–August Visits Plombières, Baden-Baden
Back in Paris, begins Act III. Rough draft of the
whole opera completed by the end of the year

> Glinka, de Musset die
> Elgar born
> Verdi: *Simon Boccanegra* (Venice)
> Flaubert: *Madame Bovary*
> Baudelaire: *Les fleurs du mal*

1858　aged 54　Full score of *Les Troyens* completed, 12 April
Wagner briefly in Paris but relations with Berlioz
strained
Postscript to the *Mémoires* dated 25 May
August Conducts at Baden-Baden, where Benazet,
manager of the casino, commissions a new opera
September Disappointing audience with the
Emperor
Serialization of the *Mémoires* in *Le monde illustré*
begins

> Puccini, Leoncavallo born
> Offenbach: *Orphée aux enfers* (Paris)
> Cornelius: *Der Barbier von Bagdad* (Weimar)

1859 aged 55 Gives readings of the libretto of *Les Troyens* and
has hopes of a performance at the Opéra
March *Les grotesques de la musique* published
Concerts in Paris, Bordeaux and Baden-Baden
September Wagner returns to Paris
November Gluck's *Orphée* at the Théâtre-lyrique
in Berlioz's version with Pauline Viardot in the
title role
Acute suffering from intestinal condition
Baden-Baden commission abandoned

> Spohr dies
> Gounod: *Faust* (Paris)
> Verdi: *Un ballo in maschera* (Rome)
> Wagner completes *Tristan und Isolde*, August
> Brahms: 1st piano concerto (Hanover)
> Darwin: *Origin of Species*

1860 aged 56 *January–February* Wagner gives three concerts
in Paris
Les Troyens accepted for performance by the
Théâtre-lyrique in its new theatre (not yet built)
2 March Berlioz's sister Adèle dies
August Annual visit to Baden-Baden, and a new
commission (for *Béatrice et Bénédict*) confirmed
Starts work at once
September Private printing of *Les Troyens* begun

> Wolf, Mahler, Chekhov born
> Garibaldi and the Red Shirts take Palermo and
> Naples
> Victor Emanuel of Sardinia invades Papal States

1861 aged 57 *March* Wagner's *Tannhäuser* creates a scandal at
the Opéra
June The new building of the Théâtre-lyrique
being hopelessly behind schedule, *Les Troyens* is
accepted for performance at the Opéra
August Last annual concert at Baden-Baden
November Gluck's *Alceste* given at the Opéra in
Berlioz's version

Victor Emanuel II proclaimed King of united Italy
Dostoevsky: *Notes from the House of the Dead*
Dickens: *Great Expectations*
Outbreak of Civil War in the United States
French troops sent to Mexico

1862 aged 58 *25 February* *Béatrice et Bénédict* completed
13 June Berlioz's second wife, Marie, dies of a
heart attack at the age of 48
9 August First performance of *Béatrice et
Bénédict* at Baden-Baden
September Publication of the last collection of
essays, *A travers chants*

Halévy dies
Debussy born
Verdi: *La forza del destino* (St Petersburg)
Flaubert: *Salammbò*
Hugo: *Les misérables*
Turgenev: *Fathers and sons*

1863 aged 59 *February Les Troyens* dropped by the Opéra but
taken up again by the Théâtre-lyrique
April Conducts *Béatrice et Bénédict* at Weimar,
concert in Löwenberg, and (June) *L'enfance du
Christ* in Strasbourg
June Rehearsals of *Les Troyens* begin, and
Berlioz reluctantly agrees to cut the first two acts
August Béatrice et Bénédict at Baden-Baden
8 October Last feuilleton for *Journal des débats*
4 November First performance of *Les Troyens à
Carthage* (i.e. the last three acts of the original
opera) at the Théâtre-lyrique. Twenty further
performances, ending 4 December

Mascagni born
Delacroix, de Vigny die
Bizet: *Les pêcheurs de perles* (Paris)
Manet: *Déjeuner sur l'herbe* at the Salon des Refusés
Abraham Lincoln: Gettysburg address
French troops enter Mexico City

1864 aged 60 *January* Concert version of the *Marche troyenne*
After thirty years, resigns as the music critic of the
Journal des débats. In continual pain, often in bed
for much of the day, taking increasing doses of
laudanum
August–September Visits nieces in the Dauphiné
Meets Estelle again [see 1816] and begins a regular
correspondence with her

> Meyerbeer dies
> Richard Strauss born
> Offenbach: *La belle Hélène* (Paris)
> Tolstoy begins *War and Peace*
> Ludwig II crowned King of Bavaria

1865 aged 61 'Postface' to the *Mémoires* dated 1 January
July 1,200 copies of the finished book privately
printed, to be published after his death
August Visits Estelle and her family in Geneva,
and his own relatives in Grenoble

> Dukas, Glazunov, Sibelius born
> Meyerbeer: *L'africaine* (Paris)
> Wagner: *Tristan und Isolde* (Munich)
> Lincoln assassinated

1866 aged 62 *January* Coaches the title role in Gluck's *Armide*
for the Théâtre-lyrique (performance abandoned)
March Liszt in Paris, last meeting
July–August Berlioz's son Louis' last visit to Paris
September Visits Estelle in Geneva
August–October Supervises rehearsals for a
revival of *Alceste* at the Opéra
December Visits Vienna to conduct *La damna-
tion de Faust*

> Satie, Busoni born
> Offenbach: *La vie parisienne* (Paris)
> Thomas: *Mignon* (Paris)
> Smetana: *The Bartered Bride* (Prague)
> Daudet: *Lettres de mon moulin*
> Dostoevsky: *Crime and punishment*

1867 aged 63 *February* At Hiller's invitation conducts two
concerts in Cologne
Appointed to organize the closing concerts for the
second Exposition Universelle in Paris
June Louis dies of yellow fever in Havana at the
age of 32
Berlioz cancels his appearance at the Exposition
August–September Takes a cure near Vichy and
visits family in Vienne. Last meeting with Estelle
November Leaves for a concert tour in Russia;
four concerts in St Petersburg

> Ingres, Baudelaire die
> Granados, Toscanini born
> Verdi: *Don Carlos* (Paris)
> Gounod: *Roméo et Juliette* (Paris)
> Wagner completes *Die Meistersinger*
> Ibsen: *Peer Gynt*
> French troops withdraw from Mexico

1868 aged 64 *January* Two concerts in Moscow and two more
in St Petersburg
February Gets back to Paris exhausted, goes to
the Riviera for a warm holiday (March). In
Monaco slips on the rocks by the sea and falls,
cutting his face. On a visit to Nice suffers a slight
stroke and has another fall. Returns to Paris
where he is confined to bed, partially paralysed
August Visits Grenoble to address a local choral
competition but at the formal banquet is unable
to speak

> Rossini dies
> Thomas: *Hamlet* (Paris)
> Wagner: *Die Meistersinger von Nürnberg* (Munich)
> Brahms: *Deutsches Requiem* (Bremen)
> Tchaikovsky: 1st Symphony (Moscow)
> Musorgsky starts work on *Boris Godunov*

1869 aged 65 *8 March* After several days of semi-coma, Berlioz
dies in his bed at 4, rue de Calais at half past midday

> Auber 87; Liszt 57; Wagner 55; Verdi 55; Gounod 50;
> Offenbach 49; Franck 46; Smetana 45; Bruckner 44;
> J. Strauss 43; Brahms 35; Saint-Saëns 33; Delibes 33;
> Bizet 30; Musorgsky 29; Tchaikovsky 28; Chabrier 28;
> Dvořák 27; Massenet 26; Grieg 25; Rimsky-Korsakov
> 24; Fauré 23; Janáček 14; Elgar 11; Puccini 10; Wolf 8;
> Mahler 8; Debussy 6; Strauss 4; Dukas 3; Sibelius 3;
> Satie 2

I BERLIOZ REMEMBERED

What everybody remembers first is the fascination of his appearance. 'A splendid head, like an exasperated eagle' was Théophile Gautier's memorable phrase, but the fullest description is probably the much quoted one by the German pianist and composer Ferdinand Hiller:

I do not believe that anyone meeting Berlioz could fail to have been surprised by his extraordinary and individual features: the high forehead sharply cut away above deep-set eyes, the strikingly prominent hawk-like nose, the thin finely sculptured lips, the rather short chin – all this crowned by an astonishing abundance of light brown curls whose fantastic proliferation had never suffered the restraining influence of the barber's scissors. It was a head that, once seen, could not be forgotten. And with it went the unusual mobility of his face, the look now shining, yes, blazing, and then dull, almost lifeless, the expression of his mouth that switched backwards and forwards between energy, withering contempt, a friendly smile or sardonic laughter. He was of medium height, slender though not elegant, and his bearing was careless in the extreme. The sound of his speaking voice could be described as soft, though it goes without saying that it varied with his continually changing mood. He had a pleasant singing voice and could have brought out the qualities of many of his vocal compositions had he been able to restrain his excitement rather better. The overwhelming intensity of feeling interfered with the meaning of the music . . .

[Hiller 1880: 65]

This is Berlioz as most people think of him, the image of the romantic composer *par excellence*. But the earliest actual physical description suggests nothing so flamboyant. In 1821, when Dr Berlioz decided that it was time for his son to go to Paris to study medicine, a domestic passport was required for travel within French borders, and one was accordingly issued to Berlioz on 26 October, when he was seventeen years and some ten months old.

Height, one metre sixty-three centimetres. Hair fair; forehead ordinary; eyebrows fair; eyes grey; nose good; mouth average; beard incipient; chin rounded; face oval; complexion high.
    Distinguishing marks, none.

[CGB: i, 34-35n]

It is not a romantic document, and certainly a far cry from the volcanic personality described by future observers, but no doubt a fair description of the teenage son of a respected doctor in a quiet provincial town in south-east France.

2 CHILDHOOD

Apart from the *Memoirs*, the only accounts we have of Berlioz's early life are those by Hiller and Joseph d'Ortigue, but d'Ortigue's version is known to have been written largely by Berlioz himself. Hiller was the son of a wealthy Frankfurt business man and had been a close friend of Mendelssohn and a pupil of Hummel; between 1828 and 1834 he lived in Paris, where he became an intimate companion of Berlioz – and remained a friend, even though Berlioz pinched his fiancée and came close to marrying her. His memories were not put on paper till nearly fifty years later, and allowance has to be made for the different temperament and background of the two young men; yet his account draws on one of the earliest of Berlioz's friendships and, though inevitably second-hand, helps to fill out a period about which we otherwise know little.

FERDINAND HILLER
(1811–85)

. . . the sympathy I felt for him grew daily as he told me about his childhood in his parents' home and his years as a student.

He was born in a small town, La Côte-Saint-André, but his upbringing had preserved that tranquil and solitary character that is generally possible only in the country. His father, a well-regarded physician of broad interests and sound education, was the only teacher of his only son, and his tuition was certainly thorough even if, thanks to the recurring demands of an active medical practice, it must have been frequently interrupted; the boy was left a lot to his own devices, and perhaps had more opportunity to indulge his love of solitary dreaming in the open air than was altogether good for him. Latin, in particular, played a very important part in his studies, and his father's passion for the works of Virgil was passed on gradually to his son. I don't think that Berlioz ever became so intimately acquainted with any other poetry as he did with the Aeneid, and it must have been a moving experience for his friends to see him, at the end of his career, turning back to this young love and writing both the verses and the music for his opera *The Trojans*.

Of his mother Berlioz spoke with love – though a love mixed with compassionate regret for what he saw as her prejudices about religion and art; this was a source of much suffering to him when he decided to become a composer. But he kept a most tender affection for his two sisters, particularly the younger one, with whom he felt a special bond of sympathy. All in all, his childhood may be said to have been happy: he was intellectually stimulated without being overtaxed, lived a life free from care among the beauties of nature and, sheltered by the love of his family, was able to follow his innocent inclinations as he wished. The mistrust of everybody and everything, which exerted such a baleful influence on his later life, was still far in the future. The days slid by in an atmosphere of purity, faith and simplicity, untouched by the cares and anxieties of school and the disturbing encounters they so often bring with them. Above all the pursuit of music filled many blissful hours. Here too his father, earnestly concerned as ever, was his first teacher – though one or two not very distinguished musicians later added some help. He easily learned to sing at sight, and quickly achieved a degree of facility on several instruments. But what were the instruments available to him to satisfy this growing passion for music? The flageolet, the flute, and the guitar!

. . . [He never learnt to play the piano, and] it says a lot for his musical gifts (if indeed anything needs saying) that even as a boy, before he had ever heard any decent music, he was already trying his hand at composition, and in several parts too – no matter how these early efforts may actually have turned out. When did any composer, who later became famous, spend his childhood under circumstances less favourable to musical development?

[Hiller 1880: 66–8]

Hiller is wrong in implying that Berlioz was never at school, though the details of his attendance at the local *petit-séminaire* are not clear. According to the *Memoirs*, he was there for a few months when he was ten years old before being removed by his father for tuition at home, and in 1883 Edmond Hippeau, one of Berlioz's first biographers, recorded the memories of two school-fellows from seventy years earlier.

[JOSEPH FAVRE AND CHARLES BERT]

At La Côte they still preserve traditions and memories of his life as a schoolboy. They haven't forgotten that it was he who led the pupils on their school parades to the sound of the drum: he was a rattling good drummer, they say. He didn't see fit to reveal the origin of this instrumental talent to the rest of us when, after noting [in the *Memoirs*] that he was a past master on the flageolet, the flute and the guitar, he added disdainfully that he '*also* played the drum'.

[Hippeau 1889: 152–3]

> For his only other memories of Berlioz at La Côte, Hippeau cites no specific source.

There was a strain of bogus mystification in his character that made itself apparent from his earliest days. His pranks made him something of a terror at the *séminaire*. When a firecracker was dis-covered one day under a paving stone in the vestibule, Berlioz was accused of trying to blow the place up – but these are the tricks of all schoolchildren . . .

[Ibid: 142]

> And Jacques Barzun, the doyen of present-day Berlioz scholars, was told by the grandson of Berlioz's boyhood friend Antoine Charbonnel, that 'Berlioz had a passion for dancing, and that he possessed a pair of green leather boots of which he was inordinately proud'.
> But nowhere is there any mention of the incident that takes up a whole chapter in Berlioz's own descrip-tion of his childhood in the *Memoirs*: the shock of first love, and the ineffaceable memory of it that was to remain in the recesses of his heart to the very end of his

life. And along with the romantic impression left by the
eyes, the elegance, the cruel indifference of Estelle
Dubeuf, what survived above all in his mind was the
vivid image of a pair of pink dancing shoes that she was
wearing when he first saw her – though many years
later, when both Estelle and Berlioz were dead, even this
sacred memory was put in doubt by a letter from
Estelle's niece.

My memories on the subject of Berlioz consist entirely of having
heard my aunt protest energetically against the legend of the pink
shoes – which, she said, had never existed outside the fertile imagination of her young lover.

[Ménestrel 1903: 398]

3 A STUDENT IN PARIS

Early in November 1821, Berlioz arrived in Paris to
begin work as a medical student in the European capital
of the arts. He took lodgings in Rue Saint-Jacques on
the Left Bank, in the heart of the university district, and
was at once plunged into Parisian student life. There is
an early glimpse of it, and of him, in the memoirs of a
fellow student, the young actor Adolphe Laferrière.

ADOLPHE LAFERRIÈRE
(1806–77)

It had been decided that I should take a room for fifteen francs a
month in a small lodging house . . . in Rue Saint-Jacques, opposite
the college of Louis-le-Grand. This hostel, which used the same
name as the college, had thirty-five numbered rooms and drew its
supply of students from the schools of law and medicine.

In addition to the thirty-five rooms, there was a dining hall, a
large and ugly room, smoky, with straw-bottomed chairs and
panelled walls, which could seat some twenty lodgers, and a second
room, with a billiard table in the middle, which we used as a bar.
It was an arrangement that might have been invented solely to
provide a Machiavellian alternative to the courses in the lecture
theatres, and the pleasures of idleness on offer were so intoxicating
that within days of my arrival I had become friendly with a tall,
jovial young man who in four or five years had never yet succeeded
in finding a day with enough time when he wasn't playing a match –
best of three – to complete his first term at the School of Law. He
was called Gallois . . .

It was obvious that Gallois would want to be my professor in
the noble game of billiards, and if he didn't have in me a pupil he

could be particularly proud of . . . at least he could boast of having found a willing scholar: I was scarcely ever out of the billiard room, and soon made myself a reputation for incompetence that became proverbial. I was unanimously awarded the title of Grand Protector . . . because at the table the man who played before me, on whose result I would have to play my own turn, could be so sure I would miss my shot that he felt himself infallibly saved in advance . . .

After a month of this protectorate I became the object of a most flattering attention. It was decided, without my knowledge, to hold a benefit sweepstake, at two francs a head, of which the proceeds would reimburse me for all the stakes I had lost. As a result, I watched, with a surprise slightly tempered by *amour propre*, as all the players round me came to grief one after another, and it was with a certain stately satisfaction that I gathered up, to general applause, the takings amounting to some fifty francs. On the score-board, someone wrote in huge letters: THE PROTECTOR HAS SWEPT THE JACKPOT!

The following morning I received a number of compliments: I was dignified, and my attitude was found to lack neither tact nor taste. But as for Gallois, he positively made himself ill: his efforts to prevent himself from laughing brought him close to an apoplectic seizure, and my triumph would have certainly been followed by a disaster if he hadn't put the preservation of his life before the protection of my honour and exploded at last in a fusillade of taunts and gibes. And so the truth was disclosed.

Though the plot had been well intentioned, and had no other purpose than to recompense me for my losses, I nursed for several days a secret grudge against its author. This was a tall, slim young man with sharp, wasted features and the grave face of a mystic, who often made jokes, but never laughed. His hair, of a fair colouring that would have been the envy of our Phrynés today, stood out like the mane of a lion. The name of this young man was Hector Berlioz. He studied Law or Medicine – I'm not sure which. But if they called me the Protector, they called *him* the Alarm Clock, because he had in his room a battered harpsichord whose decrepit keyboard he woke into life the moment dawn broke . . .

> In spite of the generosity of his fellow-students, Laferrière's debts still exceeded his resources and in this

extremity he turned for help to his old teacher, Alexandre Choron. Choron, a distinguished musicologist and the founder and director of an influential school of church music, gave the young man a vigorous piece of his mind and demanded to be taken to Laferrière's lodgings.

When we arrived at the Hôtel Louis-le Grand, Choron and I, Berlioz happened to pass by and saw us. 'Good morning, Protector,' he said to me, and raised his cap slightly to Choron who looked back at him in his turn. Berlioz went on his way.

'Who is that young man?' asked Choron. 'He's a student who lives in the same house,' I said. 'A student? What in? – music?' 'The students here are all in law or medicine.' 'Imbecile! you're studying drama yourself – or that's what you say. I tell you, that young man ought to be studying music.' 'It's true,' I replied, 'that he has a harpsichord with which he stupefies the whole household.' 'I knew it! And he's certainly going to turn out very differently from you.' 'So what is he going to be, then?' 'A great artist!'

We went in, and Choron settled my bill without further comment . . .

But Choron's remark about Berlioz had excited my curiosity, and I struck up a friendship with this future great artist. I soon discovered that I had to do with a passionate admirer of Gluck and Spontini, and also that he was already at work on a serious musical project of his own – a score drawn from [Saurin's] drama *Beverley*. I can even remember a phrase from this first operatic composition . . . What Berlioz would think now of his student music I don't know. But if he reads these pages, he will at least recognize, in the fidelity of my memory, a proof of musical sympathy, dare I say even musical fraternity, in spite of the directly opposite routes that we followed in the domain of art.

[Laferrière 1876: 49–61]

There was never really much hope for Berlioz as a medical student (though he stuck at it reluctantly for a couple of years, collecting the diploma of *bachelier-ès-sciences physiques* in January 1824). But his reaction, during those first days in the dissecting room at the Hospice de la Pitié, was one of utter revulsion to the subject he had come to study. And in any case the impact of music in Paris, opera especially, soon knocked any permanent thoughts about medicine out of his head. It was filled instead with the names he had learned to love and revere from books, and the works he could now at last hear for himself – Salieri, Méhul, above all Gluck: he had only been in Paris three weeks when *Iphigénie en Tauride* was given at the Opéra, and Berlioz had his first live experience of the master who was to be his idol and mentor to the end of his life.

FERDINAND HILLER

I don't believe it is possible for those of us who have been brought up in the world of music and the theatre to form any conception of the impact that a musical and dramatic production of this kind must have made on a man who had never in his life heard anything like it before, yet whose whole nature was tuned to respond with the deepest feeling to anything that had to do with poetry or music. It was like setting a match to a powder keg . . .

In the entire history of music there is no other example of a composer who, right up to his nineteenth year, had heard or known so little music as Berlioz, with the result that he had scarcely any conception of what a real musician means by music. And it is equally difficult to imagine any other beginner starting with such complicated experiments as he did – for after the performances he had attended at the Opéra, and the study of Gluck's scores that had excited him to such transports of admiration, he embarked straight-away on the composition of large scale vocal works with orchestra.

[Hiller 1880: 68–9, 101]

> Within just over a year of his arrival in Paris Berlioz managed to get himself taken on as a private pupil of the celebrated composer Jean-François Lesueur, and every minute he could or couldn't spare was devoted to music.

FERDINAND HILLER

Chance, which played so large a part in his early musical experience, led him to Lesueur as his first teacher. Lesueur, who is now little remembered by his fellow countrymen and in Germany was virtually unknown, nevertheless occupies a not unimportant place in the history of French music. In his younger days his musical leanings and experiments provoked violent controversy and several of his operas had great success; [*Ossian ou*] *Les Bardes* won him the favour of Napoleon who made him director of the Tuileries Chapel, a position he retained under the Restoration . . .

I knew him, and have always retained an extremely pleasant memory of his personality and the character of his family and household: he gave the impression of a benevolent patriarch, and his wife and daughters treated him with biblical respect. Over a considerable period I used to accompany Berlioz to his house every other Sunday, and walk with him and his ladies to the Tuileries Chapel where his compositions and those of his colleague Cherubini were given turn and turn about. Of his works I remember little. They were well intentioned, but the invention was mediocre and the craftsmanship (as became clear to me later when I saw the scores) inadequate. He treated his art with religious seriousness and pronounced his opinions with solemn conviction, almost in the manner of an evangelical preacher. A certain naïvety had been left unaffected by age and experience, so that his idolization of the Emperor, to whom he owed his good fortune in life, went so far that not only would he not believe in his death, but even expected him to return from St Helena. For Berlioz he cherished the warmest feelings, which Berlioz reciprocated. How much or how little Berlioz learned from him I don't know enough to say, but at all events his experience with Lesueur can only have served to strengthen him in his utterly individual search for the greatest possible precision of musical expression, which for him outweighed all other considerations.

[Hiller 1880: 101–2]

> The interest of Lesueur had done wonders for Berlioz's self-confidence, but Hector's obstinacy in wasting his time on music rather than concentrating on his medical studies

did not make for good relations with his family, and his first visits back to La Côte-St-André were not always easy.

NANCI BERLIOZ, ELDER SISTER
(1806–50)

Hector is not at all talkative this evening. With him, everything is spontaneous; he is always quite transparent – never the slightest effort to regulate the vagaries of his humour. If he is gay, so much the better; if he is gloomy, it can't be helped: it's as if he weren't there; and whatever is being talked about, he takes no part. When I think at all seriously of his position, it saddens me.

[Journal, 22 June 1824, in Cairns i, 1999: 156]

> Even so, the old high spirits could not help breaking through; only twenty-four hours earlier the story had been very different.

Hector came back from dinner with M.Deplagne in a gay humour. After supper he described some very amusing comedies and farces he had seen. He gave a brilliant account of his adventure at Auxerre [on the coach route from Paris to Lyon], where they passed themselves off as actors arrived from Paris. We laughed till we ached – mama too: it did us good to see her.

[Journal, 21 June 1824, in ibid: 153–4]

> 'He is somewhat changed for the better,' wrote Nanci, 'his manners are a little more polite, and his conversation is quite witty.' Nevertheless, student life in Paris had added a touch of wildness – as well as a new hair style – to the schoolboy of earlier days.

[ANTOINE CHARBONNEL]

> Charbonnel, son of the grocer at La Côte, was also studying medicine in Paris where he was later to share rooms with Berlioz.

Memories of their life together have been preserved by the grand-son of this comrade of carefree days. Returning home one holiday, they decided to amuse themselves with a joke or two at the expense of the good people of La Côte. During the year, to conform with the fashion of 'Les Jeunes Frances', Berlioz had allowed his hair to grow – 'this monstrous, antediluvian mop', Heine [later] called it, 'towering above his forehead like a forest on a rugged cliff' – and Charbonnel disguised himself as best he could. Having made them-selves unrecognizable, they went off one evening to the fountain of Cuissein (which is still there in the Grande-Rue), placed three lighted candles on the parapet and set about serenading the residents. Berlioz played the guitar, Charbonnel sang troubadour songs, and the passers by gathered round, bewildered, wondering what it was all about – until the moment when the spell was broken by a sharp-eyed local who suddenly cried out: 'I can see who it is – it's that devil Charbouné!'

[Tiersot: 'Berlioziana' I, in *Ménestrel*, 3 January 1904: 4]

> Back in Paris, the university still offered him a world of alternative intellectual interests, and he avidly attended lectures at other faculties – among them those of François Andrieux, the brilliant and eccentric professor of literature at the Collège de France whose memories of the *ancien régime* reached back to the passionate debate surrounding Gluck and his rival Piccinni.

DANIEL BERNARD
(1842–83)

> Bernard, who knew Berlioz personally and later edited the first collection of his letters, was told the following story 'by an intimate friend, to whom Berlioz had recounted it often'; it also appears briefly in the *Memoirs*, though it is not clear whether the livelier details of the version given here should be attributed to Berlioz, Bernard or the intimate friend.

As Andrieux talked of literature, Hector became interested especially in this professor and conceived the idea of asking him for an opera libretto. The author of *Les Étourdis* was then sixty-four years old: 'Cher Monsieur', he wrote back, 'I don't go to the theatre any more; it wouldn't look good, at my age, to write love poems, and as for music, I oughtn't really to be thinking of anything much but a Requiem'. When he had finished the letter, Andrieux decided that he would take it personally to the address of his unknown correspondent. He climbed up several floors and stopped outside a little door, through the chinks of which came a smell of sizzling onions. He knocked. A young man opened it to him, thin, bony, with red dishevelled hair: it was Berlioz, in the middle of cooking a fricassée of rabbit for his student dinner. He had the saucepan in his hand.

'Ah! Monsieur Andrieux, what an honour! . . .You have caught me just as I was preparing . . . If only I had known!'

'That's all right, don't apologize. I'm sure your fricassée will be excellent, and I would have liked to share it with you – but my stomach isn't up to it. Go on, my friend, don't let your dinner burn because you're receiving a visit from an academician who has written a few fables.'

Andrieux sat down, and they began to chat about many things, above all music. At this period Berlioz was already a fierce and intolerant admirer of Gluck:

'Yes! yes!' said the old professor, nodding his head, 'I love Gluck, you know. I love him to distraction.'

'You love Gluck, Monsieur?' cried Berlioz, flinging himself at his visitor as if he was about to embrace him, and brandishing his saucepan with a total disregard of its contents.

'Yes, I love Gluck', repeated Andrieux, who hadn't noticed his companion's gesture and, leaning on his cane, seemed to be quietly pursuing an internal conversation of his own . . . 'I love Piccinni very much too'.

'Ah!' said Berlioz coldly, and put the saucepan back on the stove.

[Bernard 1879: 11–12]

> Nothing daunted by Andrieux's refusal, Berlioz still managed to complete his first attempt at an opera before the end of 1823, and immediately started on another – only to put it aside when he was asked by the local choirmaster to write a full-scale Mass for the church

of St-Roch. Though the first rehearsal was a disaster, the Mass was successfully performed on 10 July 1825 and the press greeted the début of the young composer with encouragement. Lesueur was genuinely enthusiastic, but the reaction at La Côte-Saint-André was less so.

NANCI BERLIOZ

You have no doubt read in the papers about the success of Hector's Mass: they have practically all mentioned it – in terms that would have turned his head if the plaudits of the artists and other experts hadn't done that more effectively already. The transports of joy into which he has been thrown by this triumph are beyond anything; he has had congratulations, compliments, praise, requests, of every kind, the astonishment of his audience has driven him out of his mind, some say he has *le diable au corps*, others that he made them tremble, lose their breath, that he will go far, etc., etc. The young people who were present at the performance and are now back here claim that no one has ever seen a Mass produce such an effect or create such a stir – in short they are as carried away as he is and are envious of his lot. As for us, mademoiselle, we are completely indifferent; my father is annoyed about it, maman hasn't dared to admit that she is gratified, and I – I am very pleased, but only for him, because I sincerely believe that this 11th July will be the best day of his life. There is no limit to the illusions to which he is subject: he has no doubt that my parents will be unable to resist such a début, but in this he is singularly mistaken for my father has never been less disposed in favour of his artistic ambitions; he looks at them with the eye of strict reason and says 'What of it?'.

[Draft letter to an unknown correspondent, July 1825, in CGB I, 99–100n]

> Among the audience at the Mass was the influential musicologist and critic, F.-J. Fétis, who noted that people 'came away shrugging their shoulders and saying that what they had heard was not music'. It was not long before he had the opportunity to meet the young composer in person.

FRANÇOIS-JOSEPH FÉTIS
(1784–1871)

I remember one day . . . when I was a member of the examining jury for admission to the composition classes at the Conservatoire. Among the students who brought samples of their work was a young man who appeared to be thoroughly bored by the proceedings. He showed me some ill-gotten muddle that he believed to be double counterpoint: it was nothing but a tissue of harmonic horrors. I made a few corrections and explained the reasons for them to the young man in question. His only reaction was to tell me that he held all studies in the greatest contempt, and that he refused to believe they could be of any value to a man of genius. This confession of faith was met with fury by the director of the Conservatoire [Cherubini] and by a number of my colleagues; for myself, I took a different line and said to the young man that a knowledge of musical technique was valuable only to those who knew how to use it, and who understood its purpose. Those who despised it would make no progress in studying it – it was useless to them. And so I advised the young detractor of counterpoint and fugue to give up the studies of which he thought so little and trust freely to his own genius, if he had any. He followed my advice, left the Conservatoire, and from that day set out on his role as a reformer of music. That young man was M. Berlioz.

[Fétis 1835]

> By the time this article was written, Berlioz had unwisely antagonized Fétis, whose memory of the incident was no doubt touched with malice. He was in any case totally wrong in saying that Berlioz 'left' the Conservatoire; he enrolled in 1826 and remained a Conservatoire student for four years, a period punctuated by annual attempts to win the coveted Prix de Rome which finally brought him success in 1830. He studied composition with Lesueur and counterpoint and fugue with Antoine Reicha, in whose class one of his fellow students was the violinist Eugène Sauzay.

EUGÈNE SAUZAY
(1809–1901)

In my little room in the Faubourg Montmartre I wrote fugues of all kinds – vocal, instrumental, for 4 voices and 5. In the winter, when I had no fire, I worked into the middle of the night wrapped in an old fur coat of my mother's . . . ([In 1827] I obtained the second prize for fugue, only missing the first prize as the result of an oversight for which M. Cherubini, who took an interest in me, gave me a sharp telling off; I had forgotten to put in the dots when I was copying out my fugue) . . .

Berlioz, the composer who is so much admired today, was a pupil in Reicha's class at the same time as me. I don't know why he forced himself to this type of study, which was so foreign to his temperament. As Cherubini said: 'It isn't he that doesn't like fugue, it's fugue that doesn't like him'.

[Sauzay 1974: 165–6, 170]

> But Hiller, who first met Berlioz while he was still attending Reicha's classes, realized that Reicha's teaching and influence went far beyond dry counterpoint.

FERDINAND HILLER

It was to the regime of Cherubini (with whom he unfortunately had a number of unpleasant clashes) that Berlioz owed the most clearly structured period of his musical apprenticeship, and particularly to the lessons of Reicha, the professor of counterpoint and fugue at the Paris Conservatoire. Reicha, who had been a friend of Beethoven's as a young man, was a skilful and accomplished, if not inspired, composer who liked, as they say, to bring his pupils on quickly. This is not always the wisest course; nevertheless, confronted with a young man of Berlioz's character and abilities, already in the full fever of production, there is no doubt that he was a highly suitable teacher: Berlioz could never have endured those elementary exercises which young students are usually required to wade through. But he submitted with unwonted perseverance to the discipline of an exhaustive study which corresponded to his own inclinations

and, by providing the practical experience to match his highly individual talent, turned out to be of the greatest value. Indeed for a
number of years he was constantly at the Opéra, where he followed
the performances score in hand and made a note every time he
observed some effect of solo or combined instrumentation . . .

But the masters whom Berlioz studied at this period with an
inexhaustible persistence, and to whom he remained bound by ties
of passionate admiration throughout his life, were three: Gluck,
Spontini and Beethoven – with the addition perhaps of C. M. von
Weber. Of these, it was the first whose operas he really knew by
heart, whose every note and word were constantly in his mind. For
a man who so longed to launch himself into the world of sound,
but who was not yet fully awakened to its possibilities, or had at
most been shaped by poetic and literary influences, the interweaving
of text and music which is Gluck's outstanding achievement offered
a quick route to an understanding of the nature of musical organisation. In Spontini's works he found the same method, but now
enriched by an orchestral texture as full as it was expressive – and
this in turn prepared him to a substantial extent for an apprecia-
tion of the Beethoven symphonies. It was only later that he got to
know the great composers through whom the rest of us were led to
an understanding of Beethoven, and then only superficially: absolute
music, of which they were the leading representatives, was something that, in his heart of hearts, always remained foreign to him,
no matter how much pleasure individual works might give him.

[Hiller 1880: 103–4]

> After Berlioz had finally decided to abandon medicine in
> 1824, financial support from his father became gradu-
> ally more fitful and reluctant, and the young composer
> was in constant need of cash to live on.

JOSEPH-LOUIS D'ORTIGUE
(1802–66)

> A year older than Berlioz and one of his closest friends,
> d'Ortigue was a prolific writer on music and a staunch
> promoter of Berlioz's works. Though he didn't settle in

Paris until 1829, he heard many stories of Berlioz's youth from the composer himself, and *Le Balcon de l'Opéra*, published only four years later, is one of the earliest sources of information about the young Berlioz that we have. The following story, for instance, though clearly originating with Berlioz himself, precedes the version in the *Memoirs* by some twenty-one years.

Berlioz was already struggling with misery and despair; a letter from his father had warned him that he could expect no more from that source, and that he must provide for his needs by his own efforts. So what does our musician do? He goes off to speak to the director of the *Théâtre des Nouveautés*, which was just then being built, and asks him for a place as flautist in the orchestra. 'The flute places are already filled', replies the director. 'All right then, take me on in the chorus'. 'Monsieur, the positions are all taken; there's no way I can employ you at the moment. Though there is just a possibility that we might need a chorus bass: if that would interest you, leave us your address'.

A few days later, Berlioz was asked to present himself at the offices of the *Nouveautés*. There was to be a competition for a position in the chorus. Berlioz turned up at the theatre. The jury were assembled: it was all very impressive. His rival competitors were a blacksmith, a weaver, an old singer from the *Panorama-Dramatique* and a cantor from Saint-Eustache. This last had had a bit of a problem with the gentlemen of his parochial church council. Nevertheless, in deserting the lectern for the boards, and dropping the surplice in favour of the uniform of a comic police constable or the rags of a beggar, he believed he was taking a step in the advancement of his career.

So, the candidates sang their pieces one after the other. It came to Berlioz's turn. 'Well, monsieur, and what have you brought?' 'Why, nothing,' he replied, 'have you no music here?' 'No, there's none.' 'What, not even a book of Italian exercises?' 'No, monsieur – and in any case, you don't sing at sight, I imagine?' 'I am sorry. I will sing anything you like at sight.' 'Ah, this is different . . . Then there must be some opera aria that you know?' 'Yes, monsieur. I know by heart the entire repertoire of the Opéra, *La Vestale, Cortès, Oedipe, Les Danaïdes*, the two *Iphigénies, Orphée, Armide . . .*' 'Stop! stop! Devil take it, what a memory! All right then, since you're so well informed, sing us the big aria from the third act of *Oedipe*, with the recitative.'

Berlioz sang the recitative and the aria, accompanied by a few random chords on a violin. The candidates were dismissed. The following day, Berlioz received a letter from the administration announcing officially that he had prevailed over the blacksmith, the weaver, the singer from the *Panorama-Dramatique*, even over the cantor from Saint-Eustache, and that he was admitted to the *Théâtre des Nouveautés* as a member of the chorus at a salary of 50 francs a month. So there was Berlioz, bellowing regularly to the oompahs of a vaudeville chorus every evening. One can only imagine what our chorister must have suffered, having to sing music in which, owing to the ignorance of the composer, the voice parts written in the C clef turned out in performance to be an octave below the basses! And this from a composer who enjoyed a certain reputation in the world of music!

[D'Ortigue 1833: 300–3]

FRANÇOIS-JOSEPH FÉTIS

Fétis visited the Théâtre des Nouveautés as music critic
at just about the time Berlioz began working there.

The performance [of the music] is very inadequate. The orchestra, being too small to give compositions like the overture to *Euryanthe* in an acceptable manner, makes little effect; the cellos and violins are especially weak. As a result the overture, which is in any case a poor piece, is painful to listen to. There are some talented players in the orchestra; but nothing can be done without the proper numbers. As for the actors, they sing in the most curious manner, not excepting Mme Albert, the Pasta of the place. This artist has warmth, and even a voice, but it does not begin to be correctly placed: the notes, without being exactly out of tune, are not in tune either . . . and she hasn't the least idea of vocalisation or of phrasing . . . It would be too unkind to speak of the singing of Caseneuve and Arnaud, and I shall keep silent on the subject. It seemed to me that Bouffé was opening his mouth during the ensembles, but I cannot be sure that this was for the purpose of singing. In short, the whole performance reminded me of certain small provincial theatres in which, for my sins, I have occasionally found myself. The house, however, is full of people applauding.

[Fétis II 1828: 326–7]

JOHN ELLA
(1802–88)

Ella, an English musician and writer, studied with Fétis in Paris as a young man and maintained a wide circle of acquaintance among foreign musicians.

[Berlioz] was first known to my informant* as a chorister in a minor theatre: his reserved manners made him unsocial and unpopular with his comrades; by the musicians of the band he was remarked as eccentric in appearance, always proficient in his duties, and yet anxious to elude particular notice. My informant from motives of curiosity sought the acquaintance of this recluse, and one day adjourned to a neighbouring *estaminet* to discuss divers matters on music and sip the beverage of a *'Demie tasse'*. The humble chorister produced from his pocket a bundle of MS scores of descriptive overtures and dramatic scenes, and amidst the fumes of tobacco, the rattling of billiards and dominoes, endeavoured by singing the *motivi* of the various movements to interest his companion; when he arrived at a particular passage, the sedate and sullen chorister, having waxed warm and earnest in his gesticulations, exclaimed *'Voila! le climax!'* and down went his fist, smashing all the crockery upon the table.

[Ella 1837: 210–11]

In May 1828, still only in his second year at the Conservatoire, Berlioz organized an orchestral concert entirely of his own works, among them the overture to his unfinished opera *Les Francs Juges*.

* Unknown.

FRANÇOIS-JOSEPH FÉTIS

Chance led me to the small concert hall of the Conservatoire while [the rehearsal] was taking place. What they were playing was, I believe, an overture. The members of the orchestra were bursting with laughter as they played; every time a passage was repeated another instrument would be missing because people kept slipping out; in the end it was no longer possible to understand the composer's intentions, and the rehearsal ground to a halt. What I had just heard was horrible, and I realised that M.Berlioz was ignorant of certain basic elements of musical grammar, let alone composition. Yet there were flashes of really quite piquant orchestral effects which persuaded me that there must be something in the head that had imagined them, and I felt I should wait before making any definite judgment.

[Fétis 1835]

> By 1835, hindsight had probably coloured Fétis's memory, but at the concert itself his comments were as yet unclouded by future enmities.

FRANÇOIS-JOSEPH FÉTIS

M. Berlioz has the happiest of dispositions. He has ability; he has genius. His style is nervous and energetic. His ideas often have charm, but more often the composer, swept along by the fire of his youthful imagination, exhausts his creative power in combinations that are original and passionate in effect.

There are plenty of good things in all this; there are also some bad ones. Often M. Berlioz's originality verges on the bizarre; often his instrumentation is confused; his melodies can sometimes be arid; he is prodigal with imposing musical effects, and his exaggeration in this respect lead him to overshoot the mark – when the same means, more effectively managed, would have enabled him to achieve it with ease. His pieces are almost all too long; the overture to the *Francs Juges* would have had twice the effect if it had been half the length.

M. Berlioz is a pupil of M. Lesueur; the advice and above all the example of his master will no doubt succeed in convincing this young composer that simplicity of style and the good ordering of ideas in no way exclude the vigour and vivacity in which he takes such pleasure.

[Fétis III 1828: 423]

> Fétis was influential and, thus far at least, his attitude encouraging. Nevertheless Berlioz was fast becoming a *bête noire* to the musical establishment and it was only by the skin of his teeth that he achieved second prize in the Prix de Rome contest a couple of months later.

4 SHAKESPEARE, BEETHOVEN AND HARRIET SMITHSON

After Gluck, the two great inspirations of Berlioz's career were to be Shakespeare and Beethoven. The revelation of Shakespeare, and with it his first sight of the woman who was eventually to become his wife, burst upon the composer in September 1827.

In France in the 1820s, Shakespeare still suffered from the anathema hurled upon him by Voltaire half a century earlier; by comparison with the classical standards set by Racine and Corneille, he was seen as uncouth and barbaric, and in the years after Waterloo unpatriotic as well – even 'un aide-de-camp de Wellington' for the crustier xenophobes. But for the young enthusiasts of the new Romantic movement – Lamartine, De Vigny, Hugo, Delacroix – Shakespeare was the great unrecognized genius, as yet only known through printed translations but already a potent symbol of change. Among the youngest was the twenty-five-year-old Alexandre Dumas, later the author of *Les Trois Mousquetaires* and the most popular dramatist of his day.

ALEXANDRE DUMAS
(1802–70)

About 1822 or 1823, I think it was,* an English company had tried to give some performances at the Théâtre de la Porte-Saint-Martin, but they had been greeted with such yells and boos, and bombarded from the pit with such a profusion of apples and oranges, that the unfortunate artists had been obliged to withdraw from the field of battle plastered with missiles . . . In 1822 it was thought discreditable for a theatre which normally staged, I don't say Corneille and

* Actually 1822.

Molière, but at least MM. Caignez and Pixérécourt, to allow performing space to a barbarian like Shakspeare, and to the succession
of unsavoury works that he would bring in his wake.

Only five years later it was announced that [another] English
company was coming to present the masterpieces of Shakspeare at
the second Théâtre-Français, and the news was greeted everywhere
with the greatest interest. Five years had been enough to produce
this enlightened change of attitude, so swiftly did ideas mature in
the burning sun of the nineteenth century . . .

Indeed, utter contempt for English literature had now changed
into enthusiastic admiration. M. Guizot, who didn't know a word
of English at this period, had re-translated Shakspeare with the help
of Letourneur. Walter Scott, [Fennimore] Cooper and Byron were
in everyone's hands. M. Lemercier created a [French] tragedy out
of *Richard III*, M. Liadière another out of *Jane Shore*. They gave
Le Château de Kenilworth at the Porte-Saint-Martin . . . Decidedly,
the wind was blowing from the west and announcing the literary
revolution . . .

[Dumas 1867: 277-8]

ARMAND FERRARD DE PONTMARTIN
(1811-90)

Pontmartin, later to become an indefatigable com-
mentator on Parisian theatrical life, was at this stage a
student of only sixteen – which perhaps explains why,
sixty odd years later, his memory confused the opening
nights of *Romeo and Juliet* (at which he was present)
and *Hamlet* (at which he appears to have been an
onlooker outside the theatre). In any case, it was
Hamlet, with Charles Kemble in the title role and the
young Irish actress Harriet Smithson as Ophelia, that
opened the season on 11 September.

The devout battalion of the *claqueurs de Shakespeare*, the same
crowd who three years later would provide the claque for *Hernani*,
had arranged to assemble in the Place d'Odéon, at the Café
Voltaire, where the lady behind the bar, the legendary Madame

Irma, in the full flower of her mature beauty, encouraged the timid glances of the first year students with a smile more maternal than virginal. As a humble student of rhetoric at Saint-Louis . . . I was of course among the least of that company; its leaders included several names that were not long in becoming famous: Victor Hugo, Alfred de Vigny, Alphonse Karr, Delacroix, Alfred de Musset [*though Pontmartin was wrong about him – he was in Le Mans at the time*], the brothers Devéria, the two Johannot, Emile Deschamps, Sainte-Beuve, Chenavard, Barye, Préault, Paul Huet, Louis Boulanger, Théophile Gautier, Philarète Chasles – without mentioning those who were awaiting their moment, missed it when it came, and have since fallen back into oblivion.

It was seven o'clock, the curtain was due to go up at eight. People were chatting, shouting, discussing the possibilities of a good or bad performance: on the one hand were the philistines, the fogeys, the bourgeois, the subscribers to the *Constitutionnel*, the fuddy-duddies, the stick-in-the-muds – exploiting perhaps some old remnant of nationalist rancour; on the other Shakespeare . . . and his principal interpreters, to whom wonders were already being ascribed.

[Pontmartin 1881: 268–9]

ALEXANDRE DUMAS

I left the office at four o'clock and went to take my place in the queue . . . I knew my *Hamlet* so well that I had no need to buy the libretto; I could follow the actors, translating the words progressively as they spoke them.

I confess that the impression I received far surpassed my expectations: Kemble was marvellous in the role of Hamlet, Miss Smithson adorable in that of Ophelia. The scene on the ramparts, the scene with the fan,* the scene of the arras, the mad scene, the graveyard scene – all these bowled me over. It was only from this moment that I really began to understand the theatre, and how it was possible, out of that jumble of things past which the shock I

---

* The Mousetrap scene, in which Kemble used Ophelia's fan to point the effect of the play on Claudius and Gertrude.

had received threw up in my mind, to create a world. 'And over this chaos' says the Bible 'moved the spirit of God'. It was the first time that I saw real passions in the theatre, passions that animated men and women, of flesh and blood . . .

[Dumas 1867: 280]

Imagine a man, born blind, receiving the gift of sight and suddenly discovering an entire world of which he had had no conception; imagine Adam waking up after the Creation and finding beneath his feet the spangled earth, above his head the blazing sky, around him trees hung with golden fruit, in the distance a broad and beautiful silver river, by his side a young girl, naked and pure – and you will have some idea of the enchanted Eden upon which, for me, this performance opened the door. Oh! – this, then, is what it was that I was searching for, this that I had lacked, this that had to come; it was actors like this who forgot that they were actors, this artificial life transformed into real life by the sheer power of art, this truth of speech and gesture which turned the performers into creatures of God with all their virtues, passions and weaknesses, instead of stiff, impassive heroes spouting sententious declamations. Oh Shakspeare, my thanks! Oh Kemble, Oh Smithson! . . .

[Dumas 1863: 14–15]

EUGÈNE DELACROIX
(1798–1863)

The English . . . are working wonders, filling the Odéon with crowds that make the paving stones of the whole quarter tremble under the wheels of their carriages. They are the rage: the most stubborn of the classicists have thrown up the sponge, and our actors have gone back to school and watch wide-eyed. The consequences of this enterprise are incalculable.

[Letter to Soulier, 28 September 1827, in Delacroix 1935: 197]

It's a total invasion! Hamlet flourishes his hideous skull; Othello whets the overtly lethal dagger that threatens the end of all dramatic law and order. Who knows what will come next? King Lear will be plucking his eyes out in front of a French audience. It would become the dignity of the Académie to declare all such foreign importations incompatible with public decency. Farewell, good taste!

In any case get yourself a good solid breastplate to wear under your clothes, and beware the *poignards* of the classical set . . .

[Letter to Victor Hugo, September 1827, in ibid: 198]

> For Berlioz, Shakespeare and Harriet Smithson formed a *double coup de foudre*. 'As I came out of *Hamlet*, shaken to the depths by the experience,' he writes in the *Memoirs*, 'I vowed not to expose myself a second time to the flame of Shakespeare's genius.' But next day the playbills announced *Romeo and Juliet* and, unable to resist, he bought himself a ticket. This was the performance which the young Pontmartin actually attended.

ARMAND FERRARD DE PONTMARTIN

One would need a quill from the wing of a dove to write of the ideal beauty, the passionate chastity, the virginal – I was about to say seraphic – grace of Miss Smithson. It was a vision, a dream of Thomas Moore, a moment of magic. She would have melted the heart of a ship's hand from Trafalgar, of a veteran from the Grande Armée in the enchanting balcony scene –

Wilt thou be gone? it is not yet near day! . . .

The friend who had been sent as my companion nudged me and said in a low voice: 'Look!' On our right, in the same row of the pit, I saw a young man whose appearance, once seen for three minutes, was unforgettable. His thick shock of light auburn hair was tossed back and hung over the collar of his appropriately threadbare coat. His magnificent marmorean, almost luminous, forehead, a nose one might have supposed carved by Phidias' chisel, his fine and slender curved lips, his slightly, but not too, convex chin, his whole delicacy of mien which seemed to spell the ascetic or the poet, created an ensemble which would have been a sculptor's delight or despair. His was the ideal profile for a medallion or a cameo. But all these details vanished at the sight of those wide eyes, a pale but intense grey, fixed upon Juliet with that expression of ecstasy which the pre-Renaissance painters gave to their saints and angels. Body and soul alike were wholly absorbed in this gaze.

[Pontmartin 1880: 101–2]

JOSEPH D'ORTIGUE

It is difficult to be sure what love really means to a soul like Berlioz's. He was himself unaware that there is a period in life when love blossoms with such a degree of intensity that it expunges even the memory of those vain, ephemeral passions that one had imagined one was feeling until then. It was a lesson he was destined to learn from a celebrated Irish woman. The English theatre had brought to Paris the wonders of Shakespeare, and an actress who had been little regarded in England attempted the role of Ophelia in *Hamlet*. She was justly admired, Berlioz saw her – and from that moment a sudden passion, inexplicable in its cause or its effects, terrifying in its violence and tenacity, seized hold of his heart . . . But all the efforts he made to be loved in return, or, if that wasn't possible, at least to be understood, were futile, and he sank into profound listlessness and a pitiable state of depression. He wrote no more music, and couldn't even listen to any, for in this state of nervous, tattered exaltation the works he admired most only brought him intolerable suffering . . .

On the days when the English were not performing, Berlioz could only quiver in anticipation as he dreamed of seeing Miss [Smithson] again on the following day. Yet it was a moment he dreaded as one dreads the onset of a fit or convulsion. It was at those times that you could see him in a corner of the pit at the Odéon, ashen, dishevelled, distraught, his beard unshaven and his long hair unkempt, as he watched in gloomy silence some comedy or other of Picard which occasionally drew from him a hideous burst of laughter, like the kind of painful, involuntary muscular spasms induced by a dig in the ribs. For some of the artistic confraternity he was an object of pity, for others of mirth. The wits called him *le Père la Joie*.

'Oh, unhappy woman!' he would call out among his friends, even in the street, 'If she could only understand the meaning of a love like mine she would fling herself into my arms, no matter if she were to die, consumed by my embrace!'

[D'Ortigue 1833: 304–6]

> Although Berlioz insists in the *Memoirs* that he never dared go back to the English company after those two first experiences, it seems unlikely that he was able to absent himself entirely during the whole of the eleven months that they remained in Paris, and in any case he is known to have haunted the purlieus of the Odéon, even if he didn't go inside, in the hopes of catching a glimpse of Harriet.
>
> And Harriet, meanwhile, was being subjected to a change of fortune for which her previous experience in England had done little to prepare her.

FERDINAND HILLER

Miss Harriet Smithson . . . had achieved no very great success in England where her Irish accent had stood in her way. It was quite otherwise in Paris, where she had before her in the pit people who for the most part couldn't understand a word of English and followed the performance with a French textbook. The rich profusion of the action in Shakespeare's tragedies, which could almost be performed as pantomime, did the rest . . .

[Hiller 1880: 71]

> Her reception appears to have come as something of a surprise to her professional colleagues as well.

FANNY KEMBLE
(1809–1903)

All the most eminent members of the profession – Kean, young Macready, and my father – went over in turn to exhibit to the

Parisian public Shakespeare the Barbarian illustrated by his barbarian fellow-countrymen. I do not remember hearing of any very
eminent actress joining in that worthy enterprise; but Miss Smithson, a young lady with a figure and face of Hibernian beauty, whose
superfluous native accent was no drawback to her merits in the
esteem of her French audience, represented to them the heroines of
the English tragic drama; the incidents of which, infinitely more
startling than anything they were used to, invested their fair victim
with an amazing power over her foreign critics, and she received
from them, in consequence, a rather disproportionate share of
admiration – due, perhaps, more to the astonishing circumstances
in which she appeared before them, than to the excellence of her
acting under them.

[Kemble 1879: i, 188]

> Catty overtones of professional (or perhaps filial?) jeal-
> ousy do not alter the fact that when Harriet arrived in
> Paris she was still a relatively unsophisticated young
> woman – even if the vogue for *'La belle irlandaise'* was
> soon to effect a remarkable change.

[JOURNALIST]

A lady writes of her:

Her personal appearance had been so much improved by the
judicious selection of a first-rate *modiste* and a fashionable
corsetière, that she was soon converted into one of the most
splendid women in Paris, with an air *distingué* that com-
manded the admiration and the tears of thousands . . . I had
remembered her in Ireland and in England, but, as I now
looked at her, it struck me that not one of Ovid's fabled meta-
morphoses exceeded Miss Smithson's real Parisian one.

[Cook 1879: 744]

FERDINAND HILLER

It was a few months after I arrived in Paris, in the autumn of 1828, that I met Berlioz for the first time. The summer before, he had attracted attention with a concert in which he included several of his own compositions – and soon afterwards he had been awarded the second prize by the Institut de France. He was eight years older than I was, and had spent the last six years in the French capital where he had learned the meaning of the struggle for existence. Compared with me, at least, he was a man matured by sad experience, even if his youthful spirit still retained the southern vivacity that never entirely left him. I felt myself very strongly attracted to this overflowing personality. What I had to offer in return was of a musical kind. Only a short time before, Berlioz had discovered Beethoven, getting to know him through the symphonies which had been launched on the Parisian musical world by Habeneck at the so-called Concerts of the Conservatoire. His enthusiasm knew no bounds. We went into ecstasies together, and I had the privilege of introducing him to the sonatas of the master and the joy of watching the delight that he took in them. Our meetings became more and more frequent, and the sympathy I felt for him grew daily as he told me about his childhood in his parents' home and his years as a student . . .

. . . Not only did he know what it meant to count every penny in order to keep himself alive: he even went so far as to work, secretly and for quite some time, as a member of the chorus in a vaudeville theatre – not without a certain nervousness that he might be occasionally recognized by a friend. This was over by the time I got to know him, but he was still providing for himself by giving guitar lessons and reading proofs for publishers. I can see him before me still, in a café in the rue Richelieu (where, in that human Parisian way, he was allowed to occupy a table for half a day), correcting the proofs of Halévy's first operatic success, *The Dilettante from Avignon*. None of this bothered him particularly, though it bored him. Now and then, there would be additions to his income, as for instance when he sold the gold medal he got for winning second prize at the Institut. It fetched 200 francs.

The change that had taken place in Berlioz during the years he had lived in Paris can hardly be grasped. Not least, the change with regard to his musical talent. Out of the naïve flautist–guitarist who had attempted to compile a kind of potpourri based on assorted Italian airs had come the composer [already meditating] the *Symphonie fantastique*, out of the solitary student of the *école de médecine* a forceful young man who felt absolutely no need to prostrate himself before the eminent musical personalities of the day. But above all, the metamorphosis that his whole world of thought and feeling had undergone! In his relations with me he was something of a Mephistopheles (by which I don't at all mean that I see myself in the rôle of Faust – rather that of the poor student). All trace of his Catholic upbringing had vanished; he was haunted by doubts of every kind, and his contempt for everything that he labelled prejudice verged on the monstrous. We often met late in the evening in a café and stayed over a cup of tea till well after midnight. The things I heard then! So far as my religious beliefs were concerned, I had been brought up as a pure deist; and my artistic principles, one might say, were deistic. But Berlioz believed neither in God nor in Bach, neither in absolute beauty in art nor in pure virtue in life. Over Shakespeare, Goethe and Beethoven we raised a common hymn of praise; I followed his accounts of his experiences in a state of sympathetic suspense. But when he gave his tongue free rein, destroying everything in his path like a river in spate, sometimes a kind of fear seized my heart. 'I would like to trample on every prejudice,' he exclaimed one evening. 'If it came to it, I should be ready to marry the bastard daughter of a negress and an executioner' . . .

Yet at this period Berlioz was in the grip of an intense passion – a great, overwhelming love – which was to have a fatal influence on his whole life. To my mind there was never any doubt that his imagination was much more involved in this affair than his heart – though as regards what happened then and later, that makes little difference . . . Though Berlioz fell deeply in love [with Harriet Smithson] he never managed to approach her personally – all attempts to do so proved useless. The letters he wrote to her alarmed her – though she only knew them in translation, for she understood as few words of French as her impetuous admirer did of English. In any case Berlioz gave himself up to his passion with all the fervour of poetic rapture and, following the dictates of his nature, which made it impossible for him to bear anything in his heart without giving it expression, would fill the unresponsive boulevards and neighbouring streets on our walks together with wailings of love. His friends needed all their sympathy to enable them to listen with patience and conceal their weariness. We were given the lot – the descriptions of sleepless nights, the nervous attacks that dissolved into tears, the endless wanderings in Paris and around it, the momentary gleams of hope, the despairing renunciations. 'If it had been anyone else', said Girard, the eminent conductor and a sceptical man of the world, 'if it had been anyone else, I should have sent him packing.'

[Hiller 1880: 65–6, 69–70, 71–2]

5 SYMPHONIE FANTASTIQUE

Shakespeare and Beethoven were soon to be joined by
Goethe in Berlioz's personal pantheon. In 1828 the first
part of *Faust* came out in a new translation by Gérard
de Nerval, and that summer it was scarcely ever out of
Berlioz's hands; unable to resist the musical temptations
it offered, he published *Huit scènes de Faust* as his Opus
1 in the following year and, encouraged by Hiller, had
the temerity to send a copy to Goethe himself. Being no
musician, Goethe passed it on to Zelter, Mendelssohn's
teacher and Goethe's adviser in all musical matters.

FRIEDRICH ZELTER
(1758–1832)

There are some people who can only make their presence felt and
call attention to their activities by means of noisy puffing, cough-
ing, croaking, and spitting. One such appears to be Herr Hector
Berlioz. The smell of sulphur surrounding Mephistopheles attracts
him, so he must needs sneeze and snort till all the instruments of
the orchestra leap around in a perfect frenzy – only not a hair stirs
on Faust's head. Thank you for sending me the music all the
same. I shall certainly find an opportunity when I am teaching to
make use of this poisonous abscess, this abortion born of horrible
incest.

[Letter to Goethe, 21 June 1829 in Zelter 1918: 169–70]

> Whether or not Berlioz knew of Zelter's outburst, he
> was conscious of having taken a big step forward and
> felt encouraged to think about his next project – though
> this had probably been taking shape in his mind for
> some months already. In March 1829 Harriet Smithson

had left Paris without ever meeting her passionate admirer and the torments suffered by the young composer provided a catalyst to the turmoil stirred up by Shakespeare, Goethe, Beethoven and Harriet herself; it was upon a dream-like programme of which she was herself the protagonist that Berlioz was now to construct his first masterpiece and still his best-known work.

In real life, however, his memories of Harriet could do little to protect him from the more tangible charms with which he was surrounded. Hiller, in describing what happened next, rather touchingly attributes his own role to a fictional character, and keeps his own name out of a story which, it must be admitted, doesn't say much for Berlioz as a friend.

FERDINAND HILLER

A young German musician had been most amiably received by a charming French colleague, and the two young people made music under the eye of Frau Mama – so frequently and with such enjoyment that the desire soon arose to see one another without Frau Mama and without the piano. Nothing was easier to contrive. The young pianist was not only beautiful and obliging, but possessed an exceptional talent and was one of the most sought after of teachers; together with an indulgent chaperon, who was really more of a companion than a guardian, she went off into the remotest quarters of the city where she gave piano lessons to society ladies and young boarding-school pupils. The couple therefore met as far away from her house as possible, and did not hurry on the way home. Through me, my young compatriot had also got to know Berlioz, who was giving guitar lessons in one of the boarding-schools at which the young lady was acting as piano teacher. He was naïve enough to make Berlioz his confidant in the affair and to have recourse to his services as a *postillon d'amour*; his innocence turned out to be a piece of good luck, in that it led to his own disenchantment.

The capricious young pianist, who had heard of the grand Shakespearean passion of this messenger of love, thought it would be highly amusing to entice it away in her direction. One fine day she told him point blank that she loved him, and Berlioz at once laid on a grand seduction. Even this might have been excusable had he not at the same time taken it into his head to accompany the audacious young woman home as her lover. This was too much for Frau Mama. The daughter was henceforth chaperoned with the greatest severity – though for all that the tempestuous aspirant could not entirely be denied entry to the house.

[Hiller 1880: 76–7]

> Camille Moke was certainly a brilliant pianist (and was widely recognized as such under her later name of Marie Pleyel). The scandals in which she was involved in later life suggest that, as things turned out, both Berlioz and Hiller had a lucky escape, but at the time she clearly saw the romantic young composer as a good catch; she exerted all her considerable charms, threw in some dubious gossip about Harriet for good measure, and may even have fallen in love herself. In any case, Berlioz fell completely under her spell.
>
> Meanwhile, the *Symphonie fantastique* was rapidly approaching completion. Though some of the original ideas certainly go back further, the actual score seems to have been written down in a couple of months or less. Even so, the first performance, scheduled for 30 May, 1830, had to be postponed. Rosanne Goletty was a friend of Berlioz's sister, Nanci.

ROSANNE GOLETTY

I've left it to the end of my letter to tell you that I had the pleasure of seeing your brother, but I assure you it was a very real pleasure. I didn't dare hope for it, as it was just the time when he was arranging his concert . . . He turned up, large as life, with handsome side whiskers – I didn't recognise him, it wasn't the same person I last saw three or four years ago. He's a man now, and a man who is making his mark. I was talking the other day to my compatriot – she too is a great musician – and she said that he is singled out among the young men; when people see him pass they say, '*That's the man*'. In fact, though his concert couldn't take place, from a combination of circumstances that it was easy to foresee, the opinion is that he's made a very good start and will win a big reputation.

[Letter to Nanci Berlioz, 1 June 1830 in Cairns i, 1999: 370–1]

NANCI BERLIOZ

I am grateful for the way you write about my brother; you know from your own experience how much we welcome opinions about those close to us. I find it very funny that you should be so surprised by his side whiskers, and at finding him so much a man: he could hardly have still been the beardless youth you knew when you were here. Time and circumstances combine to make young people grow up, and I should think it was more than time to show what one is by the age of twenty-six! As for his talent and the career he has set himself, a little celebrity is all it amounts to – nothing to suggest that he is going to achieve anything more positive in the near future.

[Letter to Rosanne Goletty, 7 June 1830, MS]

> Nevertheless, the good start was confirmed later that summer when Berlioz, at the fourth attempt (and largely because he ditched his pride and wrote down to the musical level of the judges), achieved first prize in the Prix de Rome with a cantata on the death of Sardanapalus. Abraham Mendelssohn, Felix's father, was in Paris at the time.

ABRAHAM MENDELSSOHN
(1776–1835)

The day before yesterday [Hiller] introduced Hector Berlioz to me, the author or composer of 'Faust', who appeared to me agreeable and interesting, and a great deal more sensible than his music . . . Berlioz has lately obtained the *grand prix de composition*, and for five years will enjoy a scholarship of 3,000 francs for a sojourn in Italy. He does not, however, wish to go there, but intends to apply for permission to remain here . . . In all classes and trades here young peoples' brains are in a state of fermentation: they smell regeneration, liberty, novelty, and want to have their share of it. I confess that I have not yet come to a clear idea about the possible result of it all.

[Letter to his wife, 27 August 1830 in Hensel 1881: i, 257]

> But at the official performance of the prize cantata, Berlioz was bitterly disappointed when the 'conflagration' which he had added to liven up the end of the piece was bungled by the orchestra.

[JOURNALIST'S REVIEW]

It seems that the orchestra, usually so obedient to M. Grasset's bow,* was on this occasion lacking in precision and ensemble, for we saw M. Berlioz, with all the fury of an artist, fling to the ground the score he had been holding in his hand. He appeared to be overcome with violent anger, and was only with difficulty persuaded to go forward and receive the laurel crown that was his due.

[Journal du Commerce, 31 October 1830]

> The cantata had another airing (this time successful) on 5 December, when Berlioz's own much-postponed concert finally took place under the direction of François-Antoine Habeneck, the influential conductor of the Conservatoire concerts. The first version of the *Symphonie fantastique* was received with enthusiasm by a capacity audience that included figures like Meyerbeer, Spontini and Fétis, as well as Berlioz's entourage of young artists and supporters – among them the nineteen-year-old Liszt, to whom he had been introduced on the day before the concert. The author of the following article is unknown.

* Grasset, a violinist, still conducted in the old style with his bow.

[JOURNALIST'S REVIEW]

He is a slender, frail-looking young man, with long fair hair whose unruly disorder somehow carries with it a suggestion of genius. The lines on his bony face are strongly marked, and under a broad forehead the great cavernous eyes flash with light. The knot of his cravat seems to have been tightened in anger; his clothes are only elegant because his tailor made them that way, and his boots are spattered with mud because the impetuosity of his character won't tolerate the inaction of being transported in a carriage, because it is absolutely necessary that the activity of his body complements the activity of his head. He darts to and fro among the hundred musicians who fill the stage of the Conservatoire, and even though these fine artists of the Société des Concerts make up what is perhaps the most admirable orchestra that has ever been heard, he begs, he growls, he supplicates, he communicates his excitement to each one in turn. This man – this is Berlioz, this is the young composer who, in spite of his talent, has just carried off a prize at the Institut. And when the audience bursts out clapping, he makes no attempt to come politely forward, to curve his spinal column and let his arms dangle in servile humility before the public in the stalls: he simply stops wherever he happens to be, nods his head to acknowledge the applause which fills the hall, and then turns back to continue his comments to Launer [the violinist] or [the flautist] Tulou. This is what we saw at the concert which the young composer gave for the benefit of those wounded in the revolution in July.

At two o'clock precisely, Habeneck, the leader of this wonderful troupe – in which there is not a soldier who has not himself been a commander at some time or other, or who is not worthy to be a leader – Habeneck tapped his music desk with the point of his bow, and immediately the most profound silence fell upon the hall – where only moments earlier a swarm of brilliantly attired young ladies had been chatting noisily back and forth.

The overture to the *Francs-juges*, which opened the concert, is a grand symphony more remarkable for its strangeness and the power of its conception than for any particular elegance of expression. Its forms are gigantic, and I don't believe that even the trumpets of the last judgement will produce an effect more incisive than the one produced here by those thunderous trombones; nevertheless this kind of instrumentation, beautiful and striking though it is, is perhaps a little too melodramatic in character. After the overture, which was performed with the verve and perfection that is to be found only at the *société des concerts*, came the scenes from *Sardanapale*, and if the audience were not entirely convinced by the vocal sections that precede the finale, if they were justified there in reproaching the composer with a certain feebleness (no doubt because they expected so much better from him), at least the conflagration which destroyed the palace of the royal voluptuary was greeted with enthusiastic applause; you could see the flames leaping up, setting fire to the beams of the roof and howling under its long vaults, and literally hear the whole edifice come crashing down amid terrifying pandemonium . . .

But it is time to speak of the fantastic symphony entitled *Episode in the life of an artist.*

The author has described the subject of this curious composition in a programme. To begin with he imagines that a young musician, afflicted by the malady of passionate longing (1830s style), falls desperately in love and that, by some curious phenomenon, the image of the woman he loves is invariably accompanied in his mind by a musical idea, which recurrs to him again and again in whatever situation he finds himself. In the second part, he watches her admiringly at a ball, in all the tumult of the fête, and is torn alternatively by feelings of love and jealousy. In the third, a country scene brings an unaccustomed tranquillity, a warmer glow, to his imagination, and the musical idea, cleverly introduced into this concept as a reminder for the listener, sounds here more sweetly and more tenderly than ever. In the fourth, he has become convinced that his beloved is unworthy of his love; he poisons himself with opium, but the dose is not strong enough and only induces sleep accompanied by the most horrible visions. He dreams that he has assassinated his mistress, that he has been condemned to death and that he is present at his own execution. In the fifth part the dream continues: he is transported to a witches' sabbath, to the middle of a crowd of hideous shades, hags and monsters; they scream, they sing, they cackle, they grind their teeth, and the musical idea returns again – but now debased and vulgarized, transformed into a trivial, grotesque, ignoble jig. (This is a sublime idea). In the end this horrifying scene is brought to a close with a witches' round-dance, where all the misshapen creatures cavort to a parody of the *Dies irae*.

Such a conception is certainly crazy in the extreme, but all the same it is dramatic and filled with poetry. And it has to be said that the composer is bold enough not to shrink from the immense difficulties of carrying it out.

M. Berlioz's talent is preeminently dark and fantastic; he seems to aim at ferocity. His ideas are always in some way charged with anger, and he only really excels in painting violent emotions, lacerations of the soul and convulsions of nature. He hasn't been able to find happy expression for the dreams and gentle passions of the first three movements, and although his orchestra is always deployed with rare ability, the instrumentation is generally confused, devoid of meaning and insufficiently thought out. But how brilliantly he recovers in the last two parts!

How intensely everyone reacted to the impact of this solemn, funereal march, over which could be heard from far away, with a wonderful sense of aptness, the feeble memory of the musical idea! How everyone shuddered with horror at the execution, depicted in images so beautiful and so terrifying in their truthfulness that they drew, even in the middle of the performance itself, a thunder of applause that could not be repressed. How everyone smiled at the laughter of the monsters in the witches' sabbath, and how they all looked at one another in astonishment as they listened to this music that seemed so genuinely infernal, these cries, these moans, these outbursts of laughter and explosions of rage! There is a quality of despair in this extraordinary talent. There is something of Salvator Rosa, of Hoffmann, but it's darker still. I accept that this symphony is of an almost inconceivable strangeness, and that the schoolmasters will no doubt pronounce an anathema on these profanations of the 'truly beautiful'. But for anyone who isn't too concerned about the rules I believe that M. Berlioz, if he carries on in the way he has begun, will one day be worthy to take his place beside Beethoven.

[*Le Temps*, 26 December 1830]

6 ROME

It was a condition of the Prix de Rome that successful candidates were required to spend two years at the Villa Medici in Rome with other prize-winning students and send back sample compositions for approval by the Institut in Paris. Berlioz moved heaven and earth to get this condition waived: his reluctance to submit to exile at a time when his personal career seemed teeming with possibilities was made all the stronger by the fact that he had by this time become officially engaged to Camille Moke.

FERDINAND HILLER

[When] Berlioz won the Prix de Rome, Frau Martha (which was not her name) now had the game in her hands. She agreed to meet him half-way and allow a betrothal to take place and a ring to be exchanged – but she knew perfectly well that the new fiancé would shortly be obliged to absent himself across the Alps, and that these latest inclinations of her daughter's would be no more permanent than previous, or future, ones . . .

Hardly had Berlioz left [for Rome] when rumours began to circulate in our intimate musical circle about another suitor for his betrothed – an older but wealthy and distinguished man, such as a mother could only want for her daughter and the daughter could only want for good reasons of her own. I was in a position to see with my own eyes just how much or how little she minded the absence of her lover. From La Côte-Saint-André he wrote me impassioned letters describing the joy of his family, the pains of separation, his own anxieties – and when I ventured, with the best of intentions, to tell him that I suspected these loving preoccupations might not be equally shared on both sides, he thoroughly put me down. Every recollection of the frivolous manner in which the bond between them – and what a bond! – had been sealed seemed to have been completely blotted out. If his beloved had been a veritable Iphigenia he could have expressed himself in no other way.

[Hiller 1880: 77–8]

> Many years later, Hiller contributed a last, characteristically matter-of-fact postscript to the whole affair.

FERDINAND HILLER

Though it is not much in evidence in my letters to Berlioz, I was filled with a certain idealism, and thought it right to remain on friendly terms with the fiancé of the girl I had believed myself in love with. As for revenge, it was in any case useless to consider it – I am convinced (without actually knowing it) that the marriage with Pleyel had already been agreed by the time Berlioz left for Rome – and I only warned him of what everybody else was saying. Madame Moke certainly went 'Ouf!' when she knew that her putative son-in-law was out of France and I don't believe that her daughter shed any tears.

[Letter to Edmond Hippeau, 10 June 1882, in Tiersot 1936: 204]

> The publisher Camille Pleyel was obviously a good catch from Mme Moke's point of view – but Berlioz was deaf to Hiller's warnings. His efforts to get the conditions of the Prix de Rome waived having proved fruitless, he arrived in Rome in March 1831 – deeply miserable at the lack of letters from Camille and already considering returning to Paris. Next day he was introduced to Mendelssohn by a fellow student at the Villa Medici.

FELIX MENDELSSOHN
(1809–47)

[Berlioz] makes me really sad, because he is actually a cultured, agreeable man and yet composes so incredibly badly.

He is going back to Paris the day after tomorrow. He seems to be terribly in love, and has made this the basis for a symphony which he calls *Épisode de la vie d'un artiste*. When it was performed, he had 2000 copies of an explanatory note printed: in this he says that, in the first movement, the composer has imagined the main theme as representing a charming young lady who has captivated the artist, and depicts his rage, jealousy, tenderness and tears; the second movement describes a ball where everything seems empty to him because she is not there; the third is called *Scène aux champs* – the cowherds play a *ranz des vaches*, the instruments imitate the rustle of the leaves (all this is in the programme), fear and hope struggle with each other in the artist's soul. Between the third and fourth movements (so continues the programme), the artist poisons himself with opium but misjudges the quantity and, instead of dying, has the most horrible visions; the fourth movement is one of these, in which he is present at his own execution – it is called *Marche au supplice*. The fifth and last movement is called *Songe d'une nuit de sabbat*; he sees the witches dancing on the Blocksberg, his beloved among them, and hears at the same time the *cantus firmus* of the 'Dies Irae', in a parodied version, to which they dance.

How indescribably horrible all this is to me, I don't have to tell you. To see one's most cherished ideas distorted and turned into perverse caricatures would make anyone angry – and this is only the programme. The execution of it is still more wretched: nowhere a spark, nowhere warmth – cold foolishness, cold contrived passion, represented through every possible orchestral means: four timpani played with sponge sticks, two pianos for four hands which are supposed to imitate bells, two harps, lots of big drums, violins divided into eight parts, two parts for the double basses which also have solo passages, and all these effects (to which I wouldn't object if they served some purpose) used to express nothing but indifferent rubbish – mere grunting, shouting, screaming back and forth. And then you see the composer himself, that quiet, friendly, thoughtful person, going his way calmly and confidently, never for a moment in doubt of his calling, deaf to any outside criticism in his determination to follow only his inner inspiration; you see how keenly and accurately he understands and evaluates everything, while remaining in complete darkness about himself –

it is unspeakably dreadful, and I cannot tell you how much the
sight of him has upset me. I haven't been able to work since the day
before yesterday.

[Letter to his family, 1 March 1831, in Mendelssohn 1958: 119–20]

A couple of weeks later, Mendelssohn wrote again.

The two Frenchmen have again tempted me to *flâner* with them in
the last few days. When you see these two men, one beside the
other, it's really either a tragedy or a comedy – as you choose to
look at it. [Berlioz] a complete caricature, without a glimmer of
talent, groping in the dark and believing himself the creator of a
new world – writing the most horrible things while he dreams and
thinks of nothing but Beethoven, Schiller and Goethe, and at the
same time looking down on Mozart and Haydn with such boundless superiority that, for me, it makes all his enthusiasms appear
questionable. And [Monfort], who has been toiling for three
months at a little rondo on a Portuguese theme, composing everything with care, polish and a proper regard for the rules, is now
going to set about writing six waltzes and would die of happiness
if I would only play him Viennese waltzes without end – he is also
much taken with Beethoven, but with Rossini too, and equally with
Bellini, and no doubt even with Auber – in fact with everybody. And
in between them there's me, who would willingly strangle Berlioz
(that is, until he starts raving about Gluck again when I am forced
to agree with him) – there's me strolling happily along with the two
of them, because they are the only musicians here, and very pleasant, amiable people – it really makes the most comical contrast.

You say, dear mother, that there must be *something* [Berlioz]
wants, but in this I absolutely cannot agree with you. I believe he
simply wants to get married, and is actually worse than the others
because he is more affected in his behaviour. Once and for all, I
cannot endure these blatantly extrovert passions, these affectations
of despair for the benefit of the ladies, this genius proclaimed in
gothic lettering, black on white, and if he were not a Frenchman,
with whom it is always possible to have agreeable relations and
who always know how to talk and be interesting, it would really
be past all bearing.

[Letter to his family, 29 March 1831, ibid: 123–4]

A few days later, Berlioz made up his mind to return to France, but had only got as far as Florence when a letter finally reached him from Mme Moke with the news that her daughter was going to marry Pleyel. Wild with despair and determined to end the lives of Camille, her mother and himself, he set off dramatically for Paris; but by the time he got to Genoa his passion had begun to abate, and after a month in Nice he was back in Rome again.

Antoine Étex (a sculptor later known for his bas-reliefs on the Arc de Triomphe) was a student in Rome at the same time and provides a glimpse of what life there was like that summer.

ANTOINE ÉTEX
(1808–88)

After I had installed myself provisionally in a hotel room, I dined at Lepri, in Via Condotti, at the table with the French artists where I found my old friends of the École des Beaux-Arts in Paris. Because in 1831 and '32 there was an upper table and a lower table in Rome: the upper table was reserved for the *pensionnaires* of the Villa Medici; the lower one was usually occupied by the more independent artists, who were generally from better backgrounds than those of the upper table, where the *pensionnaires*, apart from the artists and architects, had little education and tended to belong to relatively undistinguished families.

After dinner, I looked into the Café Grecco, a kind of Babel where you could hear every language spoken by artists from every country under the sun. Café Grecco was then at its fullest: a few months later everyone had taken wing – the architects to Palermo, Naples, Florence, Sicily; the landscape painters to the mountains; the historical painters everywhere.

In the summer, it was only the sculptors who stayed in Rome . . .

I was overcome by a violent mood of despair. Living alone in a city as sad as Rome, never visiting the Café Grecco, abandoned by artists both foreign and French, belonging to no circle or group of friends, with no parties to go to, I fell into such profound discouragement that I even began to entertain the horrible idea of suicide . . .

I dreamed of entering a monastery with the hidden intention of pursuing my art there. Berlioz, whom I had just met in Rome, was as sad and dispirited as I was, and he came with me to the Dominican fathers, with the idea of going into retreat at a Franciscan convent. But a thousand circumstances plunged us back into our despondent mood.

One day in June he picked me up in the afternoon to make an expedition on foot to Tivoli. We suffered horribly from the sun as we crossed the Roman countryside, and this piece of folly was followed by another, more serious. After we had ordered our dinner at the tavern of the Sybilla, we went out for a walk by the side of the lake and were unable to resist the temptation to throw ourselves into its blue, limpid waters – singing as we did so the famous duet from *Guillaume Tell*, 'O Mathilde, idole de mon âme'. But in that icy water we very soon turned blue with cold; our teeth chattered and the laughter died on our lips. Without exchanging a word, we turned and made for the shore. We were very glad to eat our dinner in the warm, close to a good blaze of brushwood which they laid for us in the fireplace of the room where we had our meal. An hour later, we were both fast asleep.

The next day we got up at five in the morning, in order to reach the mountains of Lazio where we hoped to meet with a group of brigands and perhaps live with them for a while. But we never had much luck, Berlioz and I. We always arrived on the spot at the very moment when the brigands had just left. Twice some young shepherds showed us the remains of the fires they had left behind them, scarcely burned out. In the end we had just enough money to get back to Rome.

[Étex 1877: 116–21]

> Another young Frenchman at large in Rome was the poet Auguste Barbier, whose recent volume of satirical poems, *Iambes*, was much admired by Berlioz and who was later to be one of the librettists of Berlioz's first opera, *Benvenuto Cellini*.

HENRI-AUGUSTE BARBIER
(1805–82)

The features of an eagle with a great head of hair. Mostly pensive and silent, or else bursting with wild hilarity and outrageous puns. A touch of the Parisian *gamin* mixed with the countryman – he was born at La Côte-Saint-André, near the Swiss border.

I knew him at the Villa Medici in 1832, when he was in Rome as a student at the Académie de France. He was already thinking of making a musical setting of Shakespeare's *Romeo and Juliet* and asked me to write a libretto for it, but I had other ideas in mind and couldn't follow up his request. Shakespeare was then his favourite poet and he read him continually. To this passion he later added another idol, Virgil, and his entire life passed in the worship of these two mighty geniuses . . .

He had a tenor voice and sang pleasantly. He also played the piano – but sketchily. All the same, he put so much feeling into what he did play that he gave you, with a few chords, a more striking impression of his compositions than all the brilliance of a full orchestra.

His was a wonderfully constituted artistic temperament: everything that had to do with the great and the beautiful moved him deeply. As an example of this, here is an experience of my own. We were present, the two of us, at the burial of a mutual friend. During the service and at the graveside, the composer was silent and melancholy. As we left the cemetery he said: 'I'm going back home, come with me – we'll read a few pages of Shakespeare'. 'By all means'. We went up to his apartment and, once there, he read the scene by Ophelia's grave in *Hamlet*; his feelings overcame him and the tears poured from his eyes. The emotions that a real loss could not provoke had been released by a purely aesthetic experience. This doesn't mean that he was lacking in personal affection or sensitivity, but simply demonstrates the power of imagination that existed within that framework of nerves.

[Barbier 1883: 230–2]

HENRI MARÉCHAL
(1842–1924)

> Maréchal, who as a student knew Berlioz at the very
> end of his life, found Berlioz's memory still alive in Rome
> during his own period at the Villa Medici in the 1870s.

An old man whom I knew at the Académie de France in Rome told
me that, during his stay at the Villa Medici, Berlioz would deliberately cut himself off from his comrades at the communal dining
table, sitting with a volume of Homer open in front of him while
he drank out of a skull!* And you would meet him in the gardens,
bareheaded, his hair blowing in the wind, playing the guitar and
striking the most extraordinary attitudes . . .

[Maréchal 1907: 285]

> Berlioz's stay in Rome did not last the full two years; in
> the end he persuaded Horace Vernet, the amiable director
> of the Villa Medici, to allow him to leave in May 1832
> on the general understanding that he was not to be seen
> in Paris until the end of the year. He spent the interven-
> ing months with his family at La Côte-Saint-André.

ADÈLE BERLIOZ
(1814–60)

He's really merry, this lovely brother of ours, what a difference
from the last time he was here – it's not the same man. I was very
curious to know what he feels about the treacherous Camille; I was
afraid to bring up the subject, but I needn't have worried, he
brought it up himself and talked to me at great length about it. He
despises her, so much that he doesn't even think her worth hating.
I can tell you, I breathed more easily after he had said that. We
actually joke about it quite often – and about many other things.
Yesterday he told us about some of the pranks he witnessed during

---

* This was probably the skull that he picked up in the cemetery at Radicoffani
(*Memoirs*, chapter 42); he later used it to hold his writing sand, so it must have
been reasonably leak-proof.

his time in Rome – we nearly died laughing. He saw so many people and so many things that every day we hear something new. Since he's been here I've been spending my time very happily. He's working hard, and while he works I keep him company, mending his shirts, which may surprise you; but what is more extraordinary, it doesn't bore me in the least – working for *him* is delightful. I can see you laughing, you beast – but I asked for it by the naïve way I've been carrying on.

[Letter to her sister, Nanci Pal, 12 June 1832, in Cairns i, 1999: 548–9]

> But provincial life didn't suit Berlioz, and his mood changed as he became bored and restless, wanting to get on with the life that was waiting for him in Paris. A visit to his now married sister Nanci in Grenoble was not a success.

NANCI PAL

I send you back your dear Hector . . . and I send him with all his amiability untouched, for he hasn't spent a farthing of it here. At my mother-in-law's he has been continuously sullen, and you will have to forgive them if they regard him as misanthropic and unsociable, for honestly there is no reason that they should think anything else. He never once came into the house without a gloomy, morose look on his face. If the visit to Grenoble has this effect on him I can't imagine why he has stayed so long. It was really distressing for me to see him show himself all the time in such an unfavourable light. Quite often his chilling silence made me feel as if I was choking; it would be impossible to make less of an effort than he has made towards everybody here.

[Letter to her sister Adèle, July 1832, in CGB ii, 19n]

7 RETURN TO PARIS

While he chafed in La Côte-Saint-André, his supporters in Paris, apparently unaware of his imminent return, continued to champion his cause.

JOSEPH D'ORTIGUE

I said at the beginning of this article that MM. Hector Berlioz and Hiller marched at the head of the new musical generation that is on its way up. The first of these is in Rome, and we should scarcely hear of him if it weren't for some indiscreet journalist taking it into his head to mention his name from time to time when there is talk about the future of music. And I might point out, in passing, what a poor deal is offered to the prizewinners from the Conservatoire of music. The young painters who go to Rome send in the works they produce and these are exhibited. But the compositions of the young French musicians not only are not performed, they are not even read – and I use this expression advisedly because, for anyone who knows the works that M. Berlioz has already had performed at the Conservatoire, it is clear that a mere reading is not enough to appreciate them.

Well then – why not entrust young artists like this with the composition of a grand opera? But, it will be said, they should try their luck first at the Opéra-Comique. No, that would be the way to court failure. You wouldn't put a whale to swim in a millpond. Whatever opinion one may form of the quality of M. Berlioz's talent, it is impossible, after hearing his compositions and his cantatas and his romantic symphony, to deny that he is gifted with immense powers of creativity and prodigious strength of will. So give the giant the air that he needs to breathe, and instead of shutting him up within the confines of a paltry, artificial discipline, give him a broad horizon to aim at. If you want to put him to the test, don't stop him at the first step, but let him take off in a vast flight of melody, and exhaust him, if you can, with a long and unremitting run for his money. Don't start by chaining him down; on the contrary, give him all the liberty you can. But beware! don't underestimate genius! you may be able to slow down its dash and impetus, but never hope to stifle or paralyse it. There comes a moment when the colossus passes through the eye of the needle and imposes its own law. It is the story of all great men.

[D'Ortigue 1833: 274–6]

> In the event, Berlioz could bear the wait no longer. He was back in the capital on 7 November, dined with the Lesueurs that afternoon, and found himself among friends once more. Next day he set about realizing his plans for a new concert, to include the revised version of the *Symphonie fantastique* and the sequel to it, the 'mélologue' *Le Retour à la vie* (later known as *Lélio*), which had been put together during his time in Rome.

FERDINAND HILLER

In December [1832] he gave a big concert in the hall of the Conservatoire. He presented his symphony *Episode de la vie d'un artiste* together with the *Mélologue*, in which a kind of monologue binding the individual pieces together was spoken by the popular tragedian [Pierre] Bocage, and scored a great triumph. In those days the new Romantic school stood in high, if not undisputed, favour, and they saw Berlioz as their musical representative. '*C'est le Victor Hugo de la musique*,' they declared – and that's saying a lot, as well as being a lot said. Several parts of the symphony made an outstanding impression, and as spice there was also a touch of scandal, for the spoken text included a slashing attack on the most famous music critic of the day. His name was of course never mentioned, but everybody guessed who it was – and as we all know, *schadenfreude* is one of the favourite dishes of humankind.

[Hiller 1880: 85]

The famous critic was Fétis, whom Berlioz had got his knife into for his 'corrections' to the scores of the Beethoven symphonies, and the virulent hostility of one of the most influential figures in Parisian musical life really begins here. Nevertheless, the concert, conducted by Habeneck on 9 December, was such a success that it had to be repeated on 30 December 'by general demand'.

JOSEPH D'ORTIGUE

That a young artist, after satisfactorily completing his studies in harmony and composition at the Conservatoire, should enter a competition at the end of the scholastic year and carry off the first prize; that he should become a pensioner of the king and leave for Italy – nothing extraordinary in that. The young artist has only done the same as so many others, who have also carried off first prizes, but whom nobody remembers any more, their brief glory buried deep in the archives of the Institut. However this prize-winner, before leaving for Italy, gets together the artists of the Conservatoire and presents them with a symphony, which they play. The public comes to hear it and says: 'That's fine – there's a future in this young man. He'll do something; he has ideas'. That's what the public says. The successful pupil leaves for Rome, and for two years the public fills the hall of the Conservatoire to hear the symphonies of Beethoven, goes to the Opéra to applaud the music of *Robert le Diable*, the scenes in the cloisters of the nuns, of the cathedral at Palermo and the staircase of the Temptation, and admires the graceful, rhythmic movements, the aerial dance, of Mlle Taglioni. It doesn't think any more about the young prize-winner. In due course the laureate comes back from Italy. He invites this same public to hear the same symphony that he has played to it once already – to which, it is true, he has added a *mélologue*, that's to say five pieces of music for voice and orchestra, linked by a spoken recitation. And the public, which before had just said 'That's fine', is now carried away with enthusiasm. A repeat performance of the symphony and its sequel are universally demanded. A couple of weeks after the first concert a second is announced, and the name of Hector Berlioz is on everybody's lips; you hear it everywhere in the salons, in the foyers of the theatres, wherever the public is gathered together.

So what is this all about? It's about a symphony, a piece of music like many others have written, a piece of music like Haydn and Mozart wrote . . . like those which even Beethoven had to write eight or ten of in order to earn himself the reputation he enjoys in France. The symphony of Hector Berlioz, though, cannot be compared to other symphonies either in its general plan, or its musical form, or its personal character. But what matter? Whether the effect it produces arises from an extension of forms that already exist, or from some entirely new concept and the application of the resources and possibilities of art in a way never tried before, the effect itself is undeniable.

[D'Ortigue 1833: 295–7]

> This first of these concerts was one of the turning points of Berlioz's life. It marked his reestablishment in Paris, and signalled the beginning of the long struggle for recognition and the acceptance of his ideas that occupied him ceaselessly from now on. It was attended by many of the leading lights of the new Romantic movement – Liszt, Paganini, Chopin, Victor Hugo, Alexandre Dumas, Alfred de Vigny, Théophile Gautier, Heinrich Heine, George Sand, and many others. Among them was a new friend, the wealthy young literary amateur Ernest Legouvé, who half a century later was to write the most sustained memoir that we have of the young Berlioz.

ERNEST LEGOUVÉ
(1807–1903)

It was in Rome in 1832, at the Académie de France, that I first heard the name of Berlioz. He himself had just finished his time there, and had left behind him memories of a talented artist with a lively intelligence, an eccentric who gloried in his own eccentricity. There was a general inclination to regard him as a *poseur*, though Mme Vernet and her daughter defended him and were loud in his praise; women are more perceptive than we are in singling out men of exceptional quality. One day, Mlle Louise Vernet sang me a song

that Berlioz had written for her when he was staying in the mountains around Subiaco. It was called 'La Captive'. Its combination of
poetry and melancholy moved me deeply, and I felt the beginnings
of a mysterious bond of sympathy between myself and this
unknown person. I asked Mme Vernet to give me a letter of introduction, and as soon as I was back in Paris I made it my first task
to get in contact with him. But where was I to find him? He was
still so little known in those days. I was becoming desperate when
one morning, at an Italian barber's shop named Decandia in the
Place de la Bourse, I overheard one of the assistants saying to the
owner: 'This cane belongs to M. Berlioz'. 'M. Berlioz?' I cried to
the barber, 'you know M. Berlioz?' 'He's one of my best clients; he
should be coming in today'. 'Then give him this note', I said; it was
the letter from Mme. Vernet.

That evening I went to hear *Freischütz** and, the house being
packed, I could only get a place in the gangway of the second
gallery. All at once, in the ritornello in the middle of Caspar's aria,
someone near me gets to his feet, leans over towards the orchestra
and shouts in a voice of thunder: 'Those aren't two flutes, you
scoundrels! they should be piccolos! two piccolos! Oh, what pigs!'
And he sits down again indignantly. In the uproar that follows I
turn round and see, close by, a young man literally shaking with
anger, his hands clenched, his eyes flashing, with a head of hair . . .
a head of hair! . . . better call it a vast umbrella of hair, like a constantly shifting canopy overhanging the beak of a bird of prey. It
was comic and diabolical at the same time.

The next morning I hear a ring at my door. I go to open it, and
the moment I see my visitor, 'Monsieur,' I say to him, 'weren't you
at *Freischütz* last night?' 'Yes, monsieur'. 'In the second gallery?'
'Yes, monsieur.' 'Wasn't it you who yelled out "They're piccolos!"?'
'But of course! Can you believe that there are such barbarians in
existence that they can't even understand the difference between . . .'
'Then it's you, my dear Berlioz!' 'Yes, my dear Legouvé.' And there

---

* As is sometimes the case, Legouvé, at a distance of more than fifty years, is let
down by his memory. There was no performance of *Freischütz* in Paris in 1832,
so either it was a different opera at which Berlioz directed his vociferous criticisms,
or Legouvé has confused two separate occasions. But the description has an
authentic ring all the same.

we are, at our first meeting, falling on one another's necks like a couple of soul mates.

It wasn't long before we were close friends. Everything brought us together – our age, our tastes, the passion we shared for the arts . . . He adored Shakespeare as much as I did, I adored Mozart like him; when he wasn't writing music he was reading poetry; when I wasn't writing poetry I was playing music. And, as a final bond, I had just given vent to my enthusiasm in a complete translation of *Romeo and Juliet*, and he – he was madly in love with the celebrated actress who played the role of Juliet.

[Legouvé 1886: 289–91]

The reappearance of Harriet Smithson in Berlioz's life had happened by chance. After an unsuccessful season in London, she returned to Paris a couple of weeks before Berlioz himself, with the intention of setting up a permanent English company. But the venture met with little success, and to offer her some much-needed distraction a group of friends persuaded her to go with them to the concert at the Conservatoire on 9 December. It was not till she was on her way that she discovered what she was going to hear.

A few days later, Berlioz was introduced to her for the first time, and at once it was as if the intervening years had never been. He declared his passion, urged it with impatience and made no secret of it to his friends and family. But his parents, horrified by the reappearance of this dubious theatrical figure they had thought safely out of the way, were implacably opposed to any idea of marriage and used the good offices of Mme Berlioz's brother, Félix Marmion, to attempt a rapprochement with Hector.

FÉLIX MARMION
(1787–1872)

I went back to see him yesterday, to make an attempt for which I didn't really have much hope. His attitude is too unyielding, too far outside the reach of any accepted ideas. Reasoned argument just goes in one ear and out of the other. Common feelings, social conventions, family ties – he won't listen to any of them. Objections simply irritate him, and intensify still further a passion already tried and tested by five years of separation . . . Unhappy man – what a future he is laying up for himself! This woman is no longer young; I believe her to be on the verge of ruin (he knows it) and she is making vain efforts to establish an English theatre here. Her talent (which is real, and very remarkable) is likely to deteriorate as her difficulties and discouragement increase. A life of hideous poverty lies before them, and disenchantment and regret will follow all too soon. This is what I have told him over and over again – but what to everybody else is so glaringly obvious, to him is just another reason for persisting. He sees nothing alarming in the prospect . . .

I wanted to see Miss Smithson for myself yesterday. I went to the modest theatre in the rue Chanteraine where she is now appearing, *faute de mieux*, and where she has made Hector promise not to go and see her, because she regards it as a place unworthy of her talent. I was very curious to see if I could divine the secret of this powerful charm which has caused such havoc. She does in fact have remarkable features, an exquisite sensibility of voice, and nobility in her gestures. The theatre is so small that it doesn't do much to create illusion, and this inevitably puts Miss Smithson at a disadvantage; on this stage she doesn't even seem young. Even so, and without having my nephew's eyes or unique nature, I understood the impression this woman must have made upon his artist's soul . . .

[Letter to Nanci Pal, 10 February 1833, CGB: ii 75n]

ERNEST LEGOUVÉ

His love [for Miss Smithson] added fire to our friendship. It was a passion beset by storms. In the first place, he knew only a few words of English, and Miss Smithson knew even fewer of French, a circumstance which lent a certain incoherence to their dialogue. Secondly, she was actually quite a bit afraid of her frenzied admirer. And finally, Berlioz *père* put an absolute veto on any suggestion of marriage. It was a situation that could hardly have called more patently for a confidant. So he raised me to the dignity of adviser-in-ordinary and, as this was a full-time occupation which could well employ two people, he added, as joint confessor, one of my friends for whom he had a great admiration, [the novelist] Eugène Sue.

Our consultations were strange affairs, and an accident which happened to Miss Smithson (she had dislocated her ankle in getting out of her carriage) gave rise to a characteristic exchange between us. In the morning, I received a note from Berlioz written in a contorted hand:

'I must see you urgently. Warn Sue! Oh my friends, what agonies I am in!'

I immediately sent a note to Sue: 'Stormy weather ahead! Berlioz has sent for us! This evening, supper at my place, at midnight.'

At midnight, there was Berlioz, his eyes clouded with pain, his hair tumbling over his forehead like a weeping willow, heaving sighs that seemed to well up from the soles of his boots.

'Well, what's it all about?'

'Oh my friends, my life isn't worth living!'

'Is your father still relentless?'

'My father!' cried Berlioz in a fury, 'my father says "Yes"! He wrote to me this morning.'

'Well then, I should have thought . . .'

'But wait! wait! I was mad with joy at getting the letter. I rush round to tell her, I arrive wild with happiness and dissolving in tears and I cry: 'My father says "Yes", my father says "Yes"!' And do you know what she replied? "*Not yet, Hector! not yet!* My foot hurts me too much". What do you say to that?'

'What we say, my friend, is that this poor woman was undoubtedly in great pain'. 'But how can she be in pain?' he replied, 'how can pain exist when you are drunk with love? Look at me – me – if someone had plunged a knife into my chest at the moment when she told me she loved me, I wouldn't have felt it. But she . . . that she could . . . that she dared . . .' Then suddenly, interrupting himself: 'How could she have dared? Why didn't she realise that I could have strangled her?'

At this, said with such utter simplicity and conviction, Eugène Sue and I burst out laughing. Berlioz looked at us in amazement. It seemed to him that he had said the most natural thing in the world, and we had the greatest difficulty in making him understand that there was no possible connection of ideas between a woman who complains of the pain in her foot and a woman whom one strangles, and that Miss Smithson would have been totally astonished if he had hurled himself, Othello style, at her throat. The poor man listened to us without taking in anything, his head hanging forward, and the tears poured down his cheeks as he said . . . 'All the same, she doesn't love me! She doesn't love me!'

'She doesn't love you in the way you love her', replied Sue, 'that's clear enough – and just as well too, because a pair of lovers like you would make a pretty strange household!' He couldn't keep himself from smiling. 'Look, my dear friend,' I added in my turn, 'your head is full of Shakespeare's Portia, who stabs herself in the thigh to persuade Brutus to let her into his confidence. But Miss Smithson has never played Portia – she plays the Ophelias, the Desdemonas, the Juliets, the weak, gentle, timid characters, the essentially feminine ones. And I'm sure that's what her own character is like'.

'It's true!'

'I believe that she has a soul as delicate as the souls of the characters she portrays'.

'Yes, it's true! Delicate – that's exactly the word'.

'And if you had really been worthy of her, or better still worthy of yourself, instead of flinging all this joy in her face without preparation you would have applied it like a balm to her suffering. Your divine Shakespeare wouldn't have missed a chance like that if he'd been writing the scene'.

'You're right! You're right!' exclaimed the poor young man. 'I'm a brute! I'm a savage! I don't deserve the love of such a heart! If only you knew what a depth of affection lies buried there . . . Oh, how I will beg for her pardon tomorrow! But look, my friends, how right I was to consult you! . . . I came here miserable, in despair, and now here I am, happy, confident, ready to laugh again!' And suddenly, with all the innocence, the quickly changing emotions of a child, he threw himself into the joyful contemplation of his coming marriage. Observing which, I said:

'Well that's fine then, let's celebrate at once. Let's have some music'.

He agreed with enthusiasm. But how were we to make music? I

had no piano as a young man, and even if I had had one what good would it have been? Berlioz could only play with one finger. Happily we had one unfailing resource left to us – the guitar. For Berlioz the guitar was a compendium of all instruments, and he played it very well. So he picked it up and began to sing. And what did he sing? – boleros, dance tunes, popular melodies? Not a bit of it. He pitched into the finale of the second act of *La vestale*: the high priest, the vestal virgins, Julia, he sang the lot – all the characters, all the vocal lines. Unfortunately he had no voice. No matter: he produced the effect of one. Thanks to a method of singing with his mouth closed [was this humming?] which he managed with extraordinary skill, combined with the passion and sheer musical genius which animated his whole being, he drew from his chest, his throat and his guitar a whole range of unknown sounds, of penetrating moans which, mixed here and there with cries of admiration, irruptions of enthusiasm, even comments of real eloquence, produced an overall effect that was so extraordinary, a whirlwind of verve and passion so unbelievable that no performance of this masterpiece, even at the Conservatoire itself, has moved me, transported me, like this singer and his guitar.

After *La vestale* came some excerpts from his own fantastic symphony . . . And at the end, when the singing was over but as if we were still being swept along by it, the three of us launched into our ideas for the future. Eugène Sue told us his plans for future novels, I my projects for the theatre, Berlioz his dreams of opera. We tried to think of subjects for him, we constructed a scenario on Schiller's *Die Räuber* (which he adored), and we separated at four o'clock in the morning, drunk with poetry and music, in a fever of artistic exhilaration. And next day Miss Smithson saw arriving at her apartment, radiant with joy and trembling with penitence, this strange being she had watched leaving, angry and miserable, the evening before.

[Legouvé 1886: 291–6]

Once again, Legouvé's memoirs must be treated with caution: Harriet did not simply 'dislocate' her ankle, she fractured both bones in her leg and was in acute pain for several weeks, and Dr Berlioz never said 'Yes' to the marriage, then or at any other time. In fact it was only after a prolonged struggle with his parents, against whom he had in the end to initiate legal action, and with Harriet herself, in front of whom he actually took poison, that Berlioz was eventually married on 3 October 1833. The handful of friends present included Liszt (who signed the marriage certificate as principal witness), Heinrich Heine (who had become a close friend since his arrival in Paris three years before) and the faithful Hiller.

FERDINAND HILLER

His father remaining inflexible, Berlioz resorted to the means allowed by French law in such cases – the so-called *'sommations respectueuses'* – and in the late autumn the marriage was duly solemnized in the chapel of the British Embassy. Heinrich Heine and I went along with the bride and bridegroom as witnesses. It was a subdued, rather cheerless ceremony, after which the newly weds went off to their remote apartment [in Vincennes] and Heine, left alone with me, gave free rein to characteristically sardonic and melancholy reflections on the situation. It would be hard to imagine the desire of a lifetime being achieved under more unfavourable conditions.

[Hiller 1880: 87–8]

The event aroused muted enthusiasm in the English press.

Miss Smithson was married last week, in Paris, to Delrioz, the musical composer. We trust this marriage will insure the happiness of an amiable young woman, as well as secure us against her reappearance on the English boards.

[Court Journal, 12 October 1833]

But Harriet's reappearance on the French boards met with no greater success, and it soon became apparent that the financial responsibilities of married life were to fall entirely on Berlioz.

8 BERLIOZ AT THIRTY

The most direct contemporary description of Berlioz as
he approached thirty comes from d'Ortigue, who included
it in his review of the concert in December 1832.

JOSEPH D'ORTIGUE

Berlioz is of medium height, but well proportioned. However
seeing him seated, no doubt because of his virile appearance, you
would think him a lot taller than he is. His features are fine and
well marked: an aquiline nose, small and delicate mouth, prominent chin, and deep-set, piercing eyes which sometimes cloud over
with a veil of melancholy and langour. A mass of fair, curly hair
hangs over his forehead – already furrowed with lines, the legacy of
those stormy passions which have tormented his soul since childhood.

His conversation is fitful, abrupt, broken up, quick-tempered,
sometimes expansive, more often circumspect and brusque, always
honourable and loyal and, depending on the direction it has taken,
arousing in the listener feelings of lively curiosity or sympathetic
understanding.

[D'Ortigue 1833: 322–4]

> D'Ortigue knew Berlioz well: he was one of the very
> few people outside family circles whom Berlioz ever
> addressed with the familiar '*tu*'. The only other at this
> period was Liszt, whose friendship with Berlioz grew
> from a similarity of temperament that was never
> stronger than at this period.

FRANZ LISZT
(1811–86)

Poor Berlioz! . . . How I find myself, *from time to time*, reflected in his soul. He is here beside me. A few moments ago he was weeping, sobbing in my arms . . . and I have the impudence to go on writing to you! . . .

Why has day been vouchsafed to the wretched and light to those who have bitterness in their hearts?

[Letter to Marie d'Agoult, April 1833, in Liszt 1933: 19–20]

> Liszt was now being seen in the Parisian musical world
> as Berlioz's natural comrade in arms.

JOSEPH D'ORTIGUE

But Liszt – how can one describe such a phenomenon! Nothing stops him, nothing stands in his way; it is not his hands that play the piano, it is his mind, his soul, his heart . . . You have to see him, you have to hear him; you have to follow his liquid eye as it searches in the crowd for the fellow on whose sympathy it can count, for the heart where he knows he will find understanding. As he trembles there like the Delphic oracle on her tripod, his gaze falls again and again on a young artist in the audience. Do we need to say that this artist is Hector Berlioz? The target could not have been better chosen; Berlioz is the mirror image that Liszt needs. And scarcely had the last chord died away, when the pianist, shaking, panting with emotion, flung himself on the neck of his friend, who clasped him, crying over and over again: 'Oh, my dear, my sublime friend! how I love you!!' 'Dear' . . . 'sublime' – the words express everything in the artist's heart, and we understand.

After this scorching musical eruption we had to listen to a trio by M. Fétis. 'And was he pale?

Oh, very pale!' (*Hamlet*, Act 1).

[D'Ortigue 1833: 293–5]

FERDINAND HILLER

By the time Hiller left Paris in 1834 he had been largely
supplanted by Liszt as Berlioz's most intimate friend
and confidant. Nevertheless it was probably Hiller who
knew Berlioz best during his early years – he had good
reason to, after all. He certainly gives the fullest and
most temperate description of his character that we
have, even if it was not written down until more than
forty years after d'Ortigue's.

Hector Berlioz was a genuine human being of real integrity who
never betrayed his own nature. But this was made up of various
and sometimes contradictory elements. Energetic to the point of
heroism, headstrong, vehement, yet at the same time pliant – weak
even – he could be patient, deliberate, tenacious, but none the less
prone to give way to momentary impressions, good-natured, agreeable, obliging, grateful and yet bitter, caustic, indeed vindictive. He
had a healthy measure of contempt for the world and for life in
general, and with it boundless ambition. While success intoxicated
him, he made no attempt to hide his powerful disdain for the
public. To the high artistic tasks that he set himself he brought
compelling vigour – not shirking the most tedious, most trivial
occupations if they served his purpose – and yet could waste his
time like any boy and squander it on some crazy adventure. What
dominated him to an unreasonable extent was the incessant contemplation of himself, of his passionate feelings, of his behaviour
and everything he did. He was one of those people for whom it is
a necessity always to appear interesting to themselves – to give a
heightened significance to the most trifling details of what they do,
or feel, or suffer, to mull over the good or bad in everything that
happens to them. Yet he never struck you as being vain, which is
the more remarkable because he often talked almost exclusively
about himself. Not that he failed to include God and the world,
music and poetry, peoples and countries in the scope of his outpourings, but he remained always – to put it in a very German way –
subjective in the highest degree. To be sure, most people would like
to talk about themselves all the time if they were allowed to; La
Rochefoucauld said that any man would rather speak ill of himself
than say nothing at all, but I have never come across anybody,

outside the acting profession, in whom this trait was so highly developed. Fortunately his personality was so attractive, so peculiarly his own, his way of talking so lively and picturesque, his turn of mind so keen and original – now acutely logical, now humorously exaggerated, witty and pungent – his enthusiasms so fiery, his aversions so emphatic, that it was not only a pleasure to let him have his head, but a constant temptation to incite him to new 'expectorations'.

Berlioz was in the full sense of the word a man of honour. He had perhaps a few passionate weaknesses with which to reproach himself – but you were no more allowed to offend his personal dignity than he was himself. Every sort of intrigue was foreign to his nature: he would rather upset himself and others by tactless plain speaking than get what he wanted by devious means. His artistic self-confidence was very strong . . .

. . . The freedom, indeed the arbitrary independence, on which he insisted in the execution of his own musical ideas never prevented him from taking exception to the occasional harmonic quirk (if one may use the term) in the works of Beethoven, and in the same way, though generally – and particularly in the use of his mother tongue – he was a passionate purist (he abhorred the ideals of extreme liberalism too), he was in his heart of hearts an aristocrat in matters of the intellect. He disliked the republicans, and thirty years later he expressed to me his admiration for the regime of the Emperor Napoleon. '*Ma foi!*' he said, 'anyone who has power and the intelligence to go with it can always dominate the rest – that's entirely in the natural order of things'.

[Hiller 1880: 63–5, 70–1]

ERNEST LEGOUVÉ

Legouvé, writing at much the same time as Hiller, paints a more personal picture. We take up his memoirs immediately after the affair of Harriet's 'dislocated ankle'.

I do not describe this youthful scene simply for the pleasure of recalling a memory which I find affecting, but rather because it gives a vivid impression of the portrait of Berlioz that I am trying to paint; because in writing these lines I seem to see before me once again that touching, extravagant, ingenuous creature, violent, scatter-brained, vulnerable, but above all sincere. It has been said that he was a *poseur*. But to pose – that's to conceal what you really are and show the world what you are not, to pretend, to calculate, to be master of yourself. And where would he have found the strength to act such a role, this being who lived at the mercy of his nerves, who was the slave of every new impression, who dashed precipi-tately from one emotion to another, who winced, turned pale, wept in spite of himself, and could no more control his words than the muscles of his face? Reproach *him* for being a poseur! You might as well accuse him (as some have) of being envious! He was a fer-vent admirer of his own works, that I accept – but at the same time he had great enthusiasm for the works of others. You have only to re-read his admirable articles on Beethoven, on Weber, on Mozart, and, not to let it be said that he crushed the living under his praises for the dead, to remember the acclamations with which he greeted the *Désert* of Felicien David and the *Sapho* of Gounod. It was just that his antipathies were as vigorous as his adorations. He could no more hide the one than the other. The expressions of passion that welcomed the things he admired alternated with the pitiless sar-casms, like so many barbed arrows, with which he pursued those he did not like. Two incidents will illustrate the two sides of his nature.

One evening, I had invited a few friends to my apartment – Liszt, Goubaux, Schoelcher, Sue and five or six others. Berlioz was there too. 'Liszt,' he said, 'play us a Beethoven sonata.' We moved from my study into the salon; I had a salon in those days, and a piano. The lights were out, and the fire had been banked up. While Liszt went over to the piano Goubaux brought the lamp from my study and each of us found somewhere to sit.

'Turn up the wick,' I said to Goubaux, 'we can't see properly.' But instead he lowered it, and there we were, plunged into almost total obscurity. The sudden passage from light to darkness, coincid-ing with the first notes from the piano, clutched at our hearts. It was like the Scene of the Shadows in [Rossini's] *Mosé*. Liszt, whether by chance or through some unconscious association of ideas, began the melancholy, heart-rending andante of the sonata in C sharp [minor]. We all sat motionless, rooted to the spot. From time to time the fire, not quite extinguished, would pierce its covering of cinders and throw out strange, fleeting gleams of light which outlined us all like ghosts. From the armchair into which I had thrown myself I could hear above my head the sound of stifled sobs and moans: it was Berlioz. When the piece was over, we remained silent for a while; then Goubaux lit a candle and, as we went back to my study, Liszt gripped my arm and pointed to Berlioz whose cheeks were drenched with tears. 'Look at him,' he said in a low voice, 'he was listening to that as the heir apparent.'

There is Berlioz the enthusiast. Now here is the other.

We were together at the Théâtre Italien, where they were giving [Rossini's] *Othello*. In the finale of the second act there is a celebrated passage in which Desdemona, at her father's feet, cries out: '*Se il mio padre m'abbandona, Che mai più mi restera?*' 'If my father abandons me, what shall I have left?'

The first line is repeated twice, and presents Desdemona's grief in a musical phrase that is slow, expressive and genuinely touching. Then suddenly, at the second line, to picture her despair, the music bursts into a flood of runs, vocalise and roulades which to me seemed full of feeling, but which exasperated Berlioz. When the act was over, he leant towards me and sang quietly into my ear, in a voice vibrant with the emotion of the melody itself: 'If my father abandons me, If my father abandons me' – then, with a clatter of sardonic laughter, and reproducing faithfully all the roulades of the text: 'I don't care a damn! I don't care a damn! I don't care a damn!'

There are the two Berliozes, the enthusiast and the mocker.

[Legouvé 1886: 296–9]

> Now that he was married, with a wife (and ten months later, a son, Louis) to support, Berlioz embarked on a period of furious musical activity. The next eight years saw the composition of *Harold en Italie*, *Le cinq mai*, *Benvenuto Cellini*, the *Requiem*, *Roméo et Juliette*, the *Symphonie funèbre et triomphale*, *Les nuits d'été* – to name only the larger works. At the same time, his career as a journalist was beginning to take off seriously, and on top of this he started organizing, and after a couple of years conducting, a series of orchestral concerts, mainly of his own compositions, which became a regular if controversial feature of Parisian musical life.

FRANZ LISZT [OR THE COMTESSE D'AGOULT]*

Here, indeed, is a spectacle worthy of attention and one well cal-culated to restore the flagging spirits and the yielding will power of the composer whose first hearing fails to arouse the plaudits of the crowd: the sight of Berlioz spending his entire early youth in bodily combat, so to speak, with an uncomprehending public; responding with undaunted perseverance to coarse sarcasm, unintelligent prejudice, and peremptory condemnation; walking on like the philosopher who thus answered those who denied the possibility of motion; and offering as his sole argument the performance of his works, by an orchestra increasingly well rehearsed – works that the flood of critical grumbling lifted ever higher, like a noble threemaster riding out a storm.

The public complained that its patience was giving out; never-theless, attracted as if in spite of itself by the power of genius, the public kept coming back. Then, little by little, from the midst of the crowd that had almost universally condemned, there arose here and there a few individual opinions, a few voices isolated at first, but soon surrounded by partisans of the more timid sort, who are always seeking support. Thus arose a second public, as eager to defend Berlioz as the first had been to attack him. Today sarcasm and mockery are out; even the terms of the argument are different: now the question is whether the composer of the *Fantastic Symphony* is merely a talented composer or a real genius.

[*Le Monde*, 11 December 1836, in Cone 1971: 283]

> If sarcasm and mockery were out, parody was certainly
> not – though inclusion in the cabaret at the Opéra ball
> was an indication of success in its own way. Étienne
> Arnal was a well-known comedian at the Théâtre du
> Vaudeville, and his presentation of a symphony entitled
> *Episode in the life of a gambler* (with music specially
> composed by Adolphe Adam) seems to have amused
> Berlioz himself – at least to judge from his report of it
> in the *Gazette musicale*.

* Though published in Liszt's name, and no doubt expressing his views, this was probably written by Marie d'Agoult (1805–76), his mistress and the mother of his three children – who achieved her own celebrity as a novelist and literary intellectual under the pseudonum 'Daniel Stern'.

ÉTIENNE ARNAL
(1794–1872)

To put across my dramatic ideas I don't need words, or singers, or actors, or costumes, or scenery. All this, gentlemen, is in my orchestra: there you will see my hero in action, you will hear him speaking, I will paint him for you from head to foot. Why, at the second *reprise* in the first *allegro* I will even show you how he adjusts his cravate. Oh, what a wonderful thing this instrumental music is! And I'll show you a whole lot more in my second symphony, the *Symphony on the Common Law*. What a difference there is, gentlemen, in music like this, which dispenses with the thousand irrelevant details for which your real genius has no use, and makes itself understood with a mere – er – a mere three hundred musicians! What a difference from the popular ditties of Rossini! Oh! but Rossini! – don't speak to me of Rossini! An intriguer who takes it upon himself to get his music performed in the four quarters of the globe *simply to make himself a reputation*! . . . Charlatan! A man who writes things that absolutely *anybody* can understand! . . . But seriously, it really is abominable, and for me Rossini's music is plain ridiculous; it makes no effect on me, but no sort of effect at all – there, that's the effect it has on me.

[*Gazette musicale*, 18 January 1835: 23]

HEINRICH HEINE
(1797–1856)

While the *Symphonie fantastique* was beginning to achieve something almost like popularity, the romantic passion that had provided its inspiration was settling into a rather less volcanic domesticity. About the following notice however it must be said that, though Berlioz did play percussion in his earliest concerts, he would never – even at the sight of Harriet – have endangered a performance of his own music, and that in any case he was actually *conducting* the concert that Heine attended on 18 December 1836. Altogether, it is clear that Heine's much-quoted portrait of the demon timpanist owes a good deal to the poetic irony for which he was famous.

. . . One or two good concerts crop up from time to time in this cultural desert and offer much needed refreshment to the friends of music. This winter, they included the Sunday concerts at the Conservatoire, a few private soirées . . . and especially the concerts of Berlioz and Liszt. The last two are unquestionably the most remarkable phenomena in the musical world here; I say the most remarkable, not the most beautiful or the most pleasing. From Berlioz we are soon to have an opera. The subject is an episode from the life of Benvenuto Cellini – the casting of the 'Perseus'. Everyone is expecting something extraordinary, because what this composer has already accomplished is extraordinary. His natural bent is for the fantastic, not concerned so much with inner feeling as with the sentimental. He has a close affinity with Callot, Gozzi and Hoffmann, and even his outward appearance suggests this. It's a shame that he has allowed his monstrous, antideluvian locks to be cut off – that swelling mop of hair which used to tower above his forehead like a forest on a rugged cliff.   That was how he looked when I saw him for the first time six years ago,* and that's how he will always remain in my memory.

It was at the Conservatoire, where a great symphony of his was being performed – a bizarre night-piece, lighted from time to time by sentimental glimpses of a woman's dress flitting past, or else by sulphurous gleams of irony. The best thing in it is a Witches' Sabbath in which the Devil says Mass and the liturgy is parodied with the most ghastly, bloodiest grotesquerie. It is a farce which light-heartedly releases the hidden snakes that we carry in our hearts. A young man who sat next to me, talkative and lively, pointed out the composer to me – standing at the far end of the hall in a corner of the orchestra playing the kettledrum, for that is his instrument.

'Do you see', said my neighbour, 'that plump young English-woman sitting in the stage box? That is Miss Smithson. M. Berlioz has been madly in love with her for three years, and it is to this passion that we owe the wild symphony we are going to hear today'. And sure enough, in the stage box, there sat the celebrated actress from Covent Garden. Berlioz stared unswervingly in her direction, and

* Heine is referring to the concert conducted by Habeneck on 9 December 1832. Since this notice was originally written in May 1837 his 'six years ago' is not to be taken literally.

whenever her glance met his he beat upon his drum like a man in a fury.

Since then Miss Smithson has become Madame Berlioz and her husband has had his hair cut. When I heard his symphony again at the Conservatoire this winter, he sat once more behind the drums at the back of the orchestra, the plump Englishwoman sat once more in the stage box, her glances once more met his – but he no longer struck the drums so furiously.

[*Gazette musicale*, 4 February 1838, reprinted in Heine 1887: vii, 148–9]

> Only the day before this concert, Harriet, whose acting career, in spite of the efforts of herself and Berlioz, had been in steady decline since her return to France in 1832, had made her last public appearance in a Paris theatre. The fourth act of *Hamlet*, included in a miscellaneous benefit programme, had been swamped by the incongruous nature of the rest of the entertainment and her performance had gone for nothing. Yet only a few months earlier, before a fashionable audience in the private theatre at the Hôtel Castellane, the same scene had produced an ovation which showed that, even with the passing years, the magic of her performance had not entirely faded.

CHARLES JARRIN
(1813–1900)

Ophelia entered. There was general astonishment. No sign at all of the frail, diaphanous figure we had expected. No suggestion of the elfin spirit ready to take flight. We saw before us a handsome woman of perhaps a little above average height, her young breast accentuated by a nicely judged white gown, with fine bare arms, a charming, rather full, neck – all the attributes, in fact, of a young woman in the rich and abundant development of her beauty. Her features were well-proportioned, a little plump, and of a dead pallor in which the art of make-up played no part.

But it was the great blue eyes, opened wide and luminous with suffering, that transfigured her appearance. A spontaneous round of applause greeted those eyes, and Ophelia, reassured, began her desolate song. We scarcely understood her language, most of us. But straight away we all understood, as one soul to another, the meaning of her deep sobs, the utter despair that they revealed, the ominous shudders that warned of the delirium that was to come. The audience, profoundly moved, watched in silence – broken, at the first cry of madness, by the most impassioned torrent of bravos that I have ever heard.

[Jarrin, quoted in Tiersot 1886: 350–1]

Benvenuto Cellini was completed early in 1837, but before it reached the stage Berlioz had been commissioned to write another work, whose performance later the same year was to give rise to one of the most famous of all Berlioz legends. Memories of this period were left by Charles Hallé, the German pianist and conductor who later settled in Manchester and founded the orchestra that carries his name. In 1836, at the age of seventeen, Hallé arrived in Paris as a student and soon joined the circle of Berlioz's admirers.

CHARLES HALLÉ
(1819–95)

The most important friendship I formed at that time . . . was that with Hector Berlioz – *'le vaillant Hector'*, as he was often called – whose powerful dominating personality I was glad to recognise. How I made his acquaintance is now a mystery to me – it seems as if I had always known him – I also wonder often how it was he showed such interest in an artist of so little importance as I then was; he was so kind to me, and, in fact, became my friend. Perhaps it was because we could both speak with the same enthusiasm of Beethoven, Gluck, Weber, even Spontini, and, perhaps, not less because he felt that I had a genuine admiration for his own works. There never lived a musician who adored his art more than did Berlioz; he was, indeed, 'enthusiasm personified'. To hear him speak of, or rave about, a real *chef d'oeuvre*, such as 'Armida', 'Iphigenia', or the C minor Symphony, the pitch of his voice rising higher and higher as he talked, was worth any performance of the same . . . In some of the most interesting moments of Berlioz's musical career in Paris I had the privilege of being with him. Thus on December 5, 1837, I went with him to the Hôtel des Invalides to witness the first performance of his 'Requiem', and was, therefore, an eye-witness of what took place on that occasion. Habeneck, after Berlioz the most accomplished *chef d'orchestre* in Paris, conducted by rights, and Berlioz sat in a chair near him. Habeneck, who conducted not only the Grand Opera but also the 'Concerts du Conservatoire', had the habit of now and then putting his conducting stick down and listening complacently to the performance of his orchestra. It was, therefore, perhaps force of habit that made him discard the bâton at the commencement of the 'Tuba mirum', this time not to listen, but leisurely to take a pinch of snuff! To my amazement I suddenly saw Berlioz standing in Habeneck's place and wielding the bâton to the end of the movement. The moment had been a most critical one, four groups of brass instruments, stationed at the four corners of the large orchestra, which with the chorus was placed under the dome in the centre of the building, having to enter successively, and, without Berlioz's determination, disaster must have ensued, thanks to the unfortunate pinch of snuff. Habeneck, after the performance, thanked Berlioz profusely for his timely aid, and admitted that his own thoughtlessness might have caused a breakdown, but Berlioz remained persuaded that there had been no thoughtlessness, and that the breakdown was intended. I could not believe this, for the simple reason that when such a thing occurs it is always the conductor on whose shoulders the blame of the breakdown is laid, and most deservedly so; it is, therefore, most unlikely that he should himself try to provoke one.

[Hallé 1896: 64, 66–7]

> Hallé's description is a less dramatic version of the account given by Berlioz himself in the *Memoirs*, though he puts down to simple carelessness what the composer attributes to malice. But the story in the *Memoirs* has often been challenged, partly because it sounds so unlikely (at least by later performance standards), partly because there is no contemporary mention of it in the press or Berlioz's letters, and partly on the evidence provided by Charles Stanford.

CHARLES VILLIERS STANFORD
(1852–1924)

Stanford, a British composer, teacher and conductor of
Irish birth, wrote his racy and entertaining autobiography
towards the end of his life. George Osborne, his senior
by nearly half a century and also Irish, had been a close
friend of Berlioz's in his student days and later saw a
good deal of him in London at the time when the
Memoirs were being put together.

[In the *Memoirs*, Berlioz] says that with his habitual mistrust, he
had stationed himself behind Habeneck and continues: – 'Just in
the one bar where the conductor's beat is absolutely necessary,
Habeneck lowers his stick, coolly takes his snuffbox out of his
pocket, and leisurely takes a pinch. I always had my eye upon him,
turned round quickly, and stepping in front of him I put out my
arm and gave the four slow beats of the change of *tempo*. The
orchestra followed me accurately. I conducted the piece to the end,
and got the effect I wanted. When Habeneck saw that the *Tuba
mirum* was rescued, he said, "What a cold perspiration I have had!
We should have been lost without you!" "Yes I know", was my
answer, fixing him with a significant look.'

I asked Osborne if he remembered anything about this episode,
and he said that he had no reason to, for he was sitting in the nave
with Berlioz, that he never stood up, that Habeneck never put
down his bâton, did not take a pinch of snuff, and that there was
no necessity or opportunity for fixed significant flashes of the composer's eye. Moreover that when the '*Memoirs*' were published, he
asked Berlioz why on earth he had put upon record such a wholesale piece of pure invention; that Berlioz burst out laughing and
said that the story seemed to him far too good a one to be lost!

[Stanford 1914: 68–9]

> It is a question of deciding between two good story-
> tellers, the Irish and the French, though it is fair to say
> that Berlioz, while he may often have allowed himself to
> elaborate the truth, can rarely be found to have invented
> it. The incident as Berlioz recounts it makes an easy
> target, but there seems no reason to doubt the sober

testimony of Charles Hallé – except, of course, that he
was only eighteen at the time and was writing nearly
sixty years later . . . And there are two curious post-
scripts which are perhaps worth quoting here, the first
from the critic Louis Engel, who knew Berlioz personally.

LOUIS ENGEL
(b. 1828)

I now come to an incident in Berlioz's '*Memoirs*' which he has
treated rather elaborately, and which has occasionally been doubted.
I happen to know that it was exactly as he states, yet I am surprised
to find it printed. It is clear that the trick in question was not acci-
dental, but intentional; and it throws a glaring light on the jealousy
of an otherwise great conductor, so much so that after his telling
me all about it, and consulting with another friend, I advised
Berlioz to keep it out of his '*Memoirs*'; but people ask your advice
in hope that you will come to the same conclusion as they did, and
when you do not, they follow their own inspiration. After we were
all well agreed that it should not be published, he published it.

[Engel 1886: i, 87–8]

And the second from the musicologist Julien Tiersot, an
early champion of Berlioz.

JULIEN TIERSOT
(1857–1936)

Of the fact in itself . . . we have no immediate proof either way. But
I have heard from several of the artists who played in the orchestra
of the Conservatoire under Habeneck that he had the habit, when
the proper tempo for a symphony had been given and the work was
under way, of putting down his baton and taking a pinch of snuff –
sometimes even offering his snuff box to his neighbours. While this
was going on, the orchestra looked after itself. Such were the pater-
nal – or rather, perhaps, paternalistic – habits of the good old days.

[Tiersot: Berlioziana I, 7 February 1904: 44]

As it happens, even eight years later the same casual
attitude was noted on a visit to Paris by the Russian
composer Glinka.

MIKHAIL IVANOVICH GLINKA
(1804–57)

When we started rehearsing, I soon found that French musicians
are not very good at paying attention – they prefer to talk and chat
with their neighbours. I also noticed that sometimes, especially
in the heavy passages, they resort to their snuffboxes and hand-
kerchieves.

[Glinka 1963: 192]

> In any case, snuff or no snuff, the *Grande messe des*
> *morts* was a notable success, and certainly helped to
> establish Berlioz's name in serious musical circles and as
> an official composer of the regime.

ADOLPHE ADAM
(1803–56)

> Not all the Parisian musical world was persuaded, how-
> ever. Adam, a successful composer of comic operas best
> known today for his ballet *Giselle*, was an exact con-
> temporary of Berlioz and an influential figure in the
> Parisian musical world.

We have had a very curious thing here, nothing less than a Requiem
Mass by Berlioz . . .There were four hundred musicians, for which
he had been officially allocated twenty-eight thousand francs. You
cannot imagine what this music was like: apart from a considerable
orchestra with the normal proportions of instruments, it required
the addition of twenty trombones, ten trumpets and fourteen kettle-
drums. Anyhow, all this didn't make the least effect – although you
will find all the newspapers, with very few exceptions, proclaiming
the Mass a masterpiece. This is because Berlioz is a journalist him-

self: he writes in the *Journal des Débats*, the most influential of all of them, and journalists stick together.

[Letter to Samuel Heinrich Spiker, 11 December 1837, in Adam 1903: iv, 468–9]

> If there was a touch of sour grapes in Adam's attitude, he was cruelly avenged when Berlioz's first opera *Benvenuto Cellini* reached the stage of the Opéra in September the following year.

HENRI-AUGUSTE BARBIER

In 1837 [*actually 1835*], through the influence of M. Armand Bertin, director of the *Journal des débats*, M. Berlioz obtained the possibility of getting a work staged at the Paris Opéra. He conceived the idea of a lyric drama which would deal with the principal events in the life of Benvenuto Cellini, the sixteenth-century Florentine sculptor and engraver. This celebrated Italian had left some lively memoirs from which M. Berlioz took a number of striking incidents and shaped them into a grand scenario in four parts – including, as well as the struggles of the artist with his rivals and with the government authorities, the part played by the siege of Rome and the death of the constable of Bourbon.

It was a serious drama involving lengthy developments of plot. The administration of the Opéra made difficulties about accepting so substantial a work from a composer who had not worked in the theatre before, and wanted to restrict him to two acts only, less ambitious in general style, and amusing rather than tragic in mood. M. Berlioz reduced his original idea to the simple conflict between Benvenuto and the power of authority, and it was this episode of the original drama that became the subject of the piece that the Opéra accepted.

The poet whom M. Berlioz had originally wanted for the libretto of his opera was M. Alfred de Vigny. But M. de Vigny, being occupied with more important works, named M. de Wailly as the man to replace him in the job, and he in turn came to ask [me] for [my] collaboration. This was readily offered, because [I] had been a close friend of M. Berlioz for several years . . .

The story of Benvenuto Cellini had not been chosen at random.

The character and activities of Cellini had evident parallels with the
character and situation of the composer himself, and the drama
was therefore a reflection of the toil and conflicts of his own life.
Sadly, it was not also the occasion of his triumph. Before launching
himself on the operatic stage, M. Berlioz had mixed journalism
with composition. A good writer and a skilful polemicist, satirical,
pungent and witty, he had often shown himself incisive and even
excessive in his judgment of some of the best known of his colleagues. These things were not forgotten, and when he appeared
himself as a dramatic composer he was severely judged by those
who didn't share his theories and didn't like his talent. What is
more, in the work that he now presented to the public there were
traits of satire against the musical style then in fashion – the 'square
phrase' they called it – and above all against the abuse and banality
of the cadenzas in Italian opera. This imprudence was seized upon,
as was only to be expected, and the hissers and booers had a field
day with a score that was marvellously fashioned, never commonplace, and which had cost its author many hours of work. There
were faults to be found, and real ones: an excessive exuberance of
harmonic resources and a great inexperience in the art of writing
for voices – but they were amply redeemed by original beauties of
the first order. No matter! in spite of arias, ensembles and choruses
that were remarkable, in spite of the talents and the efforts of
the singers . . . the work did not succeed. Recognising failure,
M. Duprez abandoned the role [of Cellini] at the third performance. M. Alexis [Dupont], who took over from him, supported
the piece valliantly until the eighth, but it went no further and the
name of Benvenuto Cellini was struck from the lists. It was a sad
day for the musical world.

[Barbier 1874: 203–7]

> Gilbert Duprez, recently back in Paris from Italy, was
> the tenor sensation of the day, and his appearance in
> Cellini had been an important factor in Berlioz's hopes
> of success. Though the music of the opera had provoked
> growing hostility from the very beginning of the
> rehearsals, there is no doubt that it was the defection of
> Duprez that ultimately sealed the fate of Cellini and gave
> the management the excuse it needed to shelve the work.

[JOURNALIST]

Duprez has just permitted himself a *coup d'état* at the Opéra. Why? you will ask. Because our tenor wasn't applauded, encored, recalled after the performance and fêted like some Roman conqueror. This vainglorious piece of folly is a direct outrage against Berlioz, a grave insult to the public, and a rash act of rebellion against the director.

[*Le monde dramatique*, 23 September 1838, in Brenet 1889: 61–2]

Duprez's own explanation was different.

GILBERT-LOUIS DUPREZ
(1806–96)

Auber's *Le Lac des Fées* was the second important role I created – for I would never give this description to the role with which Berlioz entrusted me in *Benvenuto Cellini* . . . It is generally recognized that Berlioz, though in other respects an excellent musician, was not exactly a melodist. I had already sung, at the funeral service of Maréchal Damrémont at the Invalides, a Mass of his which sparked from my friend Monpou the comment that 'if Berlioz went to Hell, his punishment would be having to set to music a pastoral by Florian'. *Benvenuto Cellini* drew on similar sources of inspiration, which were strange to my Italian-trained ears.

At the period when this opera was staged I was about to become a father for the third time. On the evening of the third performance I set out from home leaving Madame Duprez in imminent expectation of an event which left me little peace of mind. As I had so far had only daughters I passionately wanted a son, so as I went out I asked Dr Gasnault, who was looking after the patient, to come and let me know at once if my wife gave birth to a boy.

Now, while I was on stage during the last act, I spotted my faithful doctor in the wings with his face wreathed in smiles. In my delight I completely forgot what I was doing. But when you lose your place in the kind of complicated, learned music that Berlioz writes, it isn't easy to find it again, and I didn't come too well out of the incident. However, that was certainly not the reason for the

poor success of the opera, although the composer held me responsible and always harboured resentment towards me because of it.
The fact is that Duponchel [Director of the Opéra] soon got tired
of a work which, being so novel, did less well than the established
pieces, and *Benvenuto Cellini* returned to the library shelves, never
to leave them again.

[Duprez 1880: 153–4]

> Berlioz found it difficult to forgive Duprez for what he
> regarded as a betrayal, and in fact the failure of *Cellini*
> closed the Paris Opéra to him for ever. It was a cruel
> blow: the Opéra meant so much in Parisian musical life,
> he had pinned such hopes on *Cellini*, and its failure was
> on quite a different level to the carpings of critics and
> scoffers at his earlier works.

FRANZ LISZT

. . . I heard this evening that Berlioz's opera was not a success. Our
poor friend! Fate treats him very harshly. I fear this failure will
sadden him a great deal. Have you heard his score? There must
certainly have been very beautiful things in it. What a victory for
all the malicious mediocrities who lounge about on your boulevards! That is the most intolerable aspect of failure – the insolence
of all those whippersnappers who had predicted it six months
beforehand. Be that as it may, Berlioz is and remains the most
vigorous musical brain in France.

[Letter to Ferdinand Denis, September 1838, in Liszt 1965: 204]

> Among those who looked on helpless was his colleague,
> the dramatic critic Jules Janin.

JULES-GABRIEL JANIN
(1804–74)

Between an inconsolable wife and a young child who no longer
recognised his father's voice . . . he was sad, he was ill, he no

longer read his favourite poets, he no longer enjoyed those long, intimate exchanges with Beethoven which had brought the two men into such close understanding. His friends said to him: 'Sing again, Berlioz!', but he remained obstinately silent. And we others – we too said: 'Come, defend yourself'. But Berlioz was not interested in writing any more.

[*Journal des débats*, 24 December 1838, in Prod'homme 1913: 124–5]

10 ROMÉO ET JULIETTE AND THE SYMPHONIE FUNÈBRE

Berlioz was in fact so ill that Habeneck had to conduct the first of the two concerts arranged for the winter of 1838, but for the second the composer was back on the rostrum to direct a performance of *Harold en Italie*, the symphony for viola and orchestra commissioned four years earlier by the legendary violinist Nicolò Paganini. Paganini had originally been so disappointed with the modest role given to the solo instrument in this work that he never bothered to play it. But now *Cellini* had rekindled his interest in Berlioz. He came to the concert, heard for the first time the symphony he had brought into being, and sent the astonished composer a cheque for 20,000 francs.

Parisian society was incredulous at the sudden munificence of so notorious a skinflint, and various alternative 'explanations' inevitably began to circulate.

CHARLES HALLÉ

The indifference shown by the crowd, and even by many musicians, towards his works [Berlioz] felt deeply, although he tried to make light of it, and any real success, however temporary, was eagerly welcomed, and brightened up his life for a while. So the well-known Paganini incident of the previous year had strengthened his courage for a long time, and from a morose made him a most cheerful companion. But thereby hangs a tale which, as all the actors in it are gone to their rest, may be divulged without inconvenience. Armand Bertin, the wealthy and distinguished proprietor of the 'Journal des Débats', had a high regard for Berlioz and knew of all his struggles, which he, Bertin, was anxious to lighten. He resolved therefore to make him a present of 20,000 fr., and in order to enhance the moral effect of this gift he persuaded Paganini to appear as the donor of the money. How well Bertin had judged was proved immediately; what would have been a simple *gracieuseté* from a rich and powerful editor towards one of his staff became a significant tribute from one genius to another, and had a colossal *retentissement*. The secret was well kept and never divulged to Berlioz. It was known, I believe, to but two of Bertin's friends besides myself, one of whom is Mottez, the celebrated painter; I learned it about seven years later when I had become an intimate friend of the house, and Madame Armand Bertin had been for years one of my best pupils.

[Hallé 1896: 69–70]

> But the incredulity in Paris was such that there was little hope of secrecy.

FERDINAND HILLER

The money was paid out of Rothschild's bank in Paris, there could be no doubt about that – and yet the whole business remained puzzling, unbelievable even. The key to the mystery was given to me by Rossini . . . 'But is this [the Bertin story] possible, believable, really certain?' I asked Rossini. 'I know it', replied the maestro, with that absolute seriousness which was no less characteristic of him than the jocular humour in which he so often indulged. No doubt this *fait accompli* was known to many other people, and no doubt some will question it, but I am convinced that it is true.

[Hiller 1880: 89]

> Liszt was another of those who never believed that Paganini was the true donor – and the matter has never been conclusively proved either way. But there seems no particular reason why an artist of Paganini's romantic temperament shouldn't simply have given way to a burst of sincere if somewhat uncharacteristic generosity: even Paganini's fiercest critics were prepared to see it this way.

JULES-GABRIEL JANIN

It struck us all for the first time that Paganini was really a man like the rest of us; that a really warm heart beats in his breast; that his eyes can weep; that his soul can feel; and that there is nothing supernatural in the talent of this strange being but the talent itself. From this moment on, Berlioz was saved. Hope and confidence in his own genius returned to him again and he crossed, as a conquering hero, the threshold of his home which a few hours before he had left – a desperate man.

[de Courcy 1957: ii, 286]

> In any case Berlioz himself never doubted Paganini's good faith, and the journalist Auguste Morel later reported an interview with Paganini which perhaps goes some way to reconciling the two interpretations of his behaviour.

NICOLÒ PAGANINI
(1782–1840)

I did this both for Berlioz and for myself. For Berlioz, because I saw a young man full of genius, whose strength and courage might well in the end have been broken by the desperate struggle that he had to keep up daily against jealous mediocrity or ignorant indifference, and I thought: 'I must help him'. For myself, because later on I shall be given credit for what I did, and when the time comes to reckon what claims I have to musical glory, not the least of these will be that I was the first to recognize a man of genius and to hold him up to public acclaim.

[*Journal de Paris*, 18 January 1839, in Prod'homme 1913: 127]

> And he retained his high opinion of Berlioz . . .

. . .whom you must not confuse with the common scum of [musicians] but should look on as a transcendent genius such as rises but once in every third or fourth century; a man of perfect probity and worthy of our confidence.

[Letter to Luigi Germi, 2 March 1840, in Barzun 1950: i, 345]

Determined to show his gratitude Berlioz plunged at once into composition. For years the idea of a symphonic work on the subject of Romeo and Juliet had been at the back of his mind; he had most recently thought about it after seeing Bellini's *I Capuleti e i Montecchi* in Rome (when Barbier had been too busy to undertake the text) and Berlioz turned now to the poet and translator Émile Deschamps, with whom he had first discussed the idea.

ÉMILE DESCHAMPS
(1791–1871)

It was [about 1829] that M. Hector Berlioz talked to me about his project for a dramatic symphony on *Romeo and Juliet* . . . Shakespeare fever was in the air, and it had not left me unaffected. I was delighted at this new homage to my divine poet, and at the idea of collaborating with a great artist. We worked out the plan for this poetic and musical work; the melodies and the verses came to us in floods, and the symphony appeared – ten years later.

[Deschamps 1874: v, 5–6]

In seven months Berlioz had completed the score of the symphony. Among Parisians he now had a sufficient following to sell out three performances of the new work in November and December, 1839; the Romantics and the intellectuals gathered for the occasion – '*c'était un* cerveau *que votre salle de concert*' wrote Balzac next day. There were enthusiasts from a younger generation as well: the Hungarian-born pianist and composer Stephen Heller analysed the occasion in an open letter to Schumann in Leipzig.

STEPHEN HELLER
(1813–88)

The friends and admirers of Berlioz had every reason to congratulate themselves. At the second concert, particularly, he was applauded with such enthusiasm that he could scarcely control the depth of his emotion. It is a great source of happiness for lovers of art to see this advance in the discernment of public opinion, and above all to watch a man of genius courageously hewing out a glorious path for himself, far from the vulgar highways of routine or financial speculation.

[Heller 1839: 562]

> And the young Charles Gounod gave evidence of characteristic precocity.

CHARLES GOUNOD
(1818–93)

Berlioz provided one of the most powerful emotions of my youth. He was fifteen years older than me, so he was thirty-four at the time when I, a mere boy of nineteen, was studying composition at the Conservatoire under Halévy. I remember the impression he made on me then, both in person and through his works, which he often rehearsed in the concert hall of the Conservatoire. The minute Halévy had finished correcting my exercise, I would escape from the classroom as quickly as I could and hide myself away in a corner of the concert hall, where I would let myself become intoxicated with this strange, passionate, convulsive music that opened up such new, such colourful horizons.

One day, I had been sitting in on a rehearsal of the Romeo and Juliet symphony, which was still unpublished and of which Berlioz was going to give the first performance only a few days later. I was so struck by the sweep of the great finale, the Reconciliation of the Montagues and the Capulets, that I came away with Frère Laurent's superb '*Jurez tous par l'auguste symbole!*' fixed complete in my memory.

A day or two later I went to see Berlioz and, sitting down at the piano, I played the passage to him in full. He opened his eyes wide and, staring at me, said 'Where the devil did you get that from?' 'One of your rehearsals' I replied. He couldn't believe his ears.

[Gounod 1882: viii–ix]

Visiting foreign musicians were less inclined to commit themselves and sometimes found Berlioz difficult to take, personally as well as musically. The pianist and composer Ignaz Moscheles, Mendelssohn's friend and teacher, was in Paris that summer.

IGNAZ MOSCHELES
(1794–1870)

I have now come to the end of my round of visits to artists, and have received very varied impressions. Berlioz, whose acquaintance I was anxious to make, was very cold and unsympathizing. His exquisitely penned score of *Romeo and Juliet* lay upon the table; I turned over some of the pages, but found the work so complicated, and the noise (at my very first glance) so overwhelming, that I cannot venture as yet to give any judgement on the music. One thing, however, is certain – that there must be new effects in it.

[Moscheles 1873: ii, 54]

A visitor from Germany who took Berlioz very much more seriously was Richard Wagner, who was present at one of the first performances of the *Roméo et Juliette* symphony, as well as the *Symphonie funèbre et triomphale* which followed it in 1840. Ten years younger than Berlioz, Wagner was on his first trip to Paris and supplemented his meagre income writing reports for a Dresden newspaper. But his earliest written mention of Berlioz actually occurs in a letter to his friend Ferdinand Heine in the same town.

RICHARD WAGNER
(1813–83)

I intend shortly to write an article on [Berlioz] for the *Abendzeitung*, so I hope that you will allow me to speak here only about the personal impression which my acquaintance with him has made on me. The first piece of his that I heard was the *Romeo & Juliet* symphony, where the tastelessness of the work's outward construction turned me violently against this composer of genius. The fact is, Berlioz is so completely alone among French musicians that he has nothing at all to provide him with the necessary basis of support, and is therefore compelled to grope his way through a world of labyrinthine fantasy; this makes it extremely difficult, perhaps even impossible, for him to develop his immense talents in the direction of *beauty*. He is, and remains, an incoherent phenomenon, though he is French in the fullest sense of the word. We Germans are lucky; we have our Mozart and Beethoven in our blood, and know how our pulses should beat. But Berlioz has no precursor, and is condemned to an eternal state of fever. Nevertheless, we in Germany do Berlioz the most outrageous injustice if we regard him, without the least justification, as a charlatan. On the contrary, his outward appearance is in rare accord with his inner genius. What he gives, he gives from his innermost being; he uses himself up wholly, and is the only French composer who doesn't grow fat on his own success. His is a highly poetic nature, which is all the more remarkable in that he is in other respects so utterly French, and can express himself only in the most exaggerated terms.

[Letter to Ferdinand Heine, 27 March 1841, in Wagner 1967: 465–6]

> The article in the Abendzeitung appeared a couple of
> months later.

5th May 1841 . . .
Berlioz is not the kind of composer who just happens along as a matter of course, so I cannot just happen on an occasion to discuss him. He is not associated with the ostentatious, exclusive institutions of the Parisian world of art, and will have nothing to do with them: after his first appearances, both the Opéra and the Conservatoire closed their doors on him with offended alacrity. He has been forced to become, and to remain, the stalwart exception to a longstanding convention, and this, both inwardly and outwardly, is what he now is. Anybody who wants to hear his music must go direct to Berlioz himself, for he won't find it anywhere else, not even in the places where they play Mozart next to Musard. You hear Berlioz's compositions only at the concerts that he himself gives once or twice a year. These remain his exclusive domain; here, he has his own works played by an orchestra that he has trained,

before a public he has conquered in a ten-year-long campaign. Nowhere else can you hear a note of Berlioz, except at those politico-musical state functions, in church or in the streets, at which he is occasionally required to appear.

. . . Berlioz not only possesses creative power and originality of invention, but is blessed with a virtue as rare among his composing fellow countrymen as is the vice of coquetry among us Germans. This virtue is that he doesn't write for money – and anyone who knows Paris, and the habits and behaviour of Parisian composers, knows how to value that virtue here. Berlioz is the ruthless enemy of everything common, cheap, or vulgar: he has sworn to strangle the first organ-grinder who dares to play his tunes. Terrible as that oath may be, I haven't the least anxiety for the lives of any of these street virtuosos because I can't think of anyone less likely to admire Berlioz's music than members of their widespread fraternity. But no one can deny that he has a talent for popular composition – popular, that is, in the ideal sense. When I heard the [*Symphonie funèbre et triomphale*] that he wrote for the reinterment of the victims of the July Revolution, I had the strongest feeling that every *gamin* in a blue blouse and a red cap must understand it to the core; though I ought perhaps to describe that understanding as more national than popular, for it is certainly a far cry from the *Postillon de Longjumeau** to this symphony. In truth, I am almost inclined to rank this composition above anything else in Berlioz's output: it is noble and great from the first note to the last, and all morbid emotionalism is kept at bay by a lofty, patriotic fervour which rises from lament to the heights of apotheosis . . . As regards this work at least I must . . . acknowledge with joy my conviction that this July symphony will live and exalt the hearts of men so long as there is a nation that calls itself French.

[Wagner 1914: 85, 88–9]

> After leaving Paris, Wagner's views seem to have hardened, to judge from an autobiographical sketch published in Dresden soon after his return.

My acquaintance with Habeneck, Halévy, Berlioz etc. led to no

---

* One of the most successful of Adam's *opéras-comiques*, first performed in 1836.

closer relations with any of them: in Paris artists have no time to
form friendships with one another, for everyone is in a frantic hurry
to look after his own interests. Halévy, like all the Parisian composers of our day, was fired with enthusiasm for his art only so long
as it was a question of winning a great success: once he had done
this . . . he had no thought for anything but making operas and
pocketing the money from them. Fame is everything in Paris: the
luck and the ruin of the artist. In spite of his forbidding manner,
Berlioz attracted me to a much greater extent. He differs funda-
mentally from his Parisian colleagues in that he doesn't write music
for the sake of money. But neither can he write for the sake of pure
art, for he lacks all sense of beauty and with few exceptions his
music is a grotesque caricature. He is completely isolated in his
position; on his side he has nothing but a band of devotees, shallow and without the least shred of judgment, who greet in him the
creator of a brand new musical system and completely turn his
head; everyone else avoids him as a madman.

[*Zeitung für die elegante Welt*, 1 & 8 February 1843, in Wagner 1967:
107–8]

> In a letter to Schumann, Wagner puts the blame squarely
> on Paris: 'For heaven's sake, look at Berlioz: this man
> has been so ruined by France, or rather by Paris, that it
> is no longer possible to tell what he might have become
> in Germany with talents like his'.* Nevertheless by the
> time Wagner came to dictate the 'official' account of his
> life some twenty-five years later, when a good deal of
> water had flowed under the bridge between the two men,
> the first impact of Berlioz was still vivid in his memory.

Encouraged by . . . signs of interest on his part, I tried to get to
know Berlioz more intimately. I had been introduced to him some
time before in Schlesinger's office, where I had seen him from time
to time since then. I had presented him with a copy of my *Deux
Grenadiers* but could elicit nothing more from him about it beyond
the statement that he could only strum the guitar a bit and was
unable to play it on the piano for himself. Yet his great orchestral
works, which I had heard during the previous winter under his baton,

* Wagner 1967: 577.

had made a tremendously exciting impression on me. During that winter of 1839–40, he had conducted three performances of his new *Romeo and Juliet* symphony, one of which I had attended. This was a completely new world for me, in which I had tried to find my way in an unprejudiced manner commensurate with these impressions. At first it was the impact of orchestral virtuosity, such as I had never before dreamed of, that nearly overwhelmed me. The fantastic boldness and sharp precision with which the most audacious orchestral combinations pressed almost tangibly upon me, over-awed my own musico-poetic sensibility and drove it with irresistible force back into my innermost being. I was all ears for things I had until then had no conception of and which I now had to try to explain to myself. In *Romeo and Juliet* I had nevertheless found long and frequent stretches that were empty and shallow, which pained me all the more considering that this work of art, despite being truly marred by its construction and its undue prolongation, overpowered me in its manifold brilliant moments to the point of extinguishing all reservations. Berlioz followed this new symphony with repeat performances of his *Harold en Italie* and his *Symphonie fantastique* during that winter. While I had listened to these works with rapt astonishment, being particularly impressed by the musical genre painting in the *Symphonie fantastique* and in almost every respect by *Harold*, the latest work of this extraordinary master, *Grande Symphonie funèbre et triomphale*, which he scored in the most brilliant and imaginative way for an immense military band and performed in the summer of 1840 . . . under the column in the Place de la Bastille . . ., had thoroughly acquainted me with the greatness and energy of this unique and quite incomparable artist. But I had nonetheless been unable to shake off an odd, profound feeling of oppression provoked by his work as a whole. There remained in me a residue of reserve, as if toward a foreign element with which I could never become entirely familiar, and this reserve took on the character of serious reflection as to why I could be so carried away by one of Berlioz's longer works and yet at times so undeniably repelled or even bored by it. It was only much later that I succeeded in bringing this problem, which caused me for years a certain painful tension towards Berlioz, out into the light and resolving it.

There is no question that at the time I felt myself a mere school-

boy beside Berlioz; and thus I was particularly embarrassed when
Schlesinger now . . . requested me to perform one of my own compositions at a big concert to be sponsored by the publishers of the
Gazette Musicale . . . At the rehearsal the prime source of my composition's effect proved very disheartening; not *once* were the high
and delicate passages [for trumpets] blown without cracking.
Moreover, since I was not allowed to conduct, I had to deal with a
chef d'orchestre whom I clearly perceived to be inwardly convinced
my work was nonsense, a view that seemed to be shared by all the
members of the orchestra. Berlioz, who attended this rehearsal,
remained silent throughout; he gave me no encouragement, yet also
did not try to dissuade me, but rather let me know with a weary
smile that things were very difficult in Paris.

[Wagner 1983: 191–3]

11 THE CRITIC AMONG CRITICS

Berlioz's position in the musical world of Paris was seen in a fresh perspective at this period by a new friend, the young Stephen Heller, who had arrived in Paris at the age of twenty-five and was to stay there for the rest of his life.

STEPHEN HELLER

By the time I arrived in Paris in 1838 Berlioz already occupied a place apart among the artists there. There was no longer any doubt about his celebrity as an audacious innovator, a man who aspired only to the highest goals in art.

His music, his conversation, his whole attitude to life gave him the air of a revolutionary in contrast to the '*ancien régime*' of music – which he in any case regarded as being in its last stage of decline. I don't know if he would have been a Girondist or Terrorist, but I'm sure he would cheerfully have arraigned Rossini, Cherubini, Auber, Hérold, Boieldieu, etc. – those 'Pitts' and 'Cobourgs' of the corrupted musical establishment – and committed them for trial as traitors to art. The works of these shameless aristocrats of the musical world were played in season and out, and as the profits rolled in they sucked the public dry.

But Paris is the only city in the world where every case can be accommodated, and where one can even take pleasure in searching out the most eccentric individuals, and in encouraging and helping them. Only, it is necessary that any such case must be really exceptional, that it must have some characteristic feature that makes it, so to speak, emotionally appealing. In a word, there must be some sort of legend around it. And around Berlioz there were several. His irresistible passion for music, which neither threats nor poverty

could dislodge; the necessity to which he found himself reduced –
he, the son of a rich and distinguished doctor of Grenoble – to earn
his living by joining the chorus of an insignificant theatre; his fantastic love for Miss Smithson, who had driven him into a frenzy of
emotion as Ophelia and as Juliet, although he didn't understand a
word of English; and on top of that his Fantastic Symphony, the
musical image of his passion, which aroused the love of the actress –
though she, in her turn, didn't understand a note of music; all this
had created in favour of Berlioz the background required to attract
the sympathy of a certain type of incendiary spirit. People like this,
intelligent, open, ready to offer any service, capable of any sacrifice,
will always be available in Paris to a genuine talent – provided, that
is, that it manifests itself with a suitable degree of *éclat*.

And so I realized, a few months after my first meeting with
Berlioz, that he was beginning to be considered as the chief of the
misunderstood geniuses of the time. He *was* misunderstood, it's
true, but as an artist in whom there is something to misunderstand.
Berlioz had raised the misunderstanding of talent to the level of
a dignity. The hostility of a section of the public contrasted so
strongly, so sharply, with the sympathy and genuine admiration of
the numerous circle of his friends, and appeared to them so
evidently inspired by hatred, that it brought him every day new
partisans . . .

. . . Artists of all kinds felt themselves attracted to Berlioz, not
always by his musical works in themselves, but by the poetry and
the picturesque character of his subjects. In particular, practically
all the painters (who generally have a feeling for music), the
engravers, the sculptors, the architects joined the ranks of his supporters, and these were also swelled by many of the famous poets
and novelists – Victor Hugo, Lamartine, Dumas, de Vigny, Balzac,
Theophile Gautier, and the painters Delacroix, Ary Scheffer, etc. –
who rightly saw in Berlioz a blazing star of the Romantic school.
These great writers, all of them completely ignorant of music –
people who would let a Strauss waltz be played by the orchestra as
an accompaniment to the most touching scenes of their dramas, no
doubt with the intention of adding to the emotion or the terror of
the spectator (though in this case, it is true, the waltz would be
invested with a solemn or mysterious character accentuated by
mutes and tremolos) – all these writers were, without exception,

full of enthusiasm for Berlioz and broadcast their feelings in their conversation and their writings. Added to these active popularizers was another group, not large but influential, of a superior class of amateurs: people who wanted to acquire, at small cost to themselves, the reputation of independent thinkers, while in fact being unable to tell a sonata of Wanhall or Diabelli from a sonata of Beethoven. This lot cried out vociferously against the criminal sensuality of modern music; they poked fun at their friends and peers still steeped in the music of Meyerbeer, Rossini and Auber, and above all missed no opportunity to predict the imminent demise of these ungodly, short-winded tunes and the triumph of a new art, great, noble, virile, lofty, eternal, destined to turn the world upside down.

And finally, add to these the quite large number of serious, good musicians who saw clearly what was really grand and daring in his genius, who recognized the often admirable originality of his conceptions, and who were not insensible to the wonderful charm of his orchestration.

Berlioz, then, was not as isolated and misunderstood as he himself liked to say.

[Letter to Hanslick, 1 February 1879, in Heller 1981: 247–50]

> Undoubtedly the partisan support of the devotees of the new Romanticism was an irritant to the Parisian musical establishment. In the same year that Heller arrived in Paris, the first book to be devoted entirely to Berlioz was published by the critic Joseph Mainzer; Mainzer had found much that was good and interesting in Berlioz's earlier works and said so in the press, but he had felt very differently when faced with the *Requiem*.

JOSEPH MAINZER
(1807–51)

What has struck us as being good in [M. Berlioz's] fantastic symphonies cannot oblige us to accept his *Requiem* as good, any more than the *Requiem* can in any way prejudice his reputation as a dramatist, which is to begin with *Benvenuto Cellini* . . .

The whole composition, and the way in which it was received, made such a painful impression on us that, in order not to wound the feelings of the young composer too deeply, and not to prejudice the opinion of those who had not heard the work, we resolved to abstain from making our opinion known.

But as if by magic whole hosts of enthusiasts arose: all the old masterpieces had been effaced by the new one: the *Requiems* of Jommelli, of Gossec, of Mozart, of Cherubini were nothing but pale and trivial productions beside the work of M. Berlioz. Everything that the art of past and recent times had bequeathed to us had been crushed by the immense achievement of a new genius. It was a miracle that this multitude of fanatics did not throw the statues of Buonarotti and Raphael, of Correggio and Palestrina from their pedestals, for no work created by the hand of man could find a place on the altar raised to the new Dalai-Lama! . . .

After having witnessed such comic genuflexions and heard such farcical hymns of praise, it would have been wrong to remain silent, to give credence to this overturning of the musical world, this triumph of matter over spirit . . .

[Mainzer 1838: 5, 22–4]

> It was what Berlioz stood for in music, as much as the music itself, that aroused the hostility of his colleagues, and this was to a great extent because of his activities as a musical journalist. His first articles for the press date from as early as 1823, and since 1829 he had filled an official position as critic; by 1834 he was providing reviews for the *Gazette musicale*, and only a year later he was appointed music critic (or *'feuilletoniste'*) on the *Journal des débats*, one of the most influential daily papers in France. It was a job he grew to hate.

GEORGE OSBORNE
(1806–93)

Musical composition for him was a natural function, a happiness; prose writing a labour without love. I have heard him say he would rather be a porter of a double-bass than a musical critic, if he could get as well paid for it. Although his articles, full of admiration of Gluck, Spontini, Beethoven, and Weber were most favourably received, still he began to realise the difficulties and danger of his position as composer conjointly with that of musical critic, and which, as he says, exercised so great and so deplorable an importance in his after-life. For enemies he had, not only those great conservatives who detest innovation of any kind, but also those who fell under his lash, of which he was not sparing.

[Osborne 1879: 69]

JOSEPH MAINZER

[When] M. Berlioz took to writing articles on music and became a critic, his writings, like his compositions, were interspersed with principles that nobody would dare to defend, as well as new ideas that were not without merit. Little by little, in the absence of any opposition to his views, these principles and opinions, which had been put forward in the first place with a certain degree of reserve, began to appear with greater assurance, and reached the point where M. Berlioz wanted to establish them as laws. We have followed all the steps of his literary career with interest and attention, regarding him as a man in whose soul there burned the sacred flame of that art for which he displayed an enthusiasm that amounted to fanaticism; but we were at last forced to recognize that he was straying into mistaken paths, that he was exploiting his position to turn art into an industry, and making use of the noble title of artist and of his own powerful and much respected prestige to vilify and tarnish the most illustrious celebrities . . .

Never, even when criticism was still in its tenderest infancy, has anyone dared to publish anything resembling the articles of M. Berlioz – though it is true that he appears to write more as a job than a vocation.

M. Berlioz was surely thinking of his own manner of viewing and judging when he said, à propos the duties of the 'unfortunate critic', that he could imagine nothing 'more arduous, more exhausting, more difficult, more discouraging, more detestable, more stupid and more useless' (*Gazette musicale*, 7 January 1838).

The three last adjectives, above all, seem to us perfectly chosen by
M. Berlioz, and nobody could characterize his style of criticism
more accurately than he has done himself . . .

[Mainzer 1838: 3–4, 81–2]

> *Pace* Mainzer, Berlioz retained his position on the
> *Journal des débats* for the next twenty-nine years where
> he regularly turned out some of the most distinguished
> musical criticism of the century; though it kept him
> from composition, it brought him much-needed funds
> for his vulnerable domestic life and provided the stamp
> of authority for a relentless crusade against the triviality
> of the Parisian musical scene. 'It is from there', wrote
> Adolphe Adam, 'that he hurls his anathemas against
> Auber and me – his two *bêtes noires* . . .'
>
> Poor Adam had found the commission for the
> *Symphonie funèbre* a particularly hard pill to swallow.

ADOLPHE ADAM

For the reinterment of the bodies of the July martyrs we are to have
music specially composed for the occasion by *maître* Berlioz: there
will be two hundred wind instruments and cannon fire in the
fortes – which should be charming. It is positively shameful for us
other French composers to see the favours of the government being
lavished on a man whose character and talent are so contemptible:
it is really beneath the dignity of the *Journal des débats* to allow
space for the feuilletons of M. Berlioz, who uses them to dissemi-
nate, in the worst of taste, his hatred of everything that the public
sanctions with its applause.

[Letter to Spiker, 23 July 1840, in Adam 1903: V, 143]

> The case of Fétis, another *bête noire*, was rather differ-
> ent. Like Mainzer, he made great claims (not entirely
> unjustified) to have been indulgent towards Berlioz as a
> young man, but had become a declared enemy ever
> since finding himself mercilessly pilloried in *Lélio* –
> though that is not the way he puts it himself.

FRANÇOIS-JOSEPH FÉTIS

After having ... taken a benevolent attitude towards an artist who had worked his own way up, and whose perseverance in the achievement of his objects had shown him deserving of success, the time has come for me to change roles and to take up that of critic in all the severity of the term, because the situation is now very different. The days are gone when I supported M. Berlioz against the scorn of a celebrated academic institution, against the public, and against my own distaste; today M. Berlioz has set himself up as an innovator who has already achieved the triumph of his doctrines and the defeat of his adversaries. When he became a journalist he set about converting his readers, in four periodicals and daily papers of widely differing political hues, I won't say to his new musical religion, because up until now he hasn't given much idea what that consists of (apart from the purely barbaric and irrational), but to faith in his authority. He has friends, whom he has been careful to avoid choosing from the ranks of musicians – with the exception of one or two enthusiasts of varying degrees of sincerity – and these friends, among whom are a number of influential figures, praise him to the skies and will never be happy until they succeed in persuading the powers that be that M. Berlioz is the genius of the century. You can see that such a man has no further need of my indulgence, and would even be wounded by it; he is fully ready to face criticism, for now, from the tone he adopts, it is clear that he is judging the judges.

[Fétis 1835]

> Fétis is at least right in implying that by the late 1830s Berlioz, as a writer on musical matters, was a force to be reckoned with.

HENRY FOTHERGILL CHORLEY
(1808–72)

> The regular music critic of *The Athenaeum* for thirty-five years, Chorley was a conservative journalist of recognized probity and European reputation. His opinion of Berlioz as a composer was mixed.

If it has been my disappointing fate never to hear a note of the music of M. Berlioz in Paris, it was my odd fortune to meet him for the first time in a place and a society as characteristic of his peculiar position, as a first sight of Gluck would have been if taken through the box-door of Madame St Huberti – the fascinating *prima donna* . . . who contrived to bring about an amicable interview betwixt [Gluck] and his rival Piccini.

The critics' boxes at the Conservatoire are little larger than pillboxes. To obtain a seat elsewhere, however, at one of those famed concerts was impossible; and it was with no common feelings of eagerness and anticipation that I repaired thither on a certain day in January, 1840 . . . Fortunately, it was a bitter cold day; had it been summer, the flare of the artificial lights hanging before my eyes, and the pressure from without of many beards, which seemed to sit over my shoulders, and in my pockets – here, there, and everywhere – would have made up a dear price to be paid for hearing even Beethoven's symphonies performed by the *soi-disant* most perfect orchestra in Europe. In such a masquerade of Orsons, a smooth face is at a premium; and the one which in its smoothness paired off with mine was thoughtful and shrewd-looking, with eyes at once deep and keen, and a certain sad and sardonic expression, the coming and going of which had engaged me some time before I knew that it belonged to M. Berlioz. He was sitting, almost pressed out of his hard and scanty chair, by another of the fraternity. This was M. Mainzer. Only in Paris could such a juxtaposition have presented itself! M. Mainzer had but recently published a book to prove that the genius of M. Berlioz was but quackery, and his picture-music a monstrous combination of what was with what ought to have been impossible: and M. Berlioz had only very recently retaliated, by laconically characterising M. Mainzer's 'La Jacquerie', produced at the Théâtre de la Renaissance, as 'the opera in the key of D'! There, in short, sate the romantic critic in all his formidable glory; and there sate the affronted upholder of classicism, more hurt by that one *mot*, than his antagonist had been damaged by his whole artillery of ninety-five pages.

[Chorley 1841: iii, 24–7]

Inevitably, those who had no critical or professional axe
to grind were inclined to take a less unsympathetic view
of Berlioz's journalistic activities.

ERNEST LEGOUVÉ

[His criticism] was harsh, I admit, sometimes even bitter and unfair.
I don't wish to excuse it, but I do want to explain it. To begin with,
he was soured by the struggle and the injustice that he encountered;
his sharpest attacks are often no more than revenge. Then, he
found the life of a critic intolerable; he only accepted it to earn a
living, and he never took up his pen without a movement of anger,
like a man feeling the millstone round his neck. Even the money he
earned from it distressed him, for his pride as a composer resented
the idea that his articles could bring him in more than his music.
Add to this that he was violently self-opinionated like all innova-
tors – like Beethoven, who wanted to see Rossini whipped, or
Michelangelo, who spoke with contempt of Raphael, or Corneille,
who could see no dramatic talent in Racine. Jealousy has no place
in these lapses of justice; these are the antipathies of genius which
only go to prove the presence of genius itself; the more original a
mind is, the more unfair. If Rossini, Auber and Hérold had written
what they thought of Berlioz, they would have found a lot more to
say against him than he against them.

And finally, that terrible quality that so easily becomes a weakness – Berlioz had an irrepressible sense of humour! Once he had a
pen in his hand, the witticisms that flowed from his fingers were so
funny that he burst out laughing while he was writing them down;
but his banter, even if it was often a product of pure gaiety, wasn't
any the less deadly or any the less feared for that.

Few people were at ease with him. The most eminent artists, his
own equals, felt a sort of constraint in his presence. Gounod has
often told me of the uncomfortable feeling Berlioz gave him. I have
seen Adolphe Nourrit one morning at my house embark with
enthusiasm on the performance of a Schubert song and then, suddenly flustered by seeing Berlioz enter, finish like a schoolboy the
piece he had begun as a master. Berlioz had no idea that he inspired
such feelings, and if he had known he would have been miserable.

For the smartest of his sardonic jibes would die on his lips if he feared it might inflict pain on even the most obscure recipient.

[Legouvé 1886: 314–16]

LOUIS ENGEL

Although I had the greatest personal regard for him . . . I must in truth admit that – without giving way to such violent injustice and partiality as Richard Wagner frequently, not to say perpetually, did – Berlioz, who wrote the most admirable French, the most instructive criticisms, the most brilliant and *spirituel* style, could not help being occasionally more kind to friends, and more bitter to real or imaginary adversaries, than was strictly just, especially as, on certain occasions, his satire cruelly wounded. Berlioz allowed nobody to talk him out of his opinion, which was more esteemed, as it was more penetrating, than that of any other musician. There was nothing small, nothing mean, about the man: he was a great and liberal genius, thoroughly free from petty considerations, only too enthusiastic for what he found really great, too thankful for small or great services rendered, and naturally incensed at nonentities and mediocrities pushing to the fore and demanding his complicity in proclaiming them worth the attention of the public.

Can it be wondered at that he had the majority against him, as every conscientious critic must have?

[Engel i, 1886: 107–8]

CAMILLE SAINT-SAËNS
(1835–1921)

> Saint-Saëns, who was thirty-odd years younger than
> Berlioz, later knew him well and left many perceptive
> comments about the man he so much admired.

He has been reproached for his acerbity. With him, it wasn't malevolence, but rather a kind of mischievousness, an irrepressible sense of the comic with which he laced his conversation and which he could never control. I can think of hardly anybody except

Duprez who persistently received this treatment in any considerable number of facetious articles, and frankly the great tenor had
thoroughly deserved a few arrows in his flesh. Didn't he himself
describe, in his *Memoirs*, how he had scuppered *Benvenuto Cellini*,
and was the composer likely to be grateful? Perhaps he would
have done more to support the work if Berlioz had employed the
resounding arguments used by Meyerbeer to encourage him to
prolong the run of *Les Huguenots* – as the great singer tells us in
the same book with a candour and lack of awareness that would
disarm a tiger . . .*

[Saint-Saëns 1899: 8–9]

> In spite of his admiration, however, Saint-Saëns was
> perfectly aware of the limitations of Berlioz's musical
> background.

Berlioz was, beyond any possible question, the leading music critic
of his time – in spite of the sometimes inexplicable peculiarity of his
judgments. And yet he lacked the very foundation of good criticism: musical erudition, and a knowledge of the history of the art.
A lot of people maintain that in artistic matters it is not necessary
to analyse one's impressions. That's perfectly possible, but in that
case you must limit yourself to taking your pleasure where you find
it, and not attempt any opinion as to how it arises. A critic has to
proceed differently: he must take every aspect into account, not
expect from Raphael the palette of Rembrandt or from the ancient
painters, who worked in tempera and fresco, the effects of a painting in oils. Berlioz took nothing into account except the satisfaction
or the boredom which he felt in listening to a work. For him, the
past didn't exist; he didn't understand the old masters, whom he
had only been able to get to know by reading. If he admired Gluck
and Spontini so much, it was because in his youth he had seen their
works performed at the Opéra by Mme. Branchu, the last singer to
preserve the traditions of that style. He hadn't a good word to say
for Lully, or for the *Serva padrona* of Pergolesi: 'To see this work

---

* At the 60th performance Meyerbeer bet Duprez the proceeds of his *droits
d'auteur* that the run would not reach the 80th. It did.

revived,' he said ironically, 'to be present at the first performance –
that would be a pleasure worthy of Olympus itself!'

[Ibid: 7]

STEPHEN HELLER

The music which he had really studied he could always recall at a
moment's notice. He had the orchestral works of Beethoven complete in his head, for example, – more than the quartets or the
piano works – also the operas of Gluck and Spontini; he knew
Grétry, Méhul, Dalayrac and Monsigny well, and in spite of his
unbelievable aversion to Rossini, he had a high regard for two of
his scores: *Le Comte Ory* and *Le Barbier de Séville*. Berlioz
belonged to that breed of true artists who can be genuinely
impressed, even moved to tears, by any work of art that is perfect
of its own kind. Thus, the first time Adelina Patti sang in *Le
Barbier* I was sitting next to him in the theatre, and I can state
positively that at the gayest, most charming of passages he wept
with emotion.

It was another matter at a performance of *La Flûte Enchantée*
to which we went together. Every so often, Berlioz would give way
to fits of childish anger at what he called Mozart's 'culpable concessions': for him, these included Don Ottavio's aria and Donna
Anna's in F major [in *Don Giovanni*] as well as the famous col-
oratura arias of the Queen of the Night. Nothing could persuade
him to set aside the irrelevance of these pieces from a dramatic
point of view and to recognize their intrinsic qualities as music. But
what a keen sense of satisfaction I felt that evening at seeing the
profound and powerful impression that Mozart's opera made on
him! He had often heard it before but, whether because of a hap-
pier frame of mind, or a particularly fine performance, he told me
that this music had never gone so straight to his heart. At some
moments, indeed, his exaltation became so vocally manifest that
our neighbours, who were busy picking their teeth and wanted to
digest their dinner in peace and quiet, complained sharply at this
'immoderate' display of enthusiasm.

[Letter to Hanslick, 1 February 1879, in Heller 1981: 253–4]

CAMILLE SAINT-SAËNS

I always remember his astonishment and delight at hearing a chorus of Sebastian Bach that I played him one day. He couldn't get over the idea that the great Sebastian had written things like that; he told me that he had always taken him for a sort of colossus of learning, grinding out scholarly fugues but devoid of poetry or charm. The truth was, he didn't know him.

And yet, in spite of all this, and a great deal else besides, he was a critic of the first rank, because he presented the unique phenomenon of a man of genius, endowed with a delicate, penetrating mind and an extraordinary refinement of the senses, sincerely describing impressions that were unaffected by any external preoccupation. The pages he has devoted to the symphonies of Beethoven or to the operas of Gluck are incomparable; you have always to go back to them when you want to refresh your imagination, purify your taste, wash yourself clean of all the dust that the common run of life and music leaves on our artists' souls, which have so much to suffer in this world.

[Saint-Saëns 1899: 7–8]

ERNEST LEGOUVÉ

Sure of finding at my home a piano and [in my wife] an interpreter, he used to come and chat with us about Gluck, and Beethoven, and himself. I have in my hands, and at this moment under my eyes, a copy of the score of *Alceste* in the French version, entirely covered in marginal notes and indications in Berlioz's hand. Gluck was very bad at correcting his proofs, and on this copy Berlioz corrected them again, according to the Italian edition which, as everybody knows, is the original. He restored the original tempo indications. In the aria '*Non, ce n'est pas un sacrifice*', above the phrase '*Mes chers enfants, je ne vous verrai plus*', he wrote the words 'twice as slow' in enormous letters and in a hand so tremulous that it betrays his anger and seems to say: 'Imbecile translators!' Above all the opening of the famous aria *Divinités du Styx* aroused his indignation and inspired him to his most interesting corrections . . .

Here is the French translation: '*Divinités du Styx, Divinités du Styx, ministres de la mort*' [and here is] the Italian version: '*Umbre, larve, compagne di morte*'.

As he struck out and erased the French text, and restored the Italian words over it – 'Can you understand', he said to me in fury, 'such savages as these translators! And does this great genius named Gluck really have to be the negligent, unconcerned proof corrector that we see here, to have thought up or accepted such a mutilation? "*Umbre, larve, compagne di mort*" constitute a succession of broad, sombre notes which produce a powerful effect of religious terror. Instead of that the French translator, with his hideous "*Divinités du Styx!*" – which he repeats twice, the wretch! – gives us five little skipping notes ending in this horrible word "*Styx!*" I agree that the result is certainly infernal, but infernal for the singer, infernal for the listener, and it destroys with the shriek of a whistle the funereal impression of this invocation to the gods of the underworld.'

After correcting the piece, he asked his hostess to sing it to him, and to the purely material corrections then succeeded the most delicate artistic indications. He entered, and enabled us to enter, into the mystery of the author's intentions, into all the subtleties of accent and pronunciation, with an artistry that revealed Gluck's thoughts and was capable of transforming a simple amateur into a true artist.

More poetic still was Berlioz expounding the Choral Symphony. Even his articles, admirable as they are, give an imperfect idea of what it was like, for they contain only his opinions; when he was speaking the whole of him was there. To the eloquence of words were added the look on his face, the gestures, the tone of voice, the tears, the exclamations of enthusiasm, and those spontaneous touches of feeling, those flashes of imagery which come to the speaker as the listener's expression responds to the sound of his voice. An hour spent like that taught me more about instrumental music than a whole concert at the Conservatoire. Or, to put it rather better, when I arrived at the Conservatoire on the following Sunday with my mind still full of Berlioz's commentary, Beethoven's work opened up before me like a vast temple flooded with light: I grasped its structure at a glance and walked through it freely as through a world that I knew, exploring its every byway with a confident step. Berlioz had given me the key of the sanctuary.

[Legouvé 1886: 304–7]

On Beethoven, as on Gluck or any other composers he really admired, Berlioz's critical attitudes were uncompromising. As Schumann observed: 'Berlioz does not try to be polite and elegant: what he hates, he grasps fiercely by the hair; what he loves, he nearly crushes in his fervour.'* One of the most revealing of Berlioz stories relates to the first Paris performance of Beethoven's Quartet in C sharp minor, Opus 131, in March 1829.

JOSEPH D'ORTIGUE

A composer of unquestionable merit . . . to whose talents the writer of this article has often been happy to pay homage, but who makes the mistake, in our view, of prejudging the alleged extravagance of the last works of Beethoven, was present one day at the performance of a quartet by this great master. When the piece was finished, Berlioz wanted to have the opinion of this distinguished artist.

'I don't like this music,' he replied. 'When all is said and done, apart from a few happy ideas, it lacks clarity and sequence; it doesn't give me any real sense of pleasure. And you will agree with me that the object of music is to give pleasure to the ear.'

'But I – ', cried Berlioz excitedly, ' – I want music to put me in a fever, to set my nerves on edge. *Do you imagine, Monsieur, that I listen to music for pleasure?*'

This reply left the artist in consternation; he has never been able to understand it.

[D'Ortigue 1833: 311]

And from the other end of his life comes another, equally characteristic.

STEPHEN HELLER

One day, at a chamber music recital, we were listening together to the Beethoven E minor Quartet [Op 59, No 2]. We were sitting at

* Schumann 1835.

the back of the room, in a corner. For me, hearing this admirable work was like attending a Mass for a pious Catholic, who listens in a spirit of devotion and tranquil contemplation to this essential rite of worship, made familiar by frequent observance. But Berlioz was there as a novice; for him, feelings of artistic piety were mixed with joy and a kind of fear in the presence of this secret, so rich with charm and hallowed greatness, that was being revealed to him. The rapture of pure ecstacy spread across his features during the *adagio*: it seemed as if a 'transsubstantiation' had taken place within him. Several other fine works on the programme were still to be performed, but we left without waiting for them and I accompanied Berlioz back to the door of his house. We said nothing as we walked: the sublime prayer of the *adagio* was still singing in our minds. When I left him he took my hand and said: 'That man had everything . . . and we have nothing!'

[Letter to Hanslick, 1 February 1879, in Heller 1981: 254]

Berlioz's intransigent stance as a critic and polemicist may have made him enemies, but it was his music itself that most commonly came in for attack, and in this category everything pales into insignificance beside the astonishing outpourings of the ultra-conservative musician and writer, Paul Scudo. Scudo, a Frenchman of Italian birth, began his journalistic career about 1840; six years later, he collected a number of his reviews into a publication that marks the first climax of a vicious obsession with Berlioz that was to continue throughout his life.

PAUL SCUDO
(1806–64)

The first thing that one notices about the compositions of M. Berlioz is the vast ambition of his spirit, and the futility of the efforts to which it gives rise. You see him plan the outlines of a vast structure and then not know how to fill it, spread the wings of an eagle and fail to rise from the ground. This disproportion between his desires and his abilities, between the audacity of the intention and the mediocrity of the result, is the salient feature of M. Berlioz's character, and one which has enabled him to create an instant illusion – for there is no failing more characteristic of the period in which we live. If you strip the composer's ideas of the clamorous envelope in which he seeks to conceal them, you will only find, more often than not, a body without youth and without grace. Lift but a little the heavy cloak in which he drapes himself, and you will find the limbs beneath it are feeble. M. Berlioz indulges himself with words, with empty resounding phrases, and he takes the disorderly piling up of images for strokes of genius. The author of the *Symphonie fantastique* is the first to be taken in by his own method; he deceives himself, he becomes drunk with noise, and believes he has done something marvellous because he uses twenty trombones to attack the most commonplace bass motif or even a fragment of pedal point. But if you have the tune of '*J'ai du bon tabac*' played by two hundred instruments, or the commonest of popular songs intoned by two hundred choristers, you can easily get effects like those produced by M. Berlioz – effects that are purely physical, effects of sonority, which offer no real grounds for self-congratulation. The Chinese who charm their leisure hours with the sound of the tam-tam, the savages who are driven to a frenzy by the rubbing together of two stones, make music of the same kind as the music composed by M. Berlioz . . .

M. Berlioz is perhaps the composer least endowed with melodic ideas, that is to say musical ideas, who has ever lived until now and, with the knowledge that he must have of his own sterility, he has tried to make up by efforts of will for the flashes of inspiration that visit him so rarely . . . Not only does M. Berlioz have no melodic ideas – and it is for that reason, no doubt, that he tries to cover his nakedness with the glamour of excessive sonority – but, when an idea does come to him, he doesn't know what to do with it, because he doesn't know how to write. This may perhaps surprise that group of easily moved literary and poetic amateurs who have surrounded the cradle of our reformer and proclaimed him a profound genius, but it certainly won't astonish competent musicians or men of taste . . .

M. Berlioz hardly ever writes for anything less than huge vocal or instrumental forces; he aims at the grand effect, he unleashes every piercing sound at the same time because he doesn't know how to prepare or control an idea, or how to bring it to a conclusion. His difficulty in creating orchestral dialogue is extreme . . . He brings together the most discordant colours; he groups instruments which howl at finding themselves together. He rides rough-shod over transitional motifs and incidental tonalities; he bursts through all ordered relationships, he thunders, he explodes, but there is no lightning, no storm. He uses only two effects and two colours, the *fortissimo* and the *smorzato* [fading away], the red and the black . . .

The orchestra that Beethoven used is not enough for him; to display itself in all its power his genius not only requires all known musical instruments – the ones that have been invented for fifty years – but has to get its hands on all these ill-formed experiments which the music industry turns out every day, and with which they try to revive our blunted senses. He runs the gamut of sound perceptible to our ears, he piles up the harshest dissonances and the most vexatious rhythms, he deploys an army of double basses, ophicleides and trombones; he revels in the coarsest contrasts, sets up amorous dialogues between the bass drum and the piccolo, between the oboe and the tam-tam; he uses, and wastes, the sonority produced by bringing together two or three hundred musicians; he puffs and prances, he throws himself about like a demon deprived of divine grace who wants to scale the heights of heaven by sheer force of arrogance and will power. But to gain the paradise of art you must have either the simplicity of a child or the majesty of genius. There is more wisdom in the prayer of a poor, ignorant woman, says Fénelon, than in all the stout volumes of a vain philosophy; there is more charm, more inspiration in the song of a washerwoman who sings with feeling than there is in the entire output of M. Berlioz . . .

It is evident that M. Berlioz has lost his way. He has mistaken the exaltation of youth and of a sanguine temperament for the indications of a superior vocation, the transports of fever for the transports of genius. He has been confirmed in this delusion by the blindness of his friends and by the comfortable doctrines of a school which forgives any kind of recklessness, and as a result he has never known either how to learn the art that can be taught, or how to bring himself to confess his impotence . . . Although he has received the favour of the authorities and the trumped up infatuation of public opinion, he has not managed to compose either a symphony, or a mass, or an opera, that one can acknowledge and accept without compromising oneself . . . As for the masses, the cantatas, the fragments of *Benvenuto Cellini* that have been published, their least fault is that they are unsingable. Oh! how Palestrina, Mozart and Rossini are avenged for the mockery with which M. Berlioz has honoured them!

[Scudo 1850: 46–7, 48, 50, 52, 53, 57, 61, 62]

Though the cock-eyed ferocity of Scudo's attacks may have been exceptional (Scudo himself ended his life in an asylum for the insane), the ideas that lay behind them were not uncommon in Paris. Berlioz's refusal to accept convention in his music was met by many people with genuine perplexity as well as anger – even in some cases by his friends and supporters.

ERNEST LEGOUVÉ

His *Damnation de Faust* had just been arranged for piano.

'I shall arrive at your place tomorrow at eight o'clock', he said to me one day [in January 1855], 'with my score and my pianist; he is only twelve years old* – a prodigy who will be a marvel one day. His name is Théodore Ritter'.

The next day, at the appointed time, Ritter was seated at the piano. Berlioz sat beside him, often interrupting him or making him play things over again so that he could explain to me the intention of this or that passage, the sense of this or that movement, or of this or that note. As he talked, I had a clear vision of the double aim that he has always set himself, the two contradictory objects that he has always pursued: the grandeur of the whole, and the precision of the details – Michelangelo and Meissonier.

Shall I confess it? – I felt a sort of dizziness at seeing how much he wanted the music to say, not only in its external effect but above all in the very much more mysterious domain of the soul.

Our emotions have nothing so intimate, our feelings nothing so secret, our senses nothing so fleeting, that he did not seek to express it in the language of sound. He wanted his music to be the echo of the thousand vibrations of his restless heart. A noble ambition, no doubt, but one that I believe was beyond his artistic competence. I touch here upon a very delicate point. The family of the great artists can be divided into two groups: on the one hand the simple, clear, shining geniuses – Haydn, Mozart, Rossini and, in our time, Gounod; on the other the geniuses that are complex and abstruse – Beethoven, Meyerbeer, and with them, Berlioz. The latter perhaps, even more than the former, have need of a thorough

---

* In fact, Ritter (born 1840) could not have been less than fourteen at the time.

technical expertise; the multiplicity of their ideas, the power of their conceptions, the depths of feeling to which they aspire, require an understanding of musical structure, and a flexibility in its execution, which in turn demand a degree of technical preparation that even the most naturally gifted cannot supply for themselves . . .

Well then, this is what Berlioz lacked. The resistance of his father meant that his musical studies started too late; poverty prevented him from carrying them through properly . . . and he wasn't able to acquire *the talent to match his genius*. And in his compositions, therefore, beside the most delicate and ingenious refinements of workmanship, there are moments of clumsiness, obscurities, deficiencies and oddities that result from awkwardness of technique. No doubt he was very much more skilful than practically all the others, but he wasn't skilful enough for *him* . . . To be completely himself, Berlioz would have needed the skill and technical ability of Beethoven.

[Legouvé 1886: 310–2]

> Legouvé is perhaps a bit out of his depth, but the comparison with Beethoven, which Berlioz himself encouraged by his championship of Beethoven's works, was invoked by many observers – both positively and negatively. Wagner, writing in 1841, saw it as an essential factor in Berlioz's isolation as a composer.

RICHARD WAGNER

[Berlioz's isolation] not only defines his position in the outer world but also lies at the source of his inner development. No matter how French he is, no matter how close the sympathy between his nature and his aims and those of his countrymen – he still stands alone. He sees no one before him to whom he can turn for support, no one beside him on whom he can lean. From our Germany the spirit of Beethoven wafted across to him, and certainly there must have been times when Berlioz wished he were German. It was at times like these that his genius urged him to write as the great master wrote, to express for himself what he felt was expressed in

Beethoven's works. But as soon as he took up his pen, his French blood welled up again naturally, the same blood that surged in Auber's veins when he wrote the volcanic final act of his *Muette* [*de Portici*]. Happy Auber, who knew no Beethoven symphonies! Berlioz knew them, though, and what is more he understood them. They inspired him, they intoxicated him – and yet he could not deny his French blood; he realized he could not become another Beethoven, but he also knew that he couldn't write like Auber. So he became Berlioz and wrote his *Symphonie fantastique* – a work that would have made Beethoven smile, just as it does Auber, but which sent Paganini into a positive fever of ecstasy, and assured for its creator a party of supporters who will hear no other music in this world than the Fantastic Symphony of Berlioz.

No one who hears this symphony played here in Paris by Berlioz's orchestra can fail to think himself confronted by a marvel without precedent. The power of a colossal inner richness, a heroic imagination, erupts in a morass of passions as from the crater of a volcano: what we see are gigantic clouds of smoke, parted and moulded into fleeting shapes only by flashes of lightning and tongues of flame. Everything is monstrous, daring, but infinitely painful. Nowhere is there beauty of form, nowhere the majestic stream to whose calm certainty we could trust ourselves with confident expectation. I should have found the first movement of Beethoven's C minor symphony an act of positive kindness after the *Symphonie fantastique* . . .

What is unfortunate is that Berlioz appears to enjoy his isolation, and obstinately seeks to assert it. He has no friend whom he considers worth going to for advice, or whom he would allow to point out any defects in his works. In this connection I was filled with sadness at hearing his Romeo and Juliet symphony. Alongside the most brilliant invention this work is heaped with such a load of rubbish and ineptitudes that I found myself wishing that, before having it performed, he could have shown his score to someone like Cherubini who, without doing its originality the least harm, would have had the wit to get rid of many of its imperfections. But Berlioz is so excessively sensitive that even the most intimate friend would never dare to suggest such a thing, while at the same time his hold over his audience is so powerful that they regard him as being beyond any comparison or criticism. And so Berlioz will remain always incomplete, and perhaps shine only as a transient, marvellous exception.

And this is a pity! If he could only make himself master of the many excellent qualities that have emerged with the latest brilliant period of modern French music, if he could only give up that isolation which he maintains with such arrogance of spirit and adopt the principles of any valid musical style of the past or present, then he would surely attain so vast an influence over the future of French music that his fame would never die.

[Wagner 1914: 86–8]

> One cannot help wondering what Berlioz would have said to the suggestion that Cherubini should be asked to 'tidy up' his scores. Nevertheless it was a widely held opinion that lack of technical preparation was to blame for the alleged shortcomings in Berlioz's music, even if points of reference differed – some (like Legouvé) regretting the accomplished Italianate manner that currently dominated Parisian musical taste, others (like Wagner) missing the structural and rational coherence basic to the German musical tradition. In this connection Delacroix reports a revealing conversation with Chopin – who had after all been brought up in Warsaw on the study of Bach and the earlier Viennese classics.

EUGÈNE DELACROIX

I asked [Chopin] what it was that established logic in music. He made me understand what it is that constitutes *harmony* and *counterpoint* – that it is *fugue* which best represents pure logic in music, and that to be skilled in fugue is to be in a position to appreciate the basis of all reason in music, and all its musical consequences . . .

[This led me to the difference between Mozart and Beethoven.] 'At those points,' he said, 'where Beethoven is obscure and appears to lack coherence, this is not because of the so-called, rather wild, originality with which he is credited, but because he turns his back on the eternal principles of art. Mozart never does this: each of his musical voices has its own path which, while harmonizing perfectly with the others, maintains its own melodic course and follows it

out in full: *that's* what counterpoint is – *punto contrapunto.*' He
said that it was the custom [now] to learn about harmony before
studying counterpoint – that's to say, before learning about the
succession of notes that lead to the harmonies . . . Berlioz puts his
harmonies where he wants them, and then fills up the spaces
between as best he can.

[Journal, 7 April 1849, Delacroix 1893-5: i, 364–5]

> It is a tough indictment of Berlioz's musical technique,
> but curiously wide of the mark: there are innumerable
> examples, in both the choral and symphonic works, of
> the brilliance with which he adapted fugal techniques to
> suit his own purposes. Chopin, who was in some senses
> very much a 'romantic' composer, nevertheless retained a
> reverence for an essentially eighteenth-century aesthetic
> by which Berlioz never felt himself bound, and he might
> well have found it difficult to see Berlioz's fugues as
> 'pure' – just as academics like Fétis or Cherubini had
> problems with the counterpoint in which (*pace* Chopin)
> Berlioz's scores abound. But Fétis's strictures in any case
> soon extended well beyond contrapuntal boundaries.

FRANÇOIS-JOSEPH FÉTIS

I saw that he had an aversion to melody; that he had only a feeble
notion of rhythm; that his harmony, though made up of often
monstrous aggregations of notes, was nevertheless flat and monotonous. In a word, I saw that he lacked melodic and harmonic ideas,
and I judged that he would always write in a barbarous manner.
But I saw that he had an instinct for instrumentation, and I thought
that he could fulfil a useful vocation in discovering new combinations of orchestral sounds which others would employ better than
he could.

[Fétis 1835]

> What Fétis grudgingly admitted to be 'an instinct for
> instrumentation' was the one positive virtue that almost
> all sane critics allowed to Berlioz. And 'instinct' is right,
> for this astonishing ability was something that nobody

could possibly have taught him, and that he worked out for himself by trial and error combined with an ear for instrumental timbre of unparalleled acuteness. 'I never met anyone with so sensitive an ear,' said Louise Viardot, and Osborne remembered the untiring curiosity that went with it.

GEORGE OSBORNE

It was his constant habit to go into orchestras and sit with the different performers watching them and turning over the pages for them. In this way he learned the capacity of each instrument. Besides which he got several instrumentalists to come to his house, where they played together little things which he wrote for them to see what they could accomplish. He also asked both Chopin and myself whether such and such passage could be played on the piano.

[Osborne 1879: 75]

But since orchestration was regarded as a secondary talent in the early nineteenth century, Berlioz's inability to play a keyboard instrument was often held responsible for what was seen as his fallibility in other areas of composition.

CHARLES HALLÉ

Berlioz was no executant upon any instrument (for being able to strum a few chords on the guitar does not count), and he was painfully aware how much this was a hindrance to him, and to his knowledge of musical literature, which, indeed, was limited. I was often astonished to find that works, familiar to every pianist, were unknown to him; not merely works written for the piano, such as Beethoven sonatas, of which he knew but few, but also orchestral works, oratorios, &c., known to the pianist through arrangements, but of which he had not chanced to see a score. Perhaps many undoubted crudities in his works would have been eliminated had he been able to hear them before committing them to paper, for I had several proofs that the eye alone was not sufficient to give him a clear idea of the effect of his musical combinations. Thus at the time when he scored Weber's '*Invitation à la Valse*' for the orchestra [*in 1841*], he made me play it to him, and when I had come to the point where, after the digression into C major, the theme is resumed in the original key, D flat, he interrupted me with the words, '*Après tout, cela va*,' confessing that from the perusal of the piece he had thought the modulation too harsh, and almost impossible. On another occasion, much later, he arrived at my house and eagerly told me he had found a new cadence to end a movement with. 'The last chord,' he said, 'is the chord of G major, and I precede it by the one in B minor.' When I told him there were hundreds of examples of such an ending, he would not believe me, and was greatly astonished when we searched for and found them.

[Hallé 1896: 65–6]

FERDINAND HILLER

Berlioz often expressed a certain satisfaction that he had never learnt to play the piano, and believed that this deficiency allowed him greater freedom to indulge his love of instrumental combinations without thinking about the keyboard or being affected by its influence. Certainly there is no need to be a brilliant pianist in order to become a great composer – though we have no reason to regret that Bach and Handel, Mozart and Beethoven, Weber and Meyerbeer, Mendelssohn and Schumann, were all outstanding performers. However, an absolute inability to experiment with harmonies at the keyboard can never really be an advantage, and Berlioz was surely making a virtue of necessity when he allowed himself to indulge his illusions on this subject.

[Hiller 1880: 67–8]

> Hiller was in fact one of the very few people who was in a position to observe Berlioz's methods of composition. He left tantalizingly little about them in his recollections, and what he did leave tends to emphasize the gap that separated the exploratory nature of Berlioz's approach, with its deliberate rejection of accepted

Copy of a sketch of Berlioz by Horace Vernet, Director of the French Academy
Rome, c 1831

2 Théâtre de l'Odéon, scene of Harriet Smithson's Shakespearean triumphs (engraving, early 19th century)

3 Harriet Smithson as Ophelia in *Hamlet* (lithograph, A. de Valmont, 1827)

4 Harriet Smithson at the height of h Parisian fame (painting by C. M. Dubufe, c 1828)

MARIE PLEYEL

Medallion by Dantan Aîné, made in
[R]ome in 1831, which Berlioz thought
['v]ery like me'

6 Camille Moke after her marriage to
Pleyel (lithograph after M. Alophe)

(Salle des Concerts du Conservatoire.)

[C]oncert hall of the Paris Conservatoire, the scene of many of Berlioz's early
[c]oncerts. (The figure conducting appears to be Habeneck)

8 Ferdinand Hiller after he had settled in Cologne (engraving, c 1855)

9 Franz Liszt at about the time he first met Berlioz (lithograph, A. Devéria, 1832)

10 Ernest Legouvé in the 1860s (lithograph, after a photograph by P. Petit)
11 Charles Hallé (lithograph, after H. Lehmann 1844)
12 Richard Wagner on his first visit to Paris (drawing, E. B. Kietz, 1840–42)

Marie Recio, who accompanied lioz on his foreign travels from 1842 vards, and became his wife in 1854

14 Berlioz, when he was in Vienna with Marie Recio (lithograph, A. Prinzhofer, December 1845)

Eine matinée bei Liszt (lithograph after J. Kriehuber, Vienna 1846). t to right: Kriehuber, Berlioz, Czerny, Liszt and the celebrated violinist Ernst o played *Harold en Italie* with Berlioz on this visit

16 Berlioz conducting the Société Philharmonique (engraving after G. Doré, in *Journal pour rire*, 27 June 1850). Berlioz was not in fact a left-handed conducto (cf. plate no 24), but this is the way in which the engraving was originally printe

Berlioz in London, 1851 (lithograph by C. Baugniet)
Berlioz, caricature by Nadar (in *Journal pour rire*, 18 September 1852)
Stephen Heller, c 1854 (drawing, J. J.-B. Laurens)

Berlioz, c 1863 (photograph, Petit)

21 A less formal shot taken at about the same time (photograph, P. Petit, c 1863)

22 *Les Troyens*, carica-
ture by Grévin (in *Journal
amusant*, 28 November
1863)

24 Berlioz in St
Petersburg, 1867–8
(photograph, Lewitzky).
The pose may be a little
stilted, but this is one of
the few known full-
length photographs

23 Estelle Fornier at
about the time she
first met Berlioz again

formulas, from the structured attitude of the more conventional musical mind.

FERDINAND HILLER

During the period when I saw Berlioz every day he was writing a number of works, of very different kinds, which I so to speak watched come into being. To begin with, there was a collection of songs for one or more voices with keyboard accompaniment – almost the only vocal compositions for which he was content to use the piano as an accompanying instrument, for on the whole he wrote very few short lyrical pieces. The texts are translations of some of the famous Irish Melodies of Thomas Moore: ballads, pious and warlike songs, passionate love songs – even rollicking drinking songs, too. Generally, the mood is caught with vigour, with characteristic rhythmic invention, no trace of triviality, the word setting irreproachable in the French manner. And yet there are only two or three songs that produce a deep or even a satisfying effect. They are made up of short, declamatory melodic phrases that are obviously drawn from the depths of the soul, but they are not held together by that magic bond which is so essential if a work of art is to appear an organic whole. They lack spontaneity. By this I don't mean that sort of spontaneity displayed by certain poets in word or tone through the speed with which they write – producing something quickly is just as characteristic of superficial artists as slowness is of the greatest. But whenever the way in which a composition is constructed can be felt by the listener, his concentration, that sense of being gripped, is lost; the shorter the work of art, the more one longs for inner and outer unity and evenness of invention. 'La Belle Voyageuse', a ballad in song form, is the most rounded and attractive piece in the Irish collection – and it was precisely of this song that Berlioz said, as he held it out to me laughing: 'I've been writing this for the last fourteen days – every morning a couple of bars, like a counterpoint exercise!'

It is not only in the melody of the songs that this piecemeal process is disagreeably evident – the accompaniments fare no better. All too often, the harmony appears to be far-fetched, like something acquired and not sufficiently absorbed, and the figurations of the piano writing are laboriously put together. In the latter case it could not have been otherwise, because the very nature of the piano demands that anyone who employs it as a composer should have made himself familiar with it as a performer. But the former peculiarity has a deeper defect at its source, about which I must be equally frank. The painful consequences of his late entry into the world of music make themselves felt throughout more or less the whole of Berlioz's artistic life. Music was never entirely his mother tongue. He translated the poetic idea – whether he had dreamed it up for himself or whether he had been confronted with it in the work of some other poet – into the sound of music, and he often did so with astonishing success. But the rich colouring which music offered him, and which he knew how to deploy with the freedom and prodigality of a proud and self-assured favourite of fortune, only occasionally disguised the absence of that elementary training and practice which shows itself in the lack of the skill necessary for the highest purity and beauty in handling the tonal language.

[Ibid: 104–6]

> Strange that even a musician as intelligent and as well-disposed as Hiller should have failed to see beyond the apparent technical shortcomings to the originality and freedom of imagination that lay behind them. Of all the ways in which this freedom expressed itself, the treatment of melody provided one of the most persistent stumbling-blocks. Curiously enough, it was another German who, in the flush of his early enthusiasm for the *Symphonie fantastique*, was among the first to tackle the essential point about Berlioz's melodic style.

ROBERT SCHUMANN
(1810–56)

His melodies are distinguished by such intensity of almost every note that, like many old folk-songs, they often defy harmonic accompaniment, indeed would even lose their full tonal effect by it . . . And certainly, they are not to be listened to with the ear alone; they will always be misunderstood and dismissed by people who do not know how to sing them inwardly, in their hearts – and that not just faintly, but with full and utter conviction. Then they will take on a meaning whose significance seems to grow deeper at every hearing.

[Schumann, 11 August 1835: 47]

> For most listeners, it was the irregularity of phrase length that was upsetting – particularly in comparison with the predictable melodic outlines of contemporary French opera – which may explain why a composer like Adam, whose bitterness about the commissioning of the *Symphonie funèbre et triomphale* has already been noted, was prepared to relax his habitual sniping when the piece actually came to performance.

ADOLPHE ADAM

I like neither the man nor his style, but justice forces me to admit that in [this work] there is a peroration which produces a great effect and is far superior to anything he has done up till now. The first movement and the first part of the second are an incomprehensible jumble, but the last movement is really very good; there is no melodic invention, but the rhythm is strongly marked, the harmony new and the thematic re-entries most happy. In short, there is a big advance, because the phrases are clearly laid out in groups of four bars and can be easily understood. I could have wished that the papers had done the piece justice as I have done, and given a proper indication of the progress it reveals. But they have done nothing of the kind. They have all gone off into exaggerated eulogies and said that this latest composition is up to the level of its predecessors, whereas in fact it is far superior.

[Letter to Spiker, 10 August 1840, in Adam 1903: v, 144]

> But the *Symphonie funèbre* was an exception; it belongs to a tradition of ceremonial music which has lost a good deal of its appeal today, and few would now be prepared to include it among Berlioz's best or most characteristic works. It is ironic that it should have been the first work of Berlioz to be an undoubted popular success – as well as being the only one to bring about the unlikely alliance of Adolphe Adam and Richard Wagner.

With the performance of the *Symphonie funèbre et triomphale* in 1840, and the publication of *Les nuits d'été* the following year, Berlioz's decade of intensive composition came to an end. By now, all the big orchestral works had been written, and the choral or dramatic pieces still to come were few and relatively far between: *La Damnation de Faust* was not performed until 1846, *L'enfance du Christ* followed in 1854, the *Te Deum* in 1855, *Béatrice et Bénédict* in 1862 and finally, after an agonizing wait of five-and-a-half years, *Les Troyens* in 1863. Among the reasons for this diminution of output were certainly the stress of his domestic situation and the need to earn a living as a music critic. But another factor was his growing success as a conductor – and the long periods of travelling that were to result from it.

The idea of standing up in front of an orchestra with a baton and full score, instead of leading it with a bow from the first violin's desk, was still a new one. The reaction of orchestral players to the novelty of his orchestral writing had soon persuaded Berlioz that he must master this art for himself, if only to ensure that his works were heard by the public as he intended them, and his success, first in Paris and later abroad, eventually came near to obscuring his fame as a composer. But it had been a long haul from the days of the Mass in the church of St-Roch.

LOUIS ENGEL

When this mass . . . was executed a second time (1827), Berlioz picked up his courage and conducted it himself. He, in later days the greatest conductor known – not 'although' but 'because' his nerves were in such an over-excited state that he nearly heard the impossible – speaks of himself thus on this occasion: 'How far was I from possessing the thousand qualities of precision, flexibility, fire and calm combined with that indefinable instinct which together constitute the talent of the real conductor!'

So many people fancy, and many unfortunately have given way to their fancy, that a conductor need only take up a stick and beat time! Certainly, in very easy instances, this may be sufficient; but in such cases, without any conducting at all, the band would go on, as the German street bands go on without any conductor . . . But if it came to playing great and difficult scores, the reading of which is in itself a great difficulty, the judging of the right movement, the entry of instruments that have sometimes fifty, sixty bars to count, when the look of the conductor's eye must guide them at the precise moment of entry – when it comes to making the orchestra understand and execute the sometimes not quite clear intentions of the composer, then it is that the great conductor shows the stuff he is made of. I remember having seen Berlioz – and this is what I meant when alluding to his over-excited nerves – jumping down from the conductor's desk, pouncing upon the clarinets and exclaiming: 'Your two instruments are not in tune'. Then each of them gave his A, when with unfailing certainty not only did he perceive an infinitesimal difference, but instantly told them, there and then, how to remedy it.

[Engel 1886: i, 68–70]

Throughout the thirties, Berlioz's concerts in Paris were a continual struggle against ingrained attitudes. To begin with, inexperience played a part. At his next appearance before the public, a benefit concert for Harriet in 1833, an overlong programme and a misunderstanding about the hours for which the musicians had been engaged resulted in a disaster that he described graphically in the *Memoirs*, and is here corroborated, rather less sympathetically, by a disaffected participant.

EUGÈNE SAUZAY

Not long after we left the Conservatoire – I don't remember the exact dates – I took my place at the first violin desk, right next to him, for a concert at which he intended to give, along with other unpublished works, the first performance of the *Symphonie fantastique*.*

The outcome was more than dubious. The audience, irritated by the length of the pieces being played, or upset by their strangeness, rose to its feet in a fearful uproar, while in the orchestra some cried 'Enough!' and others simply disappeared taking their instruments with them. But in order to get out into the street the players had to squeeze their way through the theatre, and the unfortunate harpist, in a hurry to get away, tripped up with his instrument and so blocked the way for all those coming behind him, who were also hurrying for fear of being called back by the composer – so that people were crying out from above and below. In the face of this tumult Berlioz put up a bold front; he apologised to the audience for the desertion of his orchestra and, since he found it impossible to continue with the concert that evening, pledged himself to give the same concert again the following week. I don't any more remember whether he kept his promise, but I made one as well – that I wouldn't again attempt to initiate the public into the music of my friend. And I kept mine . . .

[Sauzay 1974: 170]

> But even eight years later, when Berlioz was no longer a novice, the organization of an orchestral concert remained a problematic affair. Heller has left a brief glimpse of the trials that Berlioz suffered when Heller's *Caprice symphonique* for piano solo was being played by Charles Hallé at a Berlioz concert in February 1842.

STEPHEN HELLER

At 8 o'clock I went into the Salle Vivienne by the artists' entrance. I had to cross a kind of courtyard covered with ditches filled with

* Sauzay's memory is mistaken: this was not the first performance.

muddy water. After this agreeable promenade I arrived at a little door locked on the inside, where I knocked for a good quarter of an hour without being able to get anyone to hear me. In the end I applied my boots to the door, which produced a sort of funereal underground rumbling.

The door was opened. It led into a small room strewn pell-mell with cloaks, ophicleides, lamps, bunches of keys and great volumes of accounts. I could also make out, by the light of a sweet-scented candle with an inordinately long wick, two men in a furious state of agitation.

One of them was Berlioz, wrapped in his carbonaro's cloak, the other the unfortunate Hallé, victim of my *Caprice*. They both looked pale, upset, and occupied with gloomy thoughts. They were shivering with cold and had red noses. I went over and added my nose to theirs.

Berlioz cried out 'S[acré] n[om] d[e] D[ieu]!' (I crave pardon in the interests of historical accuracy) 'Forestier, the first flute, is missing, and one horn and one double-bass still haven't arrived!' It was a quarter of an hour before everything was ready. The concert began . . . The turn came for the *Caprice*. Scarcely had it begun when the little room I was in began to fill up with the musicians who were going to play the *Symphonie funèbre*. I was immersed in a tidal wave of drums, bass drummers, flageoletants, triangulars, piccolophonists, fifers and serpents. They made such a racket setting up their armoury of brass that I could hardly catch a note of what the piano was playing.

[Letter to Eugénie de Froberville, 16 February 1842, in Heller 1981: 102–3]

> Most descriptions of Berlioz conducting, at least in the earlier part of his career, suggest a flamboyant style. In 1843 Spontini wrote to congratulate him and his 'gallant and courageous army' on their 'perfect and admirable performance – in the extremest sense of the words!'

GASPARE SPONTINI
(1774–1851)

And yet, they would have brought you an equally resounding victory, and carried you with their invulnerable weapons to an equal triumph, even at the direction of a baton that was *not white*, and a foot *shorter*. Producing narrower, less expansive movements, this would cover less space and be less fatiguing for your arm, your head, and the whole of your body, and would have given greater clarity and precision in balancing arm movements that were sometimes excessively varied, as well as helping the overall steadiness of your direction.

[Letter to Berlioz, 20 November 1843, in CGB: iii, 138]

CAMILLE SAINT-SAËNS

Berlioz had an unhappy ability to create his own suffering, by searching always for the impossible and demanding it in spite of everything. He had the idea, a very false one which thanks to him has unfortunately become widespread in the musical world, that the will of the composer should not have to reckon with material obstacles. He was determined to disregard the fact that a musician is not like a painter, who can manipulate the inert materials on his canvas to his own liking, that the musician must take account of the tiredness of his executants, and of their greater or lesser abilities. In his younger days he demanded, from orchestras far inferior to those of today, efforts that were positively superhuman. If there are some difficulties in all new and original music that are impossible to avoid, there are others which can be mitigated for the performers without damage to the work. But Berlioz didn't bother himself with these practical details. I have seen him take twenty, thirty rehearsals for a single work, tearing his hair, wrecking batons and music desks, without getting the result he wanted. The poor orchestra players did everything they could, but the task was beyond them. Our orchestras have had, with time, to become more skilled before this music could at last reach the ear of the general public.

[Saint-Saëns 1899: 9–10]

ANTON SEIDL
(1850–98)

Seidl, a protégé of Wagner's and himself a distinguished conductor, was too young to have seen Berlioz conduct, but he recorded the memories of Cosima Wagner, who was thirty-one when Berlioz died and, as Liszt's daughter and the wife of both von Bülow and Wagner himself, had various opportunities of seeing him in action.

As conductor of his own compositions he was incomparable. Cosima Wagner has often related that he brought to his rehearsals a tremendous command of the minutiae of orchestral technics, a wonderful ear for delicate effects and tonal beauty, and an irresistible power of command. Upon all who heard or played under him he exerted an ineradicable influence. His music, frequently rugged in contrasts and daring leaps, is also insinuating and suave at times, and so too was his conducting; one moment he would be high in the air, the next crouched under his desk; one moment he would menace the drummer, and the next flatter the flutist; now he would draw long threads of sound out of the violinists, and anon lunge through the air at the double basses, or with some daring remark help the violoncellists to draw a cantilena full of love-longing out of their thick-bellied instruments. His musicians feared him and his demoniac, sarcastic face, and wriggled to escape unscathed from his talons.

[Seidl 1912: 125]

Both Saint-Saëns and Cosima Wagner are talking mainly about rehearsals, not performances – in Cosima's case, probably rehearsals in Germany where Berlioz, not knowing a word of the language, would be desperately trying to convey an unfamiliar meaning by every kind of gesture and mimicry. Hiller's summary is perhaps a more balanced one.

FERDINAND HILLER

As a conductor, particularly of his own compositions, Berlioz had an extraordinary gift. His personality quickly won him the sympathy of his players, which grew as they came to recognize the fire, the clear-sightedness, the utter devotion, body and soul, that he dedicated to the job in hand. If he sometimes appeared, from the outside, to be exerting himself more than was necessary, and if in so doing he attracted the attention of the listener to his platform behaviour, this was entirely without self-consciousness; he had no desire to present himself as a virtuoso conductor (the worst species of virtuoso that exists), but was solely interested in giving his music the importance it deserved. Perhaps he didn't have enough confidence in his players and felt himself too much obliged to bring in every entry – not by a look only, but by physical gestures as well. His immense inner tension, his anxiety that everything might not go as he wanted it, perhaps made itself too much felt; he didn't simply stimulate the musicians, he drove them to a frenzy, and even the excellent orchestral players in London complained to me that they were nervous under his direction. But that was their affair – the outcome was superb. There are some composers who, when they are conducting their own works, are only too happy if they can avoid making fatiguing demands on the performers. But this kind of modest restraint was not for him – besides, the difficulties which his compositions present put it completely out of the question. A good orchestra, of the kind that he generally had to deal with, is in any case not easily tired – provided the demands made on it work: unnecessary effort only irritates the players.

[Hiller 1880: 98–9]

VLADIMIR STASOV
(1824–1906)

> Stasov was the most influential Russian music critic of his day, a forceful champion of the Russian nationalist school of composers and a keen supporter of Berlioz, whom he met on the composer's first visit to Russia in 1847.

What the piano is to Liszt, the orchestra is to Berlioz. Just as Liszt knows all the innermost secrets of the piano, so Berlioz knows the orchestra. He compels it to venture upon new paths, to produce sounds such as have never been heard before. He forces it to bow before his baton and to play in such a way as no one has ever been able to play before . . . Probably no one else has ever delved so deeply into the art of musical performance as he has; no one else has ever experienced the joy he does when 'playing the orchestra' (as he himself puts it). His amazing ear catches every nuance, even the most elusive. He never permits a single one to slip by; he brings each one out through the thunder of the entire orchestra. Under Berlioz's direction the orchestra is like a steed that feels the full power of its rider. Leading it, Berlioz is a veritable general, adored by all his forces, inspiring them by some kind of extraordinary power to accomplish unprecedented feats. Under him, they do things it would have seemed no one on earth could have made them do. It is as though the musicians seated before him were not men but a row of keys; he plays on them with his ten fingers, and each one produces just the sound, just the degree of tone that is needed.

Berlioz arrives in a city. He gathers together musicians of all kinds and calibres. He seldom has more than two or three rehearsals – sometimes, very rarely, four (here, I am proud to say, there were only two rehearsals for each concert). Then suddenly this group is transformed into an orchestra; it becomes one man, one instrument, and plays as though all of its members were finished artists. Berlioz's concerts end. He leaves. And everything is as it was before – each man for himself. The mighty spirit that had inspired everyone for a moment is gone.

[Musical events of the year 1847, in Stasov 1968: 25]

RICHARD POHL
(1826–96)

Pohl was a German critic who had numerous opportunities of hearing Berlioz conduct on his visits to Weimar
and Baden-Baden.

Berlioz's achievements as an orchestral conductor are well known . . . I know of no more dependable, but also no more self-willed conductor. He lets nothing through, no *ritardando* or *accelerando* that is not in the score, no ornamentation, absolutely no cadenzas, and of course no suggestion of any changes; the words *'ad libitum'* don't exist for him. Whether in the orchestra or on the stage only one controlling view is permitted, and that an inflexible one – his own. Yet at the same time each player can feel a reassuring sense of security, and have the confidence that in an emergency his commander will never abandon him or fail to help him out.

'All for one and one for all' is Berlioz's staunchly military slogan, and he works wonders with it time and again.

[Pohl iii 1884: 177–8]

> 'Berlioz has the three theological virtues of the orchestral conductor,' wrote the critic and theorist Georges Kastner: 'faith, inspiration and authority.'

CHARLES HALLÉ

What a picture he was at the head of his orchestra, with his eagle face, his bushy hair, his air of command, and glowing with enthusiasm. He was the most perfect conductor that I ever set eyes upon, one who held absolute sway over his troops, and played upon them as a pianist upon the keyboard . . .

Of his perfect command over the orchestra, Berlioz gave an extraordinary proof on the occasion of a grand concert given by him . . . in the 'Cirque Franconi'. There had been a very long rehearsal in the morning, at which I was present, as I had to play Beethoven's G major concerto, then very seldom performed. After some hours' hard work Berlioz dismissed the orchestra; I remained with him, and hardly had the last member of the band vanished when Berlioz struck his forehead, exclaiming: 'I have forgotten the overture!' He stood speechless for a few minutes, then said with determination: 'It *shall* go nevertheless.' Now this overture was the one to '*Le Carnaval Romain*', to be performed that evening *for the first time,** and never rehearsed. Musicians who know the work,

* Another case of inaccurate memory. The concert in the Cirque Olympique on 19 January 1845 at which Hallé played (it was the Fifth Concerto, not the Fourth) included a performance of *Le Carnaval romain* – but not the first, which had taken place in the Salle Herz nearly a year earlier. However it had only been played on two other occasions since, and many of the players would have been new to it, so that the incident Hallé describes was still a remarkable *tour de force*.

with its complicated rhythm and all its intricacies, will easily understand how bold the venture was, and will wonder that it could be
successful. But to see Berlioz during that performance was a sight
never to be forgotten. He watched over every single member of the
huge band; his beat was so decisive, his indication of all the
nuances so clear and so unmistakeable, that the overture went
smoothly, and no uninitiated person could guess at the absence of
a rehearsal.

[Hallé 1896: 64, 67–8]

> It has sometimes been suggested that, when conducting
> his own works, Berlioz disregarded his own tempo
> markings and took many passages faster than was indi-
> cated in the score. Saint-Saëns's memories, of the *Requiem*
> at least, seem to point in the opposite direction.

CAMILLE SAINT-SAËNS

I have never again recaptured the impression that the *Tuba Mirum*
gave me when I heard it years ago at Saint-Eustache under Berlioz's
direction. This is due to the fact that conductors fail to follow the
composer's instructions to the letter.

The opening of the [*Dies Irae*] is marked *moderato*; further on,
at the entry of the brass, the tempo broadens and the beat halves
for the *andante maestoso*.

At most performances . . . the *moderato* becomes an *allegro*, and
the *andante maestoso* a simple *moderato* – and the terrible fanfare,
if it isn't actually reduced to a '*départ pour la chasse*' as some have
dared to suggest, could well be taken for the accompaniment to a
sovereign entering his capital. For in order to give this fanfare its
Michelangelesque effect the composer has not fallen back on the
facile melancholy of the minor key, but burst into the splendours of
the major mode, and only a great breadth of movement can preserve its grandiose character and its sense of dread.

[Saint-Saëns 1913: 211–2]

> On the other hand, his memories of Berlioz conducting
> *L'enfance du Christ* suggest a reading that specifically

avoided the sentimentality into which later interpreters
were inclined to fall.

CAMILLE SAINT-SAËNS

One day at the Société Saint-Cécile the great man came in person
to conduct *L'enfance du Christ*, which he had just written, – or
rather, *La fuite en Egypte*, the only part that existed then; the rest
was composed later. I can perfectly remember the performances
that the composer himself directed: they were more lively, more
animated than the well-prepared but languid performances to
which Édouard Colonne has accustomed us; the tempi were less
slow and the nuances more clear cut . . .

[Saint-Saëns 1913: 257]

> Of the 170-odd concerts that Berlioz is known to have
> conducted during his life, about 100 seem to have
> consisted entirely of his own works, and many of the
> remainder contained only bits and pieces by other com-
> posers forced on him by circumstances. Until the very
> end of his life even Beethoven was represented in only
> about twenty-five programmes, and then by a limited
> number of works.

FERDINAND HILLER

It did not often happen that Berlioz conducted the works of other
composers, though he took an active and positively valuable part
in the staging of Gluck's *Orphée* and *Alceste*. Certainly he gave full
weight to the masterpieces of Gluck, Spontini, Beethoven and several others, but if he had taken on works that were unsympathetic
to him, simply out of a sense of duty as a conductor, I doubt if he
would have found it in himself to give them the attention they
needed. Which I don't mean as a reproach. One man's meat is
another man's poison, and there would be every reason to criticize
him if he had attempted something and done it badly.

[Hiller 1880: 100]

And a final comment from Hallé.

CHARLES HALLÉ

Mendelssohn, and certainly Berlioz, would have been amazed if they had witnessed the modern craze for conducting without the score; *they* never did so, even with their own works, which certainly they must have known better than anybody else. There can be no possible advantage in dispensing with the score, a glance at which shows to the conductor the whole instrumentation, and enables him to watch over every detail of the execution, and over the entries of the most secondary instruments. No conductor could write by heart twenty pages of the full score of a symphony, or other work, exactly with the instrumentation of the composer (perhaps the composer himself could not do it); he must therefore remain ignorant whilst conducting, of what the minor instruments, say the second clarinet, second bassoon, second flute, and many others, have to do – a serious disadvantage. The public who go into ecstacies over 'conducting by heart' do not know how very easy it is, how much easier, for instance, than playing a concerto or a sonata by heart, at which nobody wonders. Without the score the conductor has only to be acquainted with the general outline of the composition and its salient features; then, the better the band the easier the task of its chief.

[Hallé 1896: 73]

> At the age of 38, however, Berlioz's international fame as a conductor still lay in the future. Until 1842 his appearances with an orchestra had been confined exclusively to Paris, often with a degree of success, usually with a nagging undercurrent of hostility, and invariably without financial gain. It was against this background of public indifference, financial insecurity and unceasing activity that the second stage of Berlioz's domestic drama was played out.

14 HARRIET AND MARIE

ERNEST LEGOUVÉ

When Berlioz married Miss Smithson he was passionately, madly in love with her; but she, to use an expression which drove him into a frenzy, – *elle l'aimait bien*: for her, it was a conventional attachment. Little by little, however, daily life accustomed her to the wild outbursts of her lion of a lover, little by little she began to find them attractive, and after a while the originality of his mind, the charm of his imagination, the infectious warmth of his heart, gained such a hold over her that from a cool, unresponsive bride she became an ardent partner, passing from tenderness to love, from love to passion, and from passion to jealousy. Unhappily, it often happens with a husband and a wife as it does with a pair of scales: they rarely maintain a level balance – when one goes up, the other goes down. And so it turned out with the new household. In proportion as the Smithson thermometer rose, so the Berlioz thermometer sank, and while his feelings changed to a sincere friendship, quiet and correct, his wife's exploded into arbitrary demands and violent recriminations that were alas all too legitimate. Berlioz, whose activities as a performer and music critic involved him in the world of the theatre, ran into opportunities for infidelity that would have turned stronger heads than his; besides, his position as the great misunderstood artist lent him a glamour which eased the passage from musical interpretation to personal consolation. Mme Berlioz scanned her husband's concert notices for signs of his infidelities; she searched for them elsewhere too, but fragments of intercepted letters and contents of secretly opened drawers only provided her with incomplete discoveries, which were enough to make her frantic but never revealed more than half the truth. Her jealousy was always too late. Berlioz's heart moved so fast that she couldn't keep up with it; when, by dint of searching, she lighted upon the object of her husband's passion, this passion had already changed, he loved another – and then of course, his current innocence being easy to prove, the poor woman was left as confused as a bloodhound that chases a scent for half an hour and arrives to find the bird has flown. Then, of course, some new discovery would soon set her off on another trail, and lead to more fearsome domestic scenes.

Miss Smithson was already too old for Berlioz when he married her; grief hastened the ravages of time; she grew older day by day, rather than year by year, and unhappily, the older she grew in the face, the younger she grew in her heart, the more her love increased, grew bitter and became a torture to both of them. So much so that one night their young child, who slept in their bedroom, was awoken by such terrible cries of indignation and anger from his mother that he jumped out of bed and ran to her crying: 'Maman! maman! don't be like Mme Lafarge!'*

They had to separate. The woman once known as Miss Smithson, worn out before her time, obese and ill, went off in search of peace to a small, humble apartment in Montmartre, where Berlioz, hard up though he was, provided her regularly with an honourable allowance, and went on visiting her as a friend: for he loved her always, he loved her just as much, but he loved her differently, and it is that 'differently' which created the gulf between them.

[Legouvé 1886: 300–2]

> It seems likely that Legouvé's memory has again exaggerated the facts, this time as to the extent of Berlioz's infidelity to Harriet. None of Berlioz's other friends suggest this sort of philandering – which in any case isn't in character. But he himself wrote sadly, many years later, of Harriet's 'ungovernable jealousy, which in the end had cause', and it is true that with the decline of her career as an actress her personality had undergone a change. Berlioz's closer friends became increasingly aware of the problem during the early 1840s.

* A murderess whose trial in 1840 had achieved widespread publicity.

CHARLES HALLÉ

[Berlioz] came often to my humble lodgings, and I must say that his visits to me were more frequent than mine to him; for even at that time Madame Berlioz, the once charming and poetic Ophelia, had become somewhat repellent, and it was impossible to imagine her acting or anybody falling in love with her. To her honour it must, however, be said that she upheld Berlioz in his hardest struggles, always ready to endure the greatest privations when it was a question for him to save money enough for the organisation of a concert on a large scale, concerts which seldom left any profit.

[Hallé 1896: 65]

> Harriet was not cut out to be either housekeeper or mother; she was bad at dealing with servants and became bitter at her own inability to contribute to the family funds. Certainly Berlioz cannot have been easy to live with, but the demands she made on him were more and more exhausting, and it is hardly surprising if before long he did form a new attachment.

ERNEST LEGOUVÉ

One day in the spring a sudden shower caught me unprepared in the rue Vivienne. I took shelter under the colonnade in front of the Palais-Royal and ran into Berlioz. He took me by the arm; his look was gloomy, his manner curt, and he walked with lowered head. Suddenly he turned to me and said: 'My friend, there are people in hell who deserve to be there less than I do!'

I started – accustomed though I was with Berlioz to the unexpected. 'For Heaven's sake, then, what's the matter?' 'You know that my poor wife has moved into a small apartment up in Montmartre?' 'Where I also know that you often go and see her, and where you make every effort to care for her and show her respect.' 'There's not much credit there', he replied sharply; 'a man would have to be a monster not to love and admire a woman like that.' And then, with indescribable bitterness: 'But I am a monster!'

'Your conscience pricking you again?'

'Judge for yourself. I am not living alone.'

'I know.'

'Another woman has taken her place . . .What do you expect? I am weak! Now listen. A few days ago, my wife heard someone ringing at the door. She went to open it, and found herself face to face with an elegant, pretty young woman who said, with a smile on her lips: "Madame Berlioz, if you please Madame?" "That is me", replied my wife. "But you are mistaken" said the other, "I asked for Madame Berlioz". "But that is me, Madame!" "No, no, it's not you! You are speaking of the old, the abandoned Madame Berlioz! . . . But I am speaking of the young, the pretty, the preferred Madame Berlioz! And *that* – that's *me*!" And she went out, closing the door sharply on the poor creature, who fell half fainting with grief!'

At this Berlioz stopped, then after a moment of silence: 'Well then, what do you think, isn't that atrocious? Wasn't I right to say . . .'

'Who told you this abominable story?' I burst out angrily. 'It can only be the person who did it. She was boasting about it, I'm certain. And you haven't thrown her out?'

'How could I?' he replied in a broken voice, 'I love her!' His tone silenced any reply I might have made, and the rest of what he then confided gradually disarmed me as it became clear that his wife was richly avenged. The person who replaced her had a singing voice that was quite pretty but weak, and she was consumed by a passion to sing on the stage. So Berlioz found himself obliged to use his influence as a critic to get her an engagement, to bend that pen so honest, fierce and inflexible to the manipulation and flattery of directors and writers in order to get her a simple début role! She was hissed; he had to write an article which transformed her failure into a success. Rejected by the theatre, she wanted to sing in the concerts organised by Berlioz himself – and sing what? Music by Berlioz! Songs by Berlioz! And once again he had to give in – he, who could be exasperated by one false note or made ill by a lack of musical understanding, had to suffer hearing his own works wrongly sung, and even to conduct the orchestra in the very piece in which he was being assassinated as a composer!

'So you see,' he added, after enumerating all his agonies, 'isn't it truly diabolical, truly tragic and grotesque at the same time? I said that I deserved to go to hell – but I'm there already! And I'll bet you that terrible old joker Mephistopheles is laughing as he watches the crucifixion of my musical nerves! To be honest, I'm sometimes tempted to laugh myself.'

And in fact, as the tears of anger rolled down his cheeks, his face was contorted by an expression of bitter mockery that I would hardly know how to describe.

[Legouvé 1886: 318–20]

> Can Legouvé's story be true? It is not easy to believe, but there seems no reason why it should be of pure invention, and there was certainly no love lost between the contestants for Berlioz's affections. Marie Recio, born Marie Martin, was the daughter of a French father and a Spanish mother; she was ten years younger than Berlioz and really not a particularly good singer. But there is no doubt about the powerful physical attraction that she exercised over the composer.

GEORGE OSBORNE

After a few years [Berlioz's] married life was far from being a happy one, owing to an uncontrollable jealousy of a lady who eventually became his second wife. One evening after dining with me, we conversed on the usual painful subject, and, as I saw but one remedy, I frankly told him of it. Much to my surprise, he sat down and wrote a charming letter of adieu to the lady, which he left at her lodgings when walking out with me. Next day he told me that he had gone back to the house, took the letter from the servant and tore it up, his courage having failed him.

[Osborne 1879: 67]

> Writers about Berlioz have tended to give Marie a bad press. She was certainly tactless, though she didn't deserve some of Wagner's later comments, and bossy: 'She positively ill-treated him,' said Louis Engel: 'in the midst of a rehearsal at Baden-Baden, she shouted "'Ector!" with a six yards' accent on the second syllable, simply to tell him there was a draught from an open

window.'* But other contemporaries saw the positive side, among them the twenty year old Eduard Hanslick, later to become the most influential music critic in the German-speaking world, who met her when Berlioz visited Prague in 1846.

EDUARD HANSLICK
(1825–1904)

[Berlioz] had found a remarkable complement to his own character in the person of an interesting Spanish woman (now his wife). Señora Mariquita busied herself with the concerts, checking the expenses and haggling relentlessly over the cost of the triangle or the cymbals . . . Without this dark-eyed minister of finance 'Hector', honest and magnanimous as a prince of the realm, would soon have found himself without ready cash, and might easily have turned up at rehearsal one morning naked as a Highland Scot, without the most indispensable of garments.

[*Musikalische Erinnerungen* (1860), in Hanslick 1897: 546]

'*Quel bonheur pour Hector, que je suis sa femme!*' she once exclaimed, as I translated for her the estimated expenses for a concert – and she reduced them with fearless strokes of the pen. Alas, the '*bonheur*' for Berlioz was not unmixed; at the beginning of their life together she tormented him by claiming the right to sing at his concerts, something which he, being in the end more musician than he was lover, had to put a stop to after a number of unsuccessful experiments.

[Hanslick 1894: i, 57–8]

> It has to be said that Berlioz had been organizing his own concerts quite effectively for many years before Marie joined him, and it is difficult to escape the impression that she was a bit of a busybody. But in spite of appearances, the relationship endured, and when Harriet eventually died, he married Marie.

* Engel 1886: i, 85.

FERDINAND HILLER

'She made a home for me,' he said to me later. He took in her mother too, and it was she who, outliving her daughter, looked after Berlioz in the last years of his life. Mlle Recio was an intelligent person and seems to have understood how her husband must be handled; it was only that she tended to compromise the sincerity of his behaviour as a critic, although he didn't realize it – perhaps his domestic life was enough satisfaction to him, even if she didn't make the desired impression on his friends. In his *Memoirs*, Berlioz mentions her only on the occasion of her death.

[Hiller 1880: 91–2]

15 FIRST CONCERT TOURS: GERMANY AND RUSSIA

The interest shown by visiting foreign musicians, combined with the hostility with which his works were so frequently met in Paris, contributed to Berlioz's decision in the early 1840s to try the effect of his music in other countries. The hall of the Conservatoire, until now the main venue for his concerts in Paris, would in any case be unavailable to him after November 1843, when the authorities banned its use by anyone except the Société des Concerts; his unwillingness to allow others to perform his compositions meant that few of them had actually reached publication by this time, and his growing experience as a conductor gave him the confidence he now needed to take them abroad himself. Besides which, life with Harriet had become increasingly difficult to bear. Fearing the scene she would make, he did not have the courage to tell her when he left for Brussels in September 1842, though when he set out on a longer trip to Germany a few months later she at least knew where he was going. But not necessarily who he was going with: in both cases, he took Marie.

FERDINAND HILLER

Towards the end of the year 1841 [*actually 1842*] Berlioz began his first concert tour in Germany. I had returned to Frankfurt from Italy only a short time before, and we bumped into one another at the theatre, where *Fidelio* was being given. We greeted each other as old friends. Since Kapellmeister Guhr had not thought to keep an evening free for Berlioz [on his first visit to Frankfurt], the latter had travelled on to Stuttgart, Mannheim, Karlsruhe and was now coming back through Frankfurt on his return journey. As it happened, I had a concert arranged for the following day, and I asked

Berlioz to come to it. 'Impossible,' he replied: 'you know that I am travelling in the company of a singer. She sings like a cat – which would be a matter of no great concern, but the trouble is that she insists on appearing in all my concerts. I am going from here to Weimar, where we have an ambassador, so it is out of the question for her to accompany me there. But I have laid my plans. She believes that I am invited to the Rothschilds this evening: I shall therefore leave the hotel at 7.00, my place in the coach is reserved, my bag is already at the post station, I shall set off by myself and a couple of hours later she will receive from the head porter a letter containing everything she needs for the journey home.'

In the face of such arrangements, it was hardly possible to press my invitation. The next day my time was entirely taken up by the demands of the concert, but on the third day I was so eager to hear how the matter had turned out that I took myself off to the Russische Hof where the porter willingly reported the rest of the story. The following morning, Mlle Recio, who was beside herself after receiving the letter, set off straight away to the post station and soon found out what had been going on. At that time travellers were not only numbered but their names registered, and Berlioz seems to have been so little worried that his intention might be thwarted that he had taken absolutely no further precautions, so that already his faithful companion had caught up with him. At the time I must have written him a rather frivolous letter about the whole thing, because a few days later I received a missive from Mlle Recio in which she took me soundly to task and made very clear to me the gulf that lay between egotism and love. And included with the letter, oh dear! were two lines from my friend which, making a play of my own words, said: 'we were neither trapped nor re-trapped, but rather found ourselves once again united'.

[Hiller 1880: 90–1]

> In Leipzig (to which he and Marie continued after Weimar) he was welcomed as an old friend by Mendelssohn, who was rehearsing his new cantata *Die erste Walpurgisnacht* when Berlioz arrived. In the emotion of the moment, Berlioz begged Mendelssohn to give him the baton with which he had been conducting; Mendelssohn agreed, on condition that he should receive one of Berlioz's batons in return, but when it

arrived, the Fenimore Cooper imagery in which Berlioz chose to dress up the exchange, with its references to tomahawks and the Great Spirit, had an uncertain welcome from the fastidious Mendelssohn family. (Fanny Hensel was Mendelssohn's sister.)

FANNY HENSEL
(1805–1847)

Berlioz was at Leipzig at the same time with us, and his odd manners gave so much offence that Felix was continually being called upon to smoothe somebody's ruffled feathers. When the parting came, Berlioz offered to exchange batons, 'as the ancient warriors exchanged their armour', and in return for Felix's pretty light stick of whalebone covered with white leather sent an enormous cudgel of lime-tree with the bark on, and an open letter, beginning, *'Le mien est grossier, le tien est simple'*. A friend of Berlioz who brought the two translated this sentence, 'I am coarse and you are simple', and was in great perplexity how to conceal the apparent rudeness from Felix.

[Diary in Hensel 1881: ii, 184–5]

After a brief trip to Dresden, where he met Wagner again (who later commented 'it was horrible for him to see with his own eyes how successful my operas are . . . I felt sorry for him'),* he made a return visit to Leipzig, where he at last had the opportunity of meeting Schumann. It was their only meeting of any length.

Schumann had been one of the first foreign musicians to recognise Berlioz's talent. 'We have always said', he wrote, 'that in this Frenchman's brain the flame of genius burns,' and in 1835 he devoted the longest essay of his journalistic career to an analysis of the *Symphonie fantastique*. Until now, however, his only personal contact with Berlioz had been through his fiancée Clara Wieck, who was in Paris for a series of piano recitals in 1839 and reported her impressions to Robert in Leipzig. They were not uniformly complimentary.

* Wagner 1970: 235.

CLARA WIECK
(1819–96)

I met Berlioz [at a soirée of the Bertins] after having missed him on
three previous occasions.

I was astonished to run into him accidentally like this. He started
talking about you at once. He is quiet, with monstrously thick hair,
and keeps his eyes down, looking at the floor all the time. He is
going to call on me tomorrow. To begin with I didn't know who he
was, and was so surprised when he kept talking about you that in
the end I asked him his name. When he told me I gave a delighted
start of alarm, at which he must have been flattered.

[Letter to Robert Schumann, 1 March 1839, in Schumann 1987: ii, 425]

With Berlioz I am thoroughly annoyed. He has done nothing for
me and only now, after I have visited him three times and written
to him most urgently, does he review my concert in the *Journal des
débats*, in quite cool terms. At the Schlesingers' matinée he made a
point of talking about an article he meant to write about me, but I
wait for it in vain. Yet he certainly owes you a big debt of gratitude!
However, that's what it's like in Paris – nobody understands true
friendship.

[Letter to Robert Schumann, 3 April 1839, ibid: 468]

> Clara's ideas of self-promotion and Berlioz's view of the
> role of the critic may not have mixed to Clara's advan-
> tage, but now Robert had the opportunity to see for
> himself.

ROBERT SCHUMANN

He conducted excellently. There is a lot in his music that is insuf-
ferable, but much that is extraordinarily brilliant, even touched
with genius. To me he seems the helpless King Lear to the life. Even
in his features, otherwise so distinguished, there is something weak
about the mouth and the chin. Certainly Paris has done him harm,
not to mention his dissipated youth there. Now he is travelling with

a Mlle Rezio, who is no doubt more to him than simply a concert singer. Unfortunately he speaks no German at all, so we couldn't talk much. But I had imagined him livelier, more passionate as a man. His laugh is fairly hearty. Otherwise he is a Frenchman, drinks wine only with water, and eats stewed fruit.

[Diary, in Schumann 1971: ii, 136]

CLARA SCHUMANN

Clara however, now married to Robert, saw no reason
to alter the view she had taken in Paris. After Berlioz
had spent a musical evening with them on 27 February
1843, she wrote in her diary:

[Berlioz] was unwell, but if he had behaved in a friendlier, more cordial manner he would have found the music more satisfying to his spirit. He is cold, unsympathetic, sullen, not what I like an artist to be – I can't help it. Robert feels differently and has quite taken him to his heart, which I can't understand. As for his music, there I agree with Robert: it is full of interesting and brilliant things, though at the same time I cannot suppress the feeling that it is not the kind of music that really gives me pleasure, and I have no great desire to hear more of it. Forgive me, my Robert, but why should I not say what is in my heart?

[Ibid: 258–9]

ROBERT SCHUMANN

Even Schumann's own enthusiasm soon waned: only
two and a half years later he wrote to the distinguished
musicologist August Wilhelm Ambros about a favourable review Ambros had devoted to Berlioz's *Roi Lear*
overture.

I judge Berlioz as a grown man more severely than I did when he was young: unhappily there are unbearable moments in his more recent works as well. The [overture] is, exactly as you say in your letter, 'tolerably well written' – but you can't go on saying things like that about a forty year old.

[Letter to August Wilhelm Ambros, 10 November 1845, in Schumann 1993: 24]

> The German tour continued to Brunswick, where he received the warmest welcome of anywhere on the trip, and the success of two movements of the *Roméo et Juliette* symphony elicited a double-edged tribute from the critic Wolfgang Griepenkerl.

RICHARD POHL

When, years ago, [the *Roméo et Juliette* symphony] was played for the first time in Brunswick, Griepenkerl said to Berlioz: 'You – you who have so fully understood both Shakespeare and love – you must make an opera out of *Romeo and Juliet*!' Berlioz replied with a laugh: 'If I had to compose the whole opera like that, I think I should die of it!' 'Well, if that's how it must be, then die of it – but write it!'

[Pohl iii 1884: 208]

> After Hamburg, Berlin and Hanover, Berlioz returned home via Darmstadt, where he renewed an old friendship with Louis Schloesser who had been a fellow student in Lesueur's class at the Conservatoire.

ADOLPH SCHLOESSER
(1830–1913)

When in Darmstadt [Berlioz] spent his spare time chiefly at my father's house, where in my mind's eye I see him now, sitting on the sofa in the drawing-room, drinking cup after cup of tea, of which he was very fond, until the teapot was empty!

Berlioz had an intensely interesting and fascinating personality – an aquiline nose, a shock of hair in which he frequently buried his fingers, a head one could never forget, with pronounced and intellectual features, a high forehead, and a somewhat melancholy expression, unless excited by the subject of conversation or when conducting his orchestra. During rehearsals he would stop his instrumentalists when occasion required, and would sing (without a real voice) a few notes to the bassoon, oboe, or any other instrument at fault, irrespective of pitch. Berlioz was a genius in the noblest sense of the word.

[Schloesser 1911: 6]

> After five and a half months in Germany, Berlioz came back to a Paris largely unaware of his successes abroad. He busied himself with journalism and other writings – among them the publication of the *Grande Traité d'instrumentation et d'orchestration modernes*, a ground-breaking work compiled from a series of articles written a year earlier which was to have incalculable influence on future generations of composers. He gave his last concert at the Conservatoire hall in November, and the first performance of a new overture, the *Carnaval romain*, in the following February. Though this concert, and its immediate successors, otherwise included nothing particularly new or inflammatory, that didn't prevent Heine from indulging in one of the characteristic flights of fancy that came to irritate Berlioz so much.

HEINRICH HEINE

A tout seigneur tout honneur. We begin today with Berlioz, whose first concert opened the musical season and could almost be considered as an overture to it. The more or less new pieces that were presented to the public on this occasion were received with fitting applause, and even the dullest minds were carried along by the force of the genius that all the creations of this great master display. Here is the beating of a wing that reveals no ordinary songbird – this is a colossal nightingale, a lark as big as an eagle, such as must have existed in the primitive world. Yes, for me there is always something primitive, if not antediluvian, about Berlioz's music: it makes me think of creatures and species long extinct, of fabulous kingdoms and fabulous iniquities, of towering impossibilities: it evokes visions of Babylon, of the hanging gardens of Semiramis, of Nineveh and the marvels of Mizraim as we see them in the pictures of the English painter Martin. In fact, if we are looking for an analogy in the world of painting, the affinity between Berlioz and the crazy Englishman is as close as any we can find: the same taste for the monstrous, for the gigantic, for sheer material immensity; with the one, dazzling effects of light and shade, with the other shrieking effects of instrumentation; with the one little melody, with the other little colour, with both little beauty and absolutely no feeling.

Their works are neither antique nor romantic, they recall neither ancient Greece nor the Catholic Middle Ages, rather they remind one at a far higher level of the architecture of the Assyrian–Babylonian–Egyptian period, and of the wholesale passions that they express.

[25 April 1844, in Heine 1887: vii, 215–6]

> Heine might have done better to save his ink for the concert that followed at the Palais de l'Industrie in August; given by a chorus and orchestra of over a thousand, before an audience of between seven and eight times that number, this was the first of the 'monster concerts' with which Berlioz's name later became rather unhappily identified. It was a gruelling affair, which he brought off with consummate skill, and a resounding popular success.
>
> On the domestic front, however, the situation with Harriet continued to deteriorate; she took to drinking heavily, neglected the household and treated Berlioz to a mixture of violent abuse and protestations of undying love. By 1844 a final separation had become inevitable, and for a time his living arrangements became complex; the temptation to get away from it all must have been strong – and it was with Marie, again, that he set out for Vienna in October 1845.
>
> His reception in the Austrian capital was warm, and in Pest (where his new version of the *Hungarian March* came near to causing a riot) warmer still. But it was the six concerts he gave in Prague that were the triumph of this tour.

EDUARD HANSLICK

Time and place could not have been more favourable to Berlioz . . . The constraints of a narrow classicism had weighed heavily upon the people of Prague at a time when its chief musical institution, the Conservatoire, was directed by a man (Dionys Weber) who would admit nothing of Beethoven beyond the third symphony. The Prague public clung to its Haydn, Mozart, Spohr and Onslow . . . [In 1843] the arrival of the young and enterprising Kittl as head of the Conservatoire broke the ice. The later works of Beethoven, the orchestral poems of Mendelssohn, fired the enthusiasm of audiences; Gade and Hiller soon became known, even Schumann's *La Peri* and Berlioz's *King Lear* overture were risked . . . We were playing both Schumann and Berlioz with enthusiasm at a period when, even in the most important cities, the former was known only as 'the husband of Clara Wieck' and the other was confused with Bériot . . .

Germany was beginning to make amends for the injustice that France had perpetrated against Berlioz, and in due course the great misunderstood genius turned to us in person. The brilliant impression made by his concert[s] on the Viennese public reached us with lightning speed along the tracks of the northern railway, and the vigorous clashes of opinion in the Viennese newspapers added to the interest in this controversial subject . . .

It was thus that, in Prague in 1846, Berlioz confronted a musical world already prepared and in a state of high anticipation. A happy chance soon put me into close relations with this illustrious visitor. Music is, as everyone knows, a universal language, but those who practise it persist in using their own national idiom. Berlioz didn't understand a syllable of German and had to talk a lot about music to people who couldn't be expected to know French, and since I acted as his interpreter I soon found myself more closely involved with the celebrated master than I might otherwise have done.

[*Musikalische Erinnerungen* (1860), in Hanslick 1897: 545–6]

> When Hanslick came to write his memoirs some thirty years later, he remembered the musical situation in Prague a little differently, but the image of Berlioz remained as vivid as ever.

[In 1846] the name of Berlioz was as good as unknown to the public of Prague. Only a small circle of us, whose gospel was Schumann's series of articles in the Leipzig *Neue Zeitschrift für Musik*, were already raving about the genius of this Frenchman. Of his compositions we had only the four-handed arrangement of the *Lear* overture and the Liszt piano version of the *Symphonie fantastique*, but these we thumped our way through indefatigably.

Ambros and I went every day to see Berlioz at the hotel *Blauen Stern* and accompanied him to rehearsals. We were welcomed as enthusiastic supporters – me particularly, because I was useful as translator and interpreter . . .

Berlioz was accompanied by a beautiful, fiery-eyed Spaniard, Mariquita Rezio, whom he gave out to be his wife. It was therefore understandable that we took her to be the former actress, Miss Smithson, who was already familiar to us through Heine's reports from Paris. But at the very first meeting, when Ambros expressed his joy at beholding at Berlioz's side the original of the *idée fixe* of the *Symphonie fantastique,* he received, with a menacing look, the reply: 'This lady is my second wife; Miss Smithson is dead'.

In reality, his wife was still alive; she continued to live for a long time, while Berlioz travelled all over Germany and Austria with his beautiful Spaniard. But the man with the mane of a lion, the commanding eye of an eagle, was utterly without resistance to the iron rule of the señora. In spite of all our respect for Berlioz, we still found it comic when she flung back her head imperiously and demanded: 'Hector, my *mantilla*! Hector, my gloves!' At which Hector, with the passive submission of a bashful young lover, would quickly throw her scarf over her shoulders and bring her her gloves . . .

During his visit to Prague Berlioz was our only concern, our only daily occupation. I even took him to see my teacher, [Vaclav] Tomaschek, the musical high priest of Prague, whom it was regarded as a sacred duty for all foreign musicians to visit. As if it were yesterday, I can see myself with Berlioz, strolling over the Moldau bridge on a sparkling, sunny winter's morning, to the house on the other side where 'Generalbass' lived in person. Berlioz held me firmly by the arm, and I suffered so much from the crushing awareness of this honour that I was almost afraid we should bump into somebody I knew.

A few steps before we reached the Temple of Counterpoint itself, Berlioz confided to me with nonchalant affability that he had never in his life heard the name of Tomaschek, and still less knew a note of his compositions. So now it was up to me, in the shortest possible space of time, to supply my visitor with the chapter of musical history entitled 'Tomaschek' that he was lacking. So as not to confuse him with a whole lot of of titles, I ended up by repeating insistently that there was a Requiem (in point of fact an excellent work) on which Tomaschek placed particular value. We went in, and there followed one of those half-painful, half-comic scenes usually described as interpreting sessions. This piecemeal to-ing and fro-ing of remarks that were trivial enough, yet often hard to translate, across the rather embarrassing gap that separated the old conservative from the musical revolutionary was not exactly agreeable. Mercifully, Berlioz did not miss his cue, and at once expressed his delight and gratification at making the personal acquaintance of the author of the 'masterly Requiem'. The old gentleman, who had become rather brusque as a result of living alone, accepted this homage with a slight nod of his head and the observation that he would like to come to Berlioz's next concert. But so unusual and fleeting an encounter could not be expected to afford any real insight into Tomaschek's artistic personality; 'he has the air of being pretty delighted with himself' was the only comment that Berlioz had to make on his new acquaintance.

. . .What strengthened and stimulated our passion for Berlioz in Prague was the personal relationship with him, the impression made on us by his amiable, noble personality. His artistic ideal filled him to the exclusion of all else; the realization of it, the fiery, never-satisfied drive for what he felt to be great and beautiful, was his only aim. At the core of his art, however, it may be regarded today, there was an astonishing integrity of purpose. Everything petty or self-interested was utterly foreign to this man with the head of Jove.

[Hanslick 1894: i, 56–60]

> The pressures of the Austro-Hungarian tour were the more fatiguing because Berlioz was using every minute of his spare time to work on a new score. Since the extraordinary decade of composition that ended with

the *Symphonie funèbre et triomphale* in 1840, he had produced no music on a large scale. But in 1845 he had begun sketching out a dramatic cantata (or 'legend') based on Goethe's masterpiece, revising and re-using the music for the *Eight Scenes from Faust* written as far back as 1828, and now, after so long a gap, his ideas came in floods. They were noted down, words or music, wherever he happened to be, in the coach or train, in the middle of the night, or in any odd corner of his travels – even under a gas-jet outside a grocer's shop in Prague 'until the grocer, irritated by his presence, emerged and asked him to take his papers and musical treasures elsewhere', as an article in *La France musicale* reported.

As he returned through Germany to Paris, stimulated by the reception of his music in the past few months, Berlioz had high hopes for the new work and completed his score with enthusiasm. But in the event the first performance of *La Damnation de Faust* in December 1846 was met with heart-breaking indifference.

ADOLPHE ADAM

You know the nice witticism of Rossini about Berlioz: 'How lucky this lad doesn't know music – he'd do it very badly'. In fact, Berlioz is everything you could want: poet, dreamer, idealist, a man of talent with an enquiring mind, even sometimes, in certain cases, an inventive mind, but never a musician.

There were very few people at this musical solemnity, and the reception was very cool. However, two pieces had the honour of an encore. One is the *marche militaire* on a Hungarian theme: here the melody (which is not by Berlioz) forced him to a rhythm and style of a broad simplicity that he usually avoids, and that brought out more clearly the skilful layout of instrumentation that he understands so marvellously. The other piece that was encored is a short movement in triple time, intended to depict the will-o-the-wisps and airy sprites conjured up by Mephistopheles. It is played by harps and muted cellos, and a few wind instruments. The effect is ravishing, and I wasn't among the last in calling for an encore. But two pieces that turn out well in a work which lasts nearly four hours [sic!] doesn't constitute a success, and I'm very much afraid that poor Berlioz won't have covered his expenses, which must have been considerable. All things considered this man is interesting because of his persistence and his conviction; he is on the wrong track, but he is determined to prove to us that it is the right one, and he will go on persisting as long as he can.

[Letter to Spiker, 7 December 1846, in Adam 1903: v, 629–30]

> Berlioz, in the *Memoirs*, blames the weather (it was snowing), the wrong theatre, the lack of fashionable singers, and these no doubt played their part. But it was now seven years since the *Roméo et Juliette* symphony, his last comparable work on a large scale, and though the Parisian critics were generally kind, the score of *Faust* was another hard nut for a public among whom, as Berlioz observed, 'apathy towards all that pertains to art and literature had made impressive strides'.

OCTAVE FOUQUÉ
(1844–83)

> Fouqué was a composer and musicologist who won the Prix de Rome in the year after Berlioz's death and later followed in his footsteps as librarian of the Conservatoire.

There was a weightier reason for this lack of success: the score of *La Damnation de Faust* was too elaborate, too densely wrought, too entirely new in its concept, for its form and its detail to be applauded at the time it appeared. How could the public have appreciated this music when even the performers only half understood it?

Now, it is certain that the artists who took part in the first performance approached this masterpiece with more astonishment than real admiration. I have the proof of this in a conversation that I had with [Gustave] Roger [the creator of the role of Faust] a little while before his death. The celebrated tenor had been the evening before to hear *La Damnation de Faust* at a concert at the Châtelet and was retailing his impressions. It had been superb, marvellous. He couldn't find enough to say in praise of the performance, which he had found perfect; he had the greatest admiration for the young conductor, who had understood how to bring out the qualities of this work, so imposing in the multiplicity of its ideas. And he finished by saying: 'This music, played like this, bowls me over completely! To me it's a genuine revelation!'

This surprised me. Roger had met the great man face to face: what new revelation could he need? I turned to him with interest: 'But didn't you sing Faust under the direction of Berlioz himself?' I asked. And he replied: 'Ah yes, a long time ago, in 1846! It's true that I sang it then, *but I didn't understand it!'*

[Fouqué 1882: 189–90]

> The failure of *Faust* was not only a bitter disappointment for Berlioz personally, it was also (as Adam had predicted) a financial disaster. Convinced by now that nothing more was to be expected of Paris, he determined to resume his foreign travels – this time as far as Russia, whence Balzac (who had recently been there) assured him he couldn't fail to bring back 150,000 francs.
>
> The idea of a Russian trip had in fact been in Berlioz's head since before the Austrian journey, partly as the result of a meeting with the Russian composer Glinka, who had been in Paris in 1845 at the time when Berlioz was beginning work on *Faust* and had immediately fallen under the Berlioz spell.

MIKHAIL IVANOVICH GLINKA

Certainly, for me, the most wonderful thing that has happened has been meeting Berlioz. One of my purposes in coming here was to study his works, which are so denounced by some and so extolled by others, and I have had the good fortune to do this. Not only have I heard Berlioz' music in concert and rehearsal, but I have also grown close to this man who, in my opinion, is the *foremost* composer of our century (in his own province, of course) – as close, that is, as one can be to an extremely eccentric man. And this is what I think: in the realm of fantastic music, no one has ever approached his colossal and, at the same time, ever new conceptions. In sum, the development of details, logic, harmonic texture and finally, powerful and continually new orchestration – this is what constitutes the character of Berlioz's music. When it comes to drama, he is so carried away by the fantastic aspect of a situation, that he becomes unnatural and consequently untrue. Of the works I have heard, the Overture to *Les Francs-Juges*, the March of the Pilgrims from *Harold in Italy*, the Queen Mab scherzo, and the *Dies Irae* and *Tuba Mirum* from the *Requiem* have made an indescribable impression on me. At present I have a number of Berlioz's unpublished manuscripts and I am studying them with inexpressible delight.

[Letter to N. Kukolnik, 6 April 1845, in Stasov 1968: 147]

Souza [an attaché at the Spanish Embassy] . . . introduced me to Berlioz, who was then planning a trip to Russia, counting on a rich harvest, not of applause alone, but also of rubles. Berlioz treated me most kindly (which was not the rule among Paris musicians, who were usually unbearably arrogant and supercilious), and I called on him two or three times a week, talking frankly with him about music and especially about his own compositions . . .

In March, Berlioz gave two prodigious concerts at the amphitheatre on the Champs Elysées. He liked my *Lezghinka*, which I had transcribed for orchestra alone . . . [But] at Berlioz's concert in the amphitheatre my *Lezghinka* did not have its hoped-for success because many of the effects had been designed to be played between two orchestras – one on the stage, consisting of wind instruments, and another below the stage (in the orchestra) in which the strings predominated. Berlioz had a total of 150 musicians – consequently, they were spread out too much and the listener could not grasp the whole, but only hear the sounds of those instruments near him . . .

I often called upon Berlioz, for I found his sharp, even caustic conversation always entertaining. Naturally, I did all I could to make his forthcoming trip to Russia a success.

[Glinka 1963: 191–4]

> Berlioz arrived in St Petersburg at the end of February 1847 and the two concerts he gave in March feature largely in the first essay in musical criticism by the twenty-three-year-old Vladimir Stasov – not yet the powerful force he later became in the Russian musical world.

VLADIMIR STASOV

But all these concerts, large and small, good and bad, were overshadowed by the two given by Berlioz in the Assembly Hall of the Nobility. These were the most magnificent, most crowded, most brilliant (in terms of both orchestra and applause) most deafening concerts that were presented this year. Everyone flocked to them; how could they do otherwise, when Berlioz has such a colossal reputation throughout all of Europe? The truth must be told, however: probably nowhere else has Berlioz's arrival been preceded by such widespread prejudice as it was in our country. No sooner did it become known that he was coming than the public began to receive reports through letters from abroad and in other ways that Berlioz is utterly worthless, that he composes in the manner of a washerwoman wringing out her laundry, that he is a noisemaker, a *tapoteur*, etc. Even after attending his concerts, some people continued to say such things

[Stasov 1968: 23]

> A visit to Moscow was less fruitful and he returned to St Petersburg for three more concerts in May. He was much fêted, and among many new acquaintances was one with particular significance for the future – Princess Carolyne Sayn-Wittgenstein, who had just met Liszt for the first time and a little over a year later was to settle down in Weimar as his mistress.

CAROLYNE SAYN-WITTGENSTEIN
(1819–87)

I want to tell you about Berlioz, who has just left my home. He has returned from Moscow, where he gave a concert and which he claims is a silly town. He seems furious with Paris and enchanted with St Petersburg. He says that the musical personnel are among the best he has met, and the public too. Perhaps he was serving up food for fools!

[Letter to Liszt, 21 April 1847 (Old Style), in Walker 1989: 38n]

> The climax of the Russian visit came with two complete
> performances of the *Roméo et Juliette* Symphony which
> moved Berlioz himself to tears, though the enthusiasm
> of the majority of the audience was qualified by some
> lack of understanding.

The beautiful ladies flocked there, but they were bored. The adagio –
that divine adagio – was absolutely not understood. Everyone
remained cold, and all round me they were saying: 'Is that all it is?'
Oh, the imbeciles! The infinite would not suffice for them. They
require several infinities. Or, my God, perhaps they need the *finite*?

[Letter to Liszt, 25 April 1847 (Old Style), in ibid: 39]

VLADIMIR STASOV

Although we fail to see a Byron in Berlioz, as some of his well-
wishers have called him ('Oh, these friends of mine, these friends!'
Pushkin used to say), we leave each of his concerts in a most extraordinary mood, a mood entirely different from that produced by
the usual concerts. We feel shaken, uplifted, as if we had been in
the presence of something great, yet we cannot account for this
greatness. We recall that for a moment we caught a glimpse of
beauty in all its splendour, something wonderful indeed – and then
everything dissolved in a mist of vague yet lofty aspiration. This
vagueness endows each work with a sense of incompleteness, of
uneasiness, a sense of reaching out for something, of futile seeking
after form. It is as though you saw before you shades wandering
disconsolately along the banks of the Lethe, finding no repose.
Who can deny Berlioz's poetic feeling, his poetic nature? Yet all
musical forms elude him; he always remains himself, leaving others
with an unquenched thirst, an unfulfilled desire. Even so, everyone
is awakened to a sense of music's enormous and inexhaustible
resources. It is this that intoxicates the wonderstruck listener. Rare
are the evenings when he finds himself so profoundly moved.

[Stasov 1968: 27–8]

16 LONDON

After successes in Germany, Austria, Hungary and Russia, Berlioz next set his sights on England. That amazing conductor, showman and flamboyant entrepreneur Louis Jullien (usually so-called, though he had thirty-five other Christian names to fall back on) had been delighting London for the last seven years with a series of promenade concerts, and had now decided to branch out into opera. He leased the Drury Lane Theatre for a season which was to include Donizetti's *Lucia di Lammermoor* and *Linda di Chamounix*, as well as a new opera by the Irish composer Michael William Balfe. As chief coach for his company, he turned to the young Czech musician Max Maretzek, later to become a leading operatic impresario in the United States but at this time working with the Italian Opera at Her Majesty's Theatre. When he heard that the season was to be conducted by Berlioz, Maretzek accepted with alacrity – but his enthusiasm was not shared by Balfe.

MAX MARETZEK
(1821–97)

A few days after, Mr. Balfe met me at the stage door . . ., took me under the collonade at the Haymarket, and told me, that he had just agreed with his editors, Messrs. Chappell & Co., to furnish an opera in three acts to Mr. Jullien for Drury Lane Theatre, but that he disliked to treat directly with Jullien, or to have to explain to Berlioz his ideas and his intentions concerning his new opera. He therefore had told Chappell that either Maretzek or Hatton would prepare his opera with the singers and chorus and when ready, he (Balfe) himself would come to preside at the last stage rehearsals.

'Why, Mr. Balfe, have you any particular objection to Jullien or Berlioz?' I asked with astonishment.

'None, whatever, as fellow-men, but as musicians and lunatics, I have. Jullien thinks his quadrilles as good as Beethoven's symphonies, and Berlioz labors under the delusion that he is the Michael-Angelo of music. He dislikes Donizetti, Verdi, and, of course, me, and two years ago he left not one spot in my opera, 'The Star of Seville,' when sung in Paris, in his criticism of it. And to avoid Jullien's friendly advices how to compose the opera, and the recommendations of Berlioz how not to compose it, I shall leave for Paris, write it there and send the score for rehearsal.'

'But he will have to conduct your opera when it is ready?'

'He may conduct it, but I don't want him, or Mme. Dorus-Gras, or any Frenchman, to patronize it. Miss Dolby, Mr. Sims Reeves, Mr. and Mrs. Weiss and Withworth – all of them born on English soil – shall sing it, and they are good enough for me and the London public.' . . .

In due time [the singers] arrived, and also Hector Berlioz. I paid him my visit the first day of his arrival, and never before, and certainly never after, that day saw him in better humor and higher spirits. He looked toward a bright future and everything appeared to him in a rose-colored hue.

With a childish simplicity, he narrated how he had lately applied to Messrs. Roqueplan and Duponchel, the directors of the Grand Opera in Paris, for a place as one of the chorus masters, in order to save him from his embarrassed circumstances, and how with many expressions of regret they had refused him on the ground that he was not able to play the piano nor the fiddle, and it would be against the established custom and decorum to have the choruses rehearsed with the accompaniment of a guitar or kettledrum or flageolet, the only instruments he could practically make use of.

He remarked with joyful *abandon* that now all his troubles were over, that he had been engaged for six consecutive seasons by Jullien for operas, and for concerts of his own compositions; that dear Jullien had promised to make his (Berlioz's) fortune, and that he had thought best to let [someone else] undertake the job, as he was utterly unable to do it for himself. Finally, he said that Jullien had paid him one month's salary in advance, and that he had not seen so much money for a long time.

Poor, honest soul! he little thought that his first month's salary would also be his last, and that Jullien, if he could again make a fortune, would remember the maxim that 'Charity begins at home.'

[Maretzek 1890: 72–4]

> To begin with, however, Berlioz's relations with his collaborators seem to have been excellent.

H. J. ST LEGER
(?–?)

During the engagement of Madame Dorus Gras at the Theatre Royal, Drury Lane, when the late celebrated Monsieur Jullien was the lessee, the author and his wife were passing the evening with Mr. and Madame Dorus Gras, who lived next door to Monsieur Jullien, in Harley Street, Cavendish Square. Mr Balfe and Monsieur Berlioz dined with Monsieur Jullien the same day; and they came in at ten o'clock at night, just as we had finished a rubber of whist and were preparing to go home. I shall never forget the fund of anecdote and the brilliant conversation that took place between these distinguished foreigners and my much-lamented friend [Balfe] . . . The talented visitors seemed to vie with one another as to who should tell the most extraordinary tale or circumstance. Balfe was full of Irish wit and humour; Berlioz was rife with adventures the most Quixotic; but, on this occasion, Monsieur Jullien bore away the palm, for the highly interesting and amusing anecdotes, which he told and acted with all the *verve* of an accomplished actor, the narration of which lasted until one o'clock in the morning; and we left the brilliant party, with deep regret, as we had some considerable distance to go.

[St. Leger nd: 17–18]

MAX MARETZEK

Berlioz, in social intercourse, was the most honest, plain-forward, open-hearted and outspoken gentleman imaginable, but his sensitiveness often tried the patience of his most devoted friends. Any polite flattery he believed to the letter; any civility shown to him he accepted as a demonstration, and repeatedly spoke and wrote about it. While on the other side a slight [slighting?] remark about him or his music, even if addressed in the shape of an inquiry, would arouse his mistrust, and draw from him a bitter and sarcastic reply. Consequently he had plenty of enemies, and, although many admirers, only a few personal friends who could stand his varying humor and his fits of despondency, to which he was subject when disappointed.

However, we went on splendidly. At the piano rehearsals he stood behind my chair beating time and expressing his opinions about Donizetti's or Balfe's music in French, more realistic than ideal, which fortunately nobody but Mme. Dorus-Gras and I understood in its true sense. And after rehearsals I served him as cicerone to show him the sights of London and to amuse him generally.

In a short time I was not only his daily companion but also his confidential friend, to whom he would pour out his secret thoughts, and who would listen for hours to the stories of his endless disappointments in love and musical pursuits. His modesty, which sometimes nearly approached timidity, did not allow him even to ask for his *entrées* to the Italian opera, which certainly would have been courteously given to him, but he preferred to ask me or some other artist to procure him tickets when he desired to visit Her Majesty's Theatre . . .

[Maretzek 1890: 74]

> Jullien's season opened with *Lucia di Lammermoor* on 6 December 1847. Berlioz conducted, and the performance went 'with flying colours' until the middle of Act 3.

Mr. Mapleson, a musical librarian . . . had agreed to furnish to Mr. Jullien the necessary orchestra parts for the different operas, but not possessing enough copies for so large an orchestra (eighty performers), he had borrowed from different parties several string quartets [i.e. sets of string parts] of 'Lucia', and it happened that the mad scene in the third act was written in different keys, according to the abilities of different prima donnas who had sung it previously. Therefore, some were written in the original key in F and others were transposed to E or E flat. At the first orchestra rehearsal I, sitting on the stage near the prompter's box, called out that Mme. Dorus would sing the andante and cabaletta in F, and the intervening allegro in D flat, the original keys, which was sufficient, as every professor in the orchestra was familiar with the opera, and it went off to perfection.

On the evening of the first performance, however, Mme. Dorus-Gras, fatigued from rehearsals, oppressed by the heat, and suffering fom the usual nervousness of a first appearance before a new audience, begged Mr. Berlioz to transpose (in the mad scene) the allegro after the andante and the following cabaletta, one-half note lower. Berlioz sent for Mr. Tolbegue [Tolbecque], the first violin and leader, and inquired whether such a thing could be done and risked, to which Tolbegue answered, 'We do this kind of thing nearly every night at Covent Garden or at Her Majesty's!' Whereupon he went down to notify the orchestra, but instead of naming the particular key in which they should play, he only ordered them to attack the allegro, after the cadenza of *Lucia*, with the flute obligato, one-half note lower. They all did as requested, but naturally those who had their parts written in D flat played in C; those who had theirs in C played in B, and others even in B flat. The effect can sooner be imagined than described.

Berlioz could not explain in English what they should do, so Tolbegue rapped with his fiddle-bow on his music-stand, stopped the infernal charivari, and, after calling out the key in which to play, the orchestra resumed and the opera went smoothly without further accidents. The enemies of Berlioz threw the blame on his shoulders, his friends pronounced it an intrigue against him, but he seemed quite indifferent about it, remarking, after all, with the exception of the sextet in the second finale, it made no difference in what key 'Lucia' was played and sung.

[Ibid: 75–6]

> Berlioz had clearly entered into the arrangement with Jullien in blind good faith, but when his first month in London was up and the season running, but no further payment was forthcoming, he began to have his doubts about his unpredictable collaborator.

Once, early on a gloomy December morning, when the London fog was lying so thick in the streets that anyone could cut off slices with a carving knife, Berlioz entered my room with a haggard face and threw himself on the lounge without saying a word for some time, but at last he broke out:

'Maretzek, have you some money?'

'Yes!' I answered, 'I have about £50 of my economies at your disposal, and if that is not enough I may obtain an advance on my salary from Mr. Nugent, the treasurer of Her Majesty's Theatre.'

'You are a lucky fellow to receive salary from Her Majesty's Theatre, without working at all, and I, working hard at Drury Lane every evening . . . But you misunderstood me. I never borrow or accept money for my own use.'

'But you accepted 20,000 francs from Paganini.'

'Yes, and used it all for the production of my symphonies, and at the same time I often procured my breakfast at the expense of ten cents.'

'Ten cents? How is that possible in Paris?'

'Very easy. A broiled pork chop from the corner pork shop, six cents; fried potatoes, two cents; a roll of bread, two cents; making in all, ten cents. How often did I live on such fare!'

'I admire you more every day, but why do you ask me whether I have money, if you will not borrow any?'

'I will tell you frankly,' he answered. 'This is my birthday, and I just feel like drowning myself either in water or wine. I would prefer in wine, but three shillings is all that is left in my pocket, and –'

'Well!' I interrupted hastily, 'you shall not go out of this room till we have celebrated your birthday in good old-fashioned style. What wine do you like?'

'Send for two bottles of Burgundy, some sugar, cloves and cinammon, and a tin pan!'

'I will send for an entire case of Burgundy and all that you desire!'

When the porter had brought all the required articles and opened the box, Berlioz changed the expression of his countenance, took off his coat, rolled up his shirt sleeves to his elbows, cleaned the tin pan and, turning toward me, said: 'We shall now rehearse the wolf-glen scene from the 'Freischütz.' I will be *Caspar*, and you, of course, *Max*! Come nearer to the fire and learn the art of preparing hot Burgundy punch, so that you may know how to cook it yourself for me next time. First, two bottles of wine thrown in the kettle, then two handfuls of cinnamon, a half-pound of powdered sugar, a dozen of cloves – *Probatum est!* – now the benediction!'

Scarcely an hour had passed, and Berlioz, again in good humour, expressed a wish for some music paper, pen and ink, and there he sat, writing without eating anything the whole day, until it was time to dress to go to Drury Lane to conduct the opera.

[Ibid: 78–9]

> In a remarkably short space of time the grand English opera season was in serious financial trouble; Jullien opportunely left London for a tour of the provinces, leaving a distinguished committee (including Berlioz) to look after the company in his absence. Meanwhile Balfe had returned from Paris and rehearsals been put in hand for the *Maid of Honour*.

Soon after [his return to London] Mr. Balfe invited me to dinner, and to a little chat about his forthcoming opera. During the dinner he said: 'I hear that Mr. Berlioz is poking fun at my music at rehearsals!'

Of course I denied knowing anything about it. 'Well,' he continued, 'you need not play the ignorant. Out of the hundred and twenty chorus singers, there are some men and plenty of women who understand enough French, and others who can read in his face the expression of pity at some passages of my opera, and you know that many of them are devoted to me and repeat his remarks.'

I observed that all such telltales out of school are usually exaggerated, and that no importance should be attached to what they might say.

'Not the slightest,' he replied. 'On the contrary, I wish to satisfy him, if possible, and have composed a new piece for the second act, and wish you to hear it.'

He handed me a roll of music to look at, opened the piano and played from memory a beautiful chorus, constructed in the shape of a motet of eight voices, and imitation of the style of Handel; the whole betraying a profound knowledge of the works of the ancient masters and of all the resources of musical science.

He told me to take the score home with me, and to rehearse it the next day with the chorus, recommending the division of the hundred and twenty singers into groups of fifteen each, and promising to send the chorus parts in time.

After half an hour's rehearsing the next day, Berlioz, who was reading some French papers in the lobby, rushed into the hall, asking:

'What are you rehearsing there?'

'A new piece for "Maid of Honor"!' I replied.

'Who wrote it?'

'Balfe, of course.'

Berlioz, with an incredulous look and a shrug of the shoulders, took the score from the piano, turned the pages, recognized Balfe's handwriting, but still doubting, said: 'Please try it again.' His curiosity soon changed into a deep interest; his interest to a gratified satisfaction, little short of an excitement. He beat the time, admonished the minding of the shading and the coloring of the principal subject; placed the groups in different places to judge of the effect; corrected every wrong intonation himself, had it repeated several times and finally, turning toward me, said: *'Mais c'est un chef d'oeuvre!'*

At that very moment, Balfe, who had probably listened outside, opened the door, and his appearance was the signal for an outburst of applause from the chorus, in which Berlioz joined.

The thanks which Balfe expressed to Berlioz, and the praises which Berlioz bestowed on Balfe, and their mutual protestations of friendship and admiration, were touching to the feelings of the cockney chorus singers, who cheered them both; but I could not help considering and enjoying the whole scene in a Pickwickian sense.

After repeating the chorus once more, Mr. Berlioz said: 'I really congratulate you; this piece will be *the* success of the new opera, and your triumph is assured.' 'Don't you think, sir,' replied Balfe, 'that the character of this chorus is not exactly in accordance with the rest of the music of the "Maid of Honor?"' 'Never mind that,' said Berlioz, honestly. *'This* will be the *pièce de resistance*; the success of your opera, and will ensure you the approbation of all critics and *connoisseurs.'*

With a sardonic smile, Balfe reached to the piano, took the score

of the new piece, folded it and stuck it in the pocket of his overcoat; then addressing Berlioz, remarked:

'I am fully satisfied to have your approbation and don't care for
the *connoisseurs*, and have decided to risk the new opera without
this new piece. Good morning, ladies and gentlemen; many thanks
for your good will.'

At last, the long promised 'Maid of Honor' was ushered before
the footlights, and Balfe's music scored a *succès d'estime*, with the
exception of a ballad in the last act, 'In This Old Armchair', which
created a genuine furore . . . Berlioz reproached Balfe for having
withdrawn his grand chorus in the second act, and Balfe retorted
that if the chorus had been sung the audience would have left
before hearing his ballad of the 'Old Arm Chair.'

Berlioz now grew morose and never pronounced the name of
Jullien or of Balfe. The first one he used to call in conversation 'My
Salary,' and the other 'My Old Arm Chair,' and it was really amusing to hear him say, with a grim humor, 'I see by the papers that
"My Salary" had a big success in Leeds,' or, '"My Salary" had a
row in Glasgow with the musicians for not paying *their* salaries,'
or, 'Have you heard any news from "My Salary"?'

At other times he would say: 'My "Old Arm Chair", it seems,
has no more attraction for the public than it has for me,' or, 'My
"Old Arm Chair" is getting played out, it needs a new frame, new
elasticity and new coverings.'

[Ibid: 77–8]

> In his contract with Jullien, Berlioz had been allowed
> four orchestral concerts for his own benefit. The first of
> these was to contain a selection of his own works,
> including Parts I and II of *La Damnation de Faust*, and
> in Jullien's absence Berlioz took Maretzek's advice and
> pressed on with preparations for the performance. But
> the salaries due to the chorus and orchestra (not to
> mention Berlioz) failed to materialize.

As is usual in such cases, the chorus organized meetings in the
green room, the orchestra in the music room, some proposing to
try for a few days longer, but the majority insisting on a general
strike unless the salary of the past week was forthcoming, and poor

Berlioz stood there, arguing, imploring, begging, till actually the tears began to run down his pale and furrowed cheeks.

At last I called another meeting of the chorus, and begged them as a personal favour not to persist in their resolution, hinted even that the engagements for the next season at Her Majesty's Theatre would be concluded within a few days, and that I should remember those who would sing, at least *for that night*, the first performance of a masterwork of their own conductor, a stranger, who had worked for two months for nothing, and thus helped them to get, so far, their own salaries, and if they desired it, I offered myself to be responsible for that night's wages sooner than allow them to be blamed by the public and the press for refusing their services on such an occasion.

They all, without further consultation, rushed on the stage, and declared they would sing that night for Mr. Berlioz without compensation, and their action soon decided the orchestra to fall into line, and the performance took place the same evening.

[Ibid: 79–80]

> It seems likely that the excellent relations already existing between Berlioz and the musicians with whom he was working had at least as much to do with the outcome as Maretzek.

J. W. DAVISON
(1813–85)

> Davison was the arch rival of the *Athenaeum* critic, H. F. Chorley; editor of the *Musical World* for forty years and chief music critic of *The Times* for thirty, he was a powerfully influential figure in musical London. His early hostility to Berlioz's music gave way to cautious admiration when the two men became friends at the time of Berlioz's London visits.

The band and chorus . . . exerted themselves with unparalleled zeal to testify their respect for the composer whose works they were interpreting, and a more perfect and magnificent performance was

perhaps never listened to . . . M. Berlioz fully realized his conti-
nental celebrity as a *chef d'orchestre*; his beating was emphatic and
intelligible, and the mass of instrumentalists followed the slightest
indication of his *baton*, the minutest shade of expression which he
desired to obtain, with marvellous accuracy . . .

Not a little of the unusual excellence of this performance is due
to the highly favourable impression which M. Berlioz has known
how to produce among the members of his orchestra, by his
polished and courteous manners; no conductor that ever entered an
orchestra was more affable in his demeanour, or more gentlemanly
in his conduct. M. Berlioz respects and loves his orchestra; and
herein he shows himself a man of head no less than heart; for without the means of expression how could a composer communicate
his genius to the world? . . . None better understands this than
M. Berlioz – who has given so many proofs of being a poet and a
philosopher.

[Davison 1848: 97]

> Among the less well-disposed there were the usual
> rumours and rumblings of hostility, but the press was
> generally enthusiastic. One notice gave Berlioz particular
> pleasure: Edward Holmes was a cultured and intelligent
> music critic, a friend of Keats and the author of the first
> English biography of Mozart.

EDWARD HOLMES
(1797–1859)

Since the first production of 'Fidelio' in England we have listened
to nothing with such excitement and enthusiasm as to some of the
compositions of M. Berlioz, performed in his very interesting concert on Monday at Drury Lane. The discovery of a new pen in the
art, exercised in the highest and most serious departments of music,
with all the grave intention of a Beethoven or a Gluck, and in this
lofty and independent walk realising effects which delight the imagination and warm the sympathies of the hearer, is no slight event.
We the more cordially acknowledge the powerful impression made
upon us by this first hearing of the compositions of M. Berlioz,

because we went among the most mistrusting and infidel of the audience. Detraction and false criticism in professional whispers and newspaper paragraphs had predisposed us to expect a critical penance on the occasion; and this, coupled with a somewhat pardonable unwillingness hastily to believe in original genius, or that the implements of the great German masters had passed in reversion to a Frenchman, rendered us anticipative of anything but pleasure. Surprise and gratification were complete, as all these prejudices were dispersed before the beautiful, the original and poetical effects of the music; and we can only say that if Berlioz is not Beethoven – he who can maintain such an activity of attention during four hours by the frequency of original and interesting conceptions, must be a worthy follower of that master, and a poet-musician of no common stamp. We left the house with an earnest desire to hear the whole of the music again, and as soon as possible.

[Holmes 1848]

> The concert confirmed Berlioz as the star figure of the London musical season, and a couple of weeks later he was the specially invited guest at the annual dinner of the Royal Society of Musicians.

[NEWSPAPER REPORT]

The health of the celebrated Hector Barlioz [sic] was drunk amidst the cheers of the room. He replied in French that the honour conferred upon him by such a meeting was as heart-cheering as it was unexpected; that he had been received by the *artistes* of England with almost fraternal affection, and that his brethren of the press had warmly held forth to him the warm hand of fellowship.

[*Morning Post*, February 1848, quoted in Edwards, July 1903: 448]

> By March, the confusion surrounding Jullien's enterprise had degenerated into bankruptcy, but Jullien himself escaped jail and absconded to the United States without even handing over the proceeds of Berlioz's one benefit concert. Meanwhile, in France events were also working to Berlioz's disadvantage: the abdication of

Louis-Philippe and the proclamation of the second
republic brought uncertainties of all kinds, financial as
well as political, and Berlioz stayed on in London, hop-
ing to be able to earn more there than he would in Paris.
To make up for the lost concerts at Drury Lane, he organized a concert himself. Roger, the distinguished tenor
who had sung the role of Faust eighteen months before,
was there.

GUSTAVE-HIPPOLYTE ROGER
(1815–79)

Thursday 29 June. We have been to Berlioz's concert: I heard the
Harold symphony and *Mélancholie*,* it was a sad occasion, a real
festival of exiles – the refugees from artistic France gathered here to
applaud this untamed genius who has been misunderstood for too
long, this Berlioz to whom justice will one day be done if only he
doesn't blow his brains out first. The concert provoked tremendous
enthusiasm – but little money. Berlioz is an eagle who lives in the
peaks, among the clouds, and the mines of gold don't stretch their
seams in that direction. We had dinner with him and tried to console him. It was a happy, pleasant reunion. We talked nonsense for
a bit – like in the old days, under the tyrant . . .

[Roger 1880: 58–9]

> Roger records another meeting soon after, at which he
> and Berlioz passed a part of the day '*à rire, polyglotter,
> boire et fumer*' with the English critic, Morris Barnett,
> but before long the draw of Paris became too strong;
> Berlioz was not making the money he had hoped for in
> London and, in spite of the uncertain political situation
> (and the bloody riots which had only just taken place in
> June), he returned to Paris in mid-July 1848.

* Possibly one or more of the three pieces soon to be assembled under the title
of *Tristia*.

17 PARIS AND LONDON, THE INTERIM YEARS

Back in France Berlioz faced an uncertain future. He had been in London for eight months, before that in Russia for four; he hadn't appeared as conductor in Paris since the ill-fated *Damnation of Faust* more than eighteen months ago, and although the Russian trip had more or less remedied the disastrous financial situation precipitated by *Faust*, London had largely undone the good work and he had lost money at home when the banks failed in the aftermath of Louis-Philippe's abdication. Two weeks after his return, he received news of his father's death in La Côte-Saint-André, and in October Harriet was paralysed by a stroke which permanently affected her speech.

Nevertheless, he was back among old friends and colleagues.

GUSTAVE-HIPPOLYTE ROGER

Saturday 23rd [December 1848]
This evening I gave a fine dinner to celebrate Meyerbeer's return to health. I had him as my guest, along with Berlioz, Halévy and Adam. Literature was represented by Alexandre Dumas, Méry, Fiorentino, Antony Béraud and Anicet Bourgeois. I have noted before how unwise it is to have men of this intellectual calibre round your table at the same time. Each of them, afflicted by a praiseworthy but unusual spasm of modesty, leaves to his colleagues the pleasure of letting off the fireworks; they are circumspect, they keep quiet, they get on with their food.

The first part of the festivity was dull. But luckily the table was long, and I had spaced the guests widely, so that when they all decided to talk at once there was room for everybody. I am not much of a conversationalist myself, particularly at big parties, but I do know how to make other people talk. Every man of spirit has one or two hobby-horses that he likes to ride: it is a question of knowing what they are and drawing them out.

You have to lead Dumas gently to Shakespeare, to M. de Kératry, to the Academy and the Revolution of 1830, Méry to England, Horace, Virgil, the Indies and tigers, Fiorentino to the actresses and theatre managers of the Parisian stage. Berlioz took up Shakespeare with Dumas, talked about everything under the sun and a good deal else besides, and cracked the most outrageous puns. He and Dumas were the noisy ones, who ended up by providing the sparkle in the general conversation.

The others – Halévy, Adam, Anicet Bourgeois – are quieter, more confiding by nature; they speak for the benefit of their neighbours, and their neighbours have no cause for complaint.

Béraud has all sorts of amusing stories to tell, only he tells them to his dinner plate; he makes up for it after dinner with his admirable pen drawings.

[Roger 1880: 184–6]

> The great musical event in Paris at the beginning of 1849 was the much heralded, much publicized first performance of Meyerbeer's opera *Le Prophète*. Berlioz, who had managed to retain some of his activities as music critic, was right in the line of Meyerbeerian fire.

RICHARD WAGNER

He told me a lot of amusing stories about Meyerbeer, and how impossible it was to escape his flattery, which in turn was dictated by his desire for incessant laudatory articles in the press. Before the first performance of *Le Prophète*, he told me, Meyerbeer had given the customary '*dîner de la veille*'; when Berlioz had excused himself from attending, Meyerbeer reproached him delicately, requesting him to compensate for the injury by writing 'nice little articles' about the opera. Berlioz informed me that it was utterly impossible to get anything unfavourable to Meyerbeer accepted by a Paris paper.

[Wagner 1983: 520]

But *Le Prophète*, when it reached the stage in April, was not to all tastes.

EUGÈNE DELACROIX

The frightful *Prophète*, which its composer no doubt thinks of as an advance, is the very annihilation of art. The imperative necessity which [Meyerbeer] has felt to do something better, or at least different, to anything that has been done before – in short the need to change – has led him to lose sight of the eternal laws of taste and logic which govern the arts. The Berliozes, the Hugos, all the would-be reformers, have not yet succeeded in abolishing these laws completely, but they have postulated the idea that it is possible to do something other than what is true and reasonable.

[23 April 1849, in Delacroix 1893: i, 371]

> Such was the Meyerbeer fever, however, that Berlioz decided not to risk a concert of his own in Paris during the 1849 season, but concentrated instead on the composition of a *Te Deum* – though with no commission, and no performance in view. It was not until February 1850 that he gave his next concert, the first of a new entreprise, the Société Philharmonique, of which he had been the moving spirit.

EUGÈNE DELACROIX

Dined with Chenevard, Meissonier . . . To the Berlioz concert afterwards. The [Beethoven] *Leonora* overture made the same confused impression on me; I concluded that it's a bad piece – full, if you like, of sparkling passages, but without unity. It's the same with Berlioz's own works: the noise is overwhelming – it's a heroic muddle.

[19 February 1850 in ibid: i, 417]

A vitality that sometimes becomes unruly, combined with a skilful veneer of reminiscence and a certain *brio* in the instrumentation, can give the illusion of fiery genius carried away by its own ideas and capable of still more. That's Berlioz's story . . . [Both he and Mendelssohn] lack ideas, and conceal this crucial deficiency as best they can by every means that their memory and their technical ability suggest.

[15 February 1851, in ibid: ii, 82–3]

> Berlioz conducted all eleven concerts of the Société Philharmonique, which ended its short life in April 1851. Soon afterwards an unexpected nomination as a member of the French delegation to the Great Exhibition in London took him back to England for a couple of months, but by the end of July he was in Paris again – this time with a more promising appointment in his pocket, as director of a new Philharmonic Society to be formed in London in the following year. Firmly setting aside memories of Jullien and Drury Lane, he set off for England again in March 1852.

WILHELM GANZ
(1833–1914)

> Ganz was a German violinist and pianist whose family had settled in London; as a conductor, he later became a staunch promoter of Berlioz's works. He had met Berlioz on a previous London visit.

A memorable event in the spring of 1852 was the first series of concerts given by the New Philharmonic Society, which was formed by Dr. Henry Wylde with the special object of producing novelties and giving concerts of the best kind. Great *éclat* attended these concerts, as Hector Berlioz, after his triumphant tours throughout Europe, was specially engaged to conduct. The orchestra consisted of 110 performers, the leaders being all well-known soloists . . . I was fortunate in being engaged as one of the second violins, and was much gratified when, during the first rehearsal, Berlioz said, 'Ganz, I want you to play the cymbals with Silas in the *scherzo*'. We were rehearsing his *Romeo and Juliet* symphony, which has a wonderfully light and fairy-like *scherzo* to represent 'Queen Mab', and he had two pairs of small antique cymbals made to give a particular effect in it. There were several orchestral rehearsals, which for England at that time was a really great innovation. Every one was intensely enthusiastic, and anxious to please Berlioz, who was a wonderful conductor. His beat was clear and precise, and he took endless trouble to get everything right. I remember his asking Silas and me to come and see him in King Street, St. James's, just to try over the passage for the little cymbals. I mention this to show the care he took over every detail.

As a result, the first concert proved a veritable triumph for him, and it was generally admitted that no such orchestral performance had ever before been heard in England. The hall was crammed, and the audience was absolutely carried away and cheered him to the echo. There were similar scenes at all the following concerts. Perhaps the finest was the fourth concert, when the hall was packed to overflowing for Beethoven's *Choral Symphony*. Up to then the work had never been properly given in England, as the old Philharmonic Society, although it owned the original score, would never give it more than their customary one rehearsal. In consequence it was still regarded as an unintelligible work. We had five rehearsals, at which Berlioz was indefatigable.

The performance at the concert was masterly, completely realising all the grandeur and beauty of the immortal work, and the effect on the audience was electrical, Berlioz being called out again and again amidst perfect storms of applause.

[Ganz 1913: 60–2]

LOUIS ENGEL

With what enthusiasm did Berlioz speak of the reception in London of the Ninth Symphony, of all the rehearsals he had; how he divided the hours of his day into periods of time to rehearse with the different groups of instruments, etc., how he conducted, and of the wonderful reception this immense work, so long misunderstood, enjoyed from the English people . . .

[Engel 1886: i, 97]

18 *CELLINI* REVISITED

The two performances of the Ninth Symphony marked the high point of Berlioz's achievement as a conductor in England. Meanwhile, events were moving in his favour in other parts of Europe. Liszt, now living in Weimar with the Princess Sayn-Wittgenstein, had decided to put on a revival of *Benvenuto Cellini* at the Court Theatre; it was scheduled for February 1852, but illness and other difficulties led to postponement and in the end Berlioz left for England without seeing the production, which eventually more or less coincided with his first London successes. In spite of a good reception, the Weimar performances revealed what Liszt felt to be weaknesses in the structure of the opera, and he set his young protegé Hans von Bülow the task of proposing detailed cuts and revisions. Back in Paris, Berlioz agreed with an enthusiasm which was not shared by all observers.

RICHARD WAGNER

Frankly, it saddens me that Berlioz still intends to revise his *Cellini*, whether it is a question of wanting to or having to! . . . Bülow is perfectly right in his analysis of where the problem lies: it lies in the *poem*, and in the unnatural position which the musician was therefore compelled to adopt in order to cover up, by purely musical means, a defect which *only* the poet can remedy. Berlioz will not, now or at any time, be able to rescue *Cellini*: but which is worth more, Cellini – or Berlioz? Let the former go, and rescue the latter! For me, there is something rather gruesome about standing by and watching these galvanic attempts at resuscitation. For heaven's sake, Berlioz must write *a new opera*; it will be his *greatest misfortune* if he does not, for there is only one thing that can save him: *drama* . . . Believe me, – I *like* Berlioz, even though he distrustfully and stubbornly keeps his distance from me: he does not *know* me, – but *I* know *him*. If I expect anything of anyone, it is of Berlioz: but not along the path that led him to the tastelessness of his Faust symphony – for if he carries on in this direction he can only end up looking completely ridiculous. If ever *a musician* needed *a poet*, it is Berlioz, and it is his misfortune that he always adapts the poet he chooses to suit his own musical whim, arranging now Shakespeare, now Goethe, as his fancy takes him. He must have a poet who completely fulfills his needs, a poet who *compels* him to rapture, who is to him what man is to woman. I look on in despair as this incomparably gifted artist goes to ruin as a result of his own egoistical loneliness. Can I help him?

[Letter to Franz Liszt, 8 September 1852, in Wagner 1979: 458–9]

> Nevertheless, the revisions were carried through and sent to Weimar for rehearsal; Liszt conducted and Berlioz was in Weimar for the occasion.

ADELHEID VON SCHORN
(1841–1916)

> Adelheid was the daughter of Henriette von Schorn, a close friend of Liszt's mistress, Carolyne Sayn-Wittgenstein.

We ran into Liszt and Berlioz in the street, and while Liszt introduced Berlioz to my mother I had time to have a good look at the Frenchman's remarkable head. The sharp, handsome, but rather birdlike cut of his features, with their bright, piercing eyes and bushy grey hair, might have been considered attractive if their expression had been a little softer. And this was all the more striking in contrast with the indescribable charm of Liszt's manner, which often suffused his face with something that one could only describe as radiance.

[Schorn 1901: 48]

> Berlioz also conducted a big concert himself and was much fêted.

IGNAZ MOSCHELES

Berlioz was very cordially received, his desk was wreathed with laurels; my expectations were not at a high pitch, but he certainly has surpassed them. A great deal is no doubt over-eccentric and disconnected, but there is much that is grandly conceived and carried out. In the 'Faust', his introduction of the Rácokzy March is electrifying; this was repeated, as well as the soldier's song, and the waltz. The music given to Queen Mab in 'Romeo and Juliet' is not only effective and charming, but worthy of being placed by the side of Mendelssohn's works of a similar kind. Berlioz's conducting inspired the orchestra with fire and enthusiasm, he carried everything as it were by storm; I am glad to have made acquaintance with him, both as a composer and conductor.

> On the following day Moscheles was at a performance
> of *Cellini*.

I was delighted by the flow of melody, and the occasionally very discreet instrumentation; a great deal, however, I find obscure, and the finale, the 'Carnival at Rome', completely unintelligible. The audience generally was in favour of the music, although there was nothing encored. Berlioz was called for after every act. After the opera, we all met at Liszt's, it was a most interesting evening, and Berlioz the hero of it. I had much conversation with him; he is a great thinker.

[Moscheles 1873: ii, 228–9]

> The success of *Cellini* at Weimar encouraged Berlioz,
> and when the suggestion of a performance in London
> was mooted, he followed it up with enthusiasm and was
> back in England for rehearsals in May 1853. He began
> his visit with a concert – this time not with the New
> Philharmonic Society but with its august predecessor.

J. W. DAVISON

The mist of prejudice, which for so long a time has hidden the merits of this original and imaginative composer from the general view, is being rapidly dispelled . . . The Old Philharmonic Society, latest in the field, as usual, has nevertheless not come too late to do itself honour and credit . . .

It is not for critics of the present time to rob posterity of its prerogative, by attempting to decide upon the actual place to which Hector Berlioz is entitled among the masters of the art. For aught we know he may either be forgotten soon after his death, or may live in his works as long as music is cultivated. He is a man too remarkable to be dismissed with a sneer, and at the same time too eccentric to be comprehended at a glance. One thing is indisputable – there is an element of originality in his music which places it apart from that of other composers, and this alone entitles it to respect and consideration. So far as our own impressions are concerned we may state, without reserve, that in every composition of M. Berlioz which we have had the advantage of hearing, our curiosity has been excited from the very beginning, and our interest sustained until the end. On Monday night, after listening for more than an hour and a half to music exclusively his, we felt so little fatigued that we could willingly have heard as much again. So much novelty of idea, such startling and unanticipated effects, and such a magical command of the orchestra, keep the attention continually on the alert; and each new surprise becomes a new source of pleasure and satisfaction.

[Davison 1853: 348–9]

> The success of the Philharmonic concert left Berlioz ill-prepared for the reception of *Cellini* at Covent Garden, though the habitués of the Royal Italian Opera were known to be traditionally conservative in their taste and mainly interested in hearing the operatic stars of the day.

FERDINAND HILLER

I [had been] present at several of [Berlioz's earlier London] concerts, like the concert of the Philharmonic Society whose hero Berlioz was. I was also at the first night of *Benvenuto Cellini* at Covent Garden – but this was not a happy occasion. The composer put the blame on a cabal of Italians – though I must confess I had the impression that the audience, for the most part anyhow, had come in the best of moods. The following morning I went to see Berlioz and found him ailing and downcast in bed. He had prepared for this performance with the care and persistence of which I have already had occasion to speak – among other things he had subjected the complete orchestral parts to the most scrupulous examination and revision (a shining example, this, to other composers), in order to spare the conductor, the celebrated Costa, any trouble on this score. It had been a wasted effort. But is not a great part of the lives of the best of men taken up with wasted efforts?

[Hiller 1880: 94]

> Hiller's memory was at fault about the conductor: it was Berlioz himself who conducted. Michael Costa, a formidable but able disciplinarian, was the musical director of the Royal Italian Opera and had opposed the production of *Cellini* from the start; though he was courteous and cooperative during rehearsals, Berlioz never really trusted him – and always suspected that he was behind the uproar that undoubtedly took place that night.

[JOURNALIST]

Why, then, was Hector Berlioz's opera, a work which it would be insulting to him to compare with those we have mentioned [Verdi's *Rigoletto* and Gounod's *Saffo*], hissed throughout with a determination which the vigorous efforts of the major portion of the audience failed to overpower?

We have had some experience in theatrical matters both at home and abroad, and must say that the conduct of a certain number of the audience on Saturday night looked extremely suspicious. The sibillations were delivered with a simultaneousness, precision, and perfectness of *ensemble*, which savoured strongly of collusion and *malice prepense*.

[*Morning Post*, June 1853, quoted in Edwards, October 1903: 654]

EDWARD HOLMES

I was in a box at the opera with [Mme. Viardot] and M. Viardot . . . on the night of the first performance of *Benvenuto Cellini*, which you know is Berlioz's opera. She said to me – 'Don't you think Sir, it is very wrong to hiss an opera like this'. I could hardly reply to her, from vexation. To see the generous work of Berlioz so crushed – the labour of months and years destroyed in a few hours quite overpowered me . . .

[Letter to Clara Novello, 9 January 1857, in Novello 1910: 213]

QUEEN VICTORIA

Dined as yesterday and then went to the opera, where we saw and heard produced one of the most unattractive and absurd operas I suppose anyone could ever have composed. *Benvenuto Cellini* by Berlioz, who conducted himself. There was not a particle of melody, merely disjointed and most confused sounds, producing a fearful noise. It could only be compared to the noise of dogs and cats! The two first acts kept us in fits of laughter, owing to their extreme foolishness.

[Victoria: 25 June 1853]

> It was the one failure of Berlioz's visits to England, and though the behaviour of the claque may have been exceptional, there is little doubt that Berlioz, as a composer, still presented a problem to the more conservative element of the London musical establishment.

HENRY FOTHERGILL CHORLEY

The tale of the triumph of *Benvenuto Cellini* at Weimar, which gathered amplitude by the way, made the trial of the opera here a natural if somewhat courageous experiment. The performance was prepared with great care, and the composer himself presided in the orchestra. The evening was one of the most melancholy evenings which I ever passed in any theatre.

Benvenuto Cellini failed more decidedly than any foreign opera I recollect to have seen performed in London. At an early period of the evening the humour of the audience began to show itself, and the painful spectacle had to be endured of seeing the composer conducting his own work through every stage of its condemnation. Be such an exercise of justice warranted or not, it is impossible to be present at any scene of the kind without real feelings of concern – concern in this case heightened by thinking how much good labour on good material had been thrown away, out of systematic perversity.

. . . It may be doubted whether, when his own personal influences as an admirable conductor of certain music, as a man notorious for wit of word and pen, as a combatant who, right or wrong, has fought for his own system, have passed away, the works of M. Berlioz, pretentious though they are, and in some sense poetical, will keep their place; and the sympathy which every generous person must feel for one so earnestly striving, so often discouraged, so partially accepted, is strengthened by the vexing conviction that his case is not one of vacant vanity mistaking its occupation, so much as of a self-will that has deluded its possessor into a labyrinth from which there is little reasonable prospect of his extrication.

[Chorley 1862: 329–31]

FRANCIS HUEFFER
(1843–89)

The quintessential Victorian, Hueffer was a music critic and writer, and a pioneer supporter of Wagner, Liszt and Berlioz.

A story which does infinite credit to the hearts of the two persons concerned, and which I have on the best authority, may be told in connection with this unfortunate *première*. It appears that Berlioz had asked the principal artists and a few friends to a supper after the performance, to celebrate the anticipated success. When that success was converted into a dismal failure, none of the *convives* liked to put in an appearance, with the sole exception of Mr. Davison. The table was spread for many guests and the two men sat down at the deserted board, Berlioz being moved to tears by the tact and true politeness shown by his solitary guest.

[Hueffer 1889: 220]

19 GERMANY: THE SECOND PHASE

Back in Paris after the *Cellini* débâcle, Berlioz had only a few weeks there before he and Marie were off again – this time to Germany. A short trip to Baden-Baden and Frankfurt was followed in October by a longer one to Brunswick, Hanover and Leipzig. But in Paris, in the hurried gap between the two, he had the unexpected opportunity of renewing his acquaintance with a German visitor whom he had not seen since Dresden ten years before. The catalyst for the meeting was Liszt.

JULES JANIN

. . . the devil and his infernal racket in person, Franz Liszt – the great Liszt, who fell on my house like a bombshell, shouting, smoking, singing and attacking the piano with such formidable vigour that the unfortunate instrument, woken for a moment by that all-powerful hand, didn't know which saint to turn to for protection. He came, anyhow – with the Princess (his wife) and the Prince (his brother-in-law) and his entire household, including the children . . . Liszt is, as always, a good, rollicking, boisterous fellow, delighted with his own fame and blissfully ignorant of everything that has been going on in Paris since he left. He is only here for five or six days, and has come expressly (and only) to see his children, whom he hasn't set eyes on since 1847 . . . [The Princess] is a good woman with a pointed nose, passably good figure, passably ugly – she smokes cigars like a trooper, has teeth as black as the bottom of a stove, and is evidently a bit mad; I'm afraid she drives the poor devil to distraction with her extravagant goings-on.

[Letter to his wife, 14 October 1853, in Janin ii, 1975: 379–80]

RICHARD WAGNER

One day Liszt invited me to spend an evening with his children, who lived a secluded life in Paris under the care of a governess . . . He himself seemed a bit bemused by his role as a father, from which over the years he has derived only the cares and none of the satisfactions. On this occasion, too, it came to a reading, namely the final act of *Götterdämmerung* [the text for which Wagner had recently completed], and thus the long-awaited close of the whole thing. Berlioz, who arrived while it was going on, behaved with admirable forbearance in the face of this misfortune. We spent the next morning with him, when he gave us a breakfast to bid us farewell; he had already packed his musical materials to embark on a concert tour of Germany. Here Liszt played for me from *Benvenuto Cellini*, and Berlioz accompanied by singing in his own rather dry way.

[Wagner 1983: 503]

JULES JANIN

This unhappy Berlioz leads the life of a vagabond; he chases after the impossible and, failing to achieve the substance, whiles his time away with the shadow – which fails him too, like everything else. He would certainly have got an excellent position if he had been prepared to marry a reasonable woman and stay in the same place; that's the only way salvation lies, and that's a fact – fair, legitimate and unchanging (?). I pity [people like this] from the bottom of my heart, above all when they are people of talent and ability.

[Letter to his wife, 16 October 1853, in Janin ii, 1975: 382]

> By this time, Berlioz was a better-known figure than he had been on his last German trip a decade before; his concerts in Leipzig, particularly, attracted the attention of the German musical world – among its younger adherents, the twenty-year-old Brahms and the poet–composer Peter Cornelius, later famous for his comic opera *The Barber of Baghdad*.

PETER CORNELIUS
(1824–74)

Very early on Thursday morning (it was ice cold), we set off, Liszt and eight Weimar musicians, to Leipzig where Berlioz was giving a concert. In this way I got to know Berlioz personally, and received twice as much pleasure at the performance because I had made a point of studying him exclusively for the last eight days.

[Letter to his sister, 5 December 1853, in Cornelius 1904: i, 149]

> Hedwig Salomon, the musical daughter of a Leipzig banker, left her impressions of Berlioz on the night of the first of his two Leipzig concerts.

HEDWIG SALOMON
(born 1822)

Concert by Berlioz. He is a philosopher of music – indeed a sophist. He makes the most hair-splitting improbabilities possible. It is quite indisputable that his genius has taken new paths and despises the old ground under its feet, but for this reason it floats in an airless space whither few can follow it. Not even myself – his music can only excite me, tear me free from myself; but it cannot inspire me and lead me to God. He claims not to care for the recognition of other people, and yet after the concert, when half the audience had applauded and the other half hissed, he said to me: '*on ne me veut plus*', and indeed he said it with such bitterness and such deep melancholy that it made him appear more human and closer to me. He happened to lay his hands on the table beside me, and I was astonished by the muscular fingers which expressed such energetic power, as if in them were sleeping all the curious rhythms which his baton reproduces with such incredible decisiveness. In appearance he is noble, distinguished and full of character; the softness of his eyes contradict the Roman nose and the determined mouth.

List [*sic*] sat opposite me at dinner and wanted to amuse himself with us; God knows what tempted him to do that – what vampire, what terrible daemon. He was in the best of moods that evening and made jokes about everything . . . Gouvy, who has recently had such great success with his symphony, was also there. Poor Brahms had a hard time. How can the poor boy help it that Schumann's intemperate praise has made him the target of all those who envy and mock him.

[Autograph journal dated 2 December, Salomon 1853]

JOHANNES BRAHMS
(1833–97)

On Thursday evening I went straight from the train station to Helbig's [restaurant]; you should have seen the surprise. Senff, Wenzel, and Sahr were there. Liszt had come to the Berlioz concert with all his disciples (also Reményi) – he did himself a great deal of harm. The exaggerated applause of the Weimar clique provoked some determined opposition . . . In spite of the violent distaste of some of the Leipzigers my first call on Friday was to Liszt. I was accorded a very friendly reception . . . Liszt also visited me with Cornelius etc. Friday I was at David's, also Liszt, Berlioz etc. On Sunday evening at Brendel's, notwithstanding the awful faces the Leipzigers made. Pohl, Berlioz, etc. were there, and before I forget, Schloenbach, Giesecke, and all the literary nobility (or nobodies?) of Leipzig. Berlioz praised me with such exceeding and heartfelt warmth that the others meekly repeated his words. He was just as friendly last night at Moscheles. I have to be very grateful to him. Liszt is coming back on Monday (to Berlioz's greatest disadvantage).

[Letter to Joseph Joachim, 7 December 1853, in Avins 1997: 28–9]

> One of the 'literary nobility' wrote a letter to the *Neue Zeitschrift für Musik* recording his own impressions of this meeting between Berlioz and the latest German prodigy.

ARNOLD SCHLOENBACH
(1807–66)

We listened now to the young Brahms from Hamburg, referred to the other day in Schumann's article in your journal . . . and when the slender, fair youth appeared, so deficient in presence, so shy, so modest, his voice still in transitional falsetto, few could have suspected the genius that had already created so rich a world in this young nature. Berlioz had, however, already discovered in his profile a striking likeness to Schiller, and conjectured his possession of a kindred virgin soul, and when the young genius unfolded his wings . . . [and] presented his scherzo . . . we all felt: Yes, here is a true genius, and Schumann was right; and when Berlioz, deeply moved, embraced the young man and pressed him to his heart, then, dear friend, I felt myself affected by such a sacred tremor of enthusiasm as I have seldom experienced.

[9 December 1853, in May 1948: i, 145]

> Berlioz's fast-growing recognition in Germany only made the return to Paris more depressing, and when he got back this time he had more personal reasons for depression as well. Harriet, who had suffered a further series of strokes in 1849 and become progressively weaker in the following years, was now clearly entering a final decline. He was ill himself, with one of the gastric attacks that had become more frequent in recent years, and he had hardly recovered by the beginning of March when Harriet died.

JULES JANIN

How sadly, how swiftly they pass, these legendary divinities, frail children of Shakespeare and Corneille. Alas, it was not so long ago – we were young then, filled with the thoughtless pride of youth – that Juliet, one summer evening on her balcony above the Verona road, with Romeo at her side, trembling with rapture, listened – and heard the nightingale, and the lark, the herald of the morn. She listened with a pale, dreamy intensity, a bewitching fire in her half-averted eyes. And her voice! a golden voice, pure and vibrant . . . When she moved, when she spoke, her charm mastered us. A whole society stirred to the magic of this woman . . .

And now she is dead. She died a week ago, still dreaming of the glory that comes so swiftly and so swiftly fades. What images lie there, what worlds of poignant regret!

[*Journal des débats*, 20 March 1854, in Berlioz 1969: 463–4]

It was with an effort that Berlioz pulled himself together for one more German trip, and only with the greatest difficulty that he managed to control his feelings as he conducted the *Symphonie fantastique* and the Love Scene from *Roméo et Juliette* in Hanover.

JOSEPH JOACHIM
(1831–1907)

[Berlioz] will have told you about his concert here, at which the standard of the orchestral playing seems to have pleased him. Truthfully, I have never heard a finer, more mellow sound from the woodwind than at this concert. The public, which is unfortunately more materialistic here than in other places, behaved with the sluggish indolence of a snail and naturally drew in its horns before the onslaught of Berlioz. The enthusiastic participation of the king and queen did something to attenuate the bad impression inflicted on the foreign master by this money-mad city. For my own part, I have found genuine refreshment in the immense strength of feeling, the broad melodic impulse and the orchestral fascination of his works – but you know well the power of this man's individuality.

[Letter to Liszt, 13 April 1854, in Joachim 1911: i, 182]

> But it was the four concerts in Dresden that were the high point of this tour, even if there were warning hints of the coming division between Berlioz and the Liszt–Wagner faction.

HANS VON BÜLOW
(1830–94)

At some point it would perhaps be a good thing to remind M. Berlioz that the first and warmest friends he found among the orchestra and audience at Dresden belong to the Wagner party and have belonged to it for a long time. These words . . . have been prompted by the memory of some gossipy remarks of Mme. Berlioz's on the subject of Richard Wagner, which rather irritated me. But Mme.

Berlioz is at heart an excellent woman who has the fault of being a bit of a chatterer and of passing on a whole load of things to which it would be wrong to pay too much attention.

[Letter to Liszt, 30 April 1854, in Bulow 1898: 79]

> Bülow's comment was probably too charitable, if Marie's later attitude to Wagner is anything to go by – but in any case, where Marie was concerned, Berlioz now had little choice, and in October, seven months after Harriet's death, he and Marie were married in Paris. The move was greeted philosophically by Berlioz's friends and family and, more importantly perhaps, by his son; after a disturbed childhood and difficult early youth, Louis, at twenty, was now embarking on a naval career and could only welcome a development that promised his father the stability and support he needed.
>
> 1854 virtually marked the end of Berlioz's German activities. After the Leipzig and Dresden visits, there were to be no more grand tours in the German-speaking countries: a couple more 'Berlioz weeks' at Weimar and an annual summer trip across the French border to Baden-Baden from 1856 to 1863, but apart from these only two short visits, to Cologne and to Vienna, in the last years of his life.

20 FRIENDS IN PARIS

The great novelty at Berlioz's concerts in Leipzig and Dresden had been the performances of a new work, *La fuite en Égypte*. Originating in the little chorus, 'L'adieu des bergers', which had been performed (under a pseudonym) as long ago as 1850, this was the first completed section of what was later to become *L'enfance du Christ*. It was introduced to Paris by François Seghers at a concert of the Société Ste Cécile on 18 December 1853, and Berlioz, who had arrived back from Leipzig on the day before the concert, rushed to the final rehearsal.

Seghers was a staunch champion of young French composers, and at this rehearsal a new symphony was being tried out for performance at the same concert.

CAMILLE SAINT-SAËNS

The modern French school, which found the door barred to it in the rue Bergère [the Conservatoire], was welcomed with open arms in the Chaussée-d'Antin [the Salle Ste Cécile] in the persons of Reber, Gounod, Gouvy and even of beginners like Georges Bizet and myself. It was there that I took the first step of my career with the Symphony in E flat that I wrote when I was seventeen. In order to get it accepted by his committee, Seghers presented it to them as the work of an unknown composer which had been sent to him from Germany; the committee swallowed the bait and the symphony, which would never had had the honour of a hearing if it had been signed with my name, was praised to the skies.

I can see myself now at a rehearsal, listening to the conversation between Berlioz and Gounod; they both displayed great interest in me, spoke freely in front of me and discussed the qualities and defects of the anonymous symphony. They took the work extremely seriously, and you can imagine how I soaked up their words.

When the secret was disclosed, the interest of these two great musicians turned to friendship . . .

[Saint-Saëns 1913: 255–6]

> Saint-Saëns's enthusiasm for Berlioz had begun early, and received magnificent confirmation at the performance of the *Requiem* at Saint-Eustache in October of the previous year.

Shall I tell you my impressions of the famous *Messe des Morts* which I had the good fortune to hear at Saint-Eustache under the direction of the composer? I knew it from reading the score, and was dying to hear the effect in performance; it surpassed all my expectations. At the *Tuba mirum* I felt as if each slim shaft in every column of pillars had become an organ pipe and the whole church one immense organ! More than anything I marvelled at the poignant feeling that runs through this astonishing work, the constant and unparalleled elevation of style that, as with all the works of this composer, is so much more evident in performance than from reading the score. My mother, who was a great admirer of Berlioz, was with me on this occasion; as we left we bumped into one of my class-mates and burst out with enthusiasm. 'Yes', he said to us coldly, 'it's attractive – but the melody . . .!!' We let out a roar like a pair of wild beasts and leapt at his throat; he took to his heels – and he was wise. We would have strangled him.

[Saint-Saëns 1903: 174–5]

> The 'young musical lion', as Berlioz called him, was to become probably the nearest thing to a pupil that Berlioz ever had, and the relationship started early.

You can imagine my delight when one day, climbing up my three storeys in the rue du Jardinet, Berlioz came to ask me to do the piano reduction of *Lélio*, which was still unpublished. It was from this moment that he favoured me with the great honour of his affection, and with his support and encouragement in the first disappointments of my career.

[Ibid: 175]

In addition to my total admiration, I had the greatest affection for him, born of the kindness he showed me of which I was properly proud, as well as those intimate qualities which I had discovered in him and which were in such complete contrast to the reputation he had in the outside world, where he was regarded as proud, mischievous and filled with hate. On the contrary he was good, good to the point of weakness, grateful for the least signs of interest that one showed in him, and of a wonderful simplicity which lent even greater value to his witticisms and caustic sallies, because you never felt that straining after effect, that desire to dazzle people, which often spoils so many good remarks . . .   .

[Saint-Saëns 1899: 12–13]

He was a good, affectionate, highly original creature, certainly sarcastic from time to time, but arousing an irresistible sympathy in anyone capable of appreciating him. And the sympathy that you offered him was all the sweeter because he was too often the victim of very different attitudes: he suffered from them visibly, although he didn't want to appear to do so.

[Saint-Saëns 1903: 174]

Berlioz has been reproached for his lack of love for mankind, to which he himself confesses in his *Mémoires*. In this he was of the same mind as Horace, who said: *Odi profanum vulgus*, and La Fontaine who wrote: '*Que j'ai toujours haï les pensers du vulgaire!*' A superior nature like his was incapable of loving the vulgarity, the coarseness, the ferocity and egoism which play such a considerable role in the world and of which he had so often been the victim. One should love that element of humanity of which one feels oneself a part, work if one can for its improvement and help it to progress. This is what, in his own sphere of activity, Berlioz did as much as anyone, by opening up new paths and preaching all his life the love of beauty and the worship of the masterpieces of art. There is nothing more you can ask of him; the rest is not the business of an artist but of a saint.

[Saint-Saëns 1899: 14]

Between ourselves, I believe that Berlioz was too much enamoured of Shakespeare, Byron and Goethe. He admitted as much himself, without realizing it: '*Hamlet*,' he says in *Lélio*, 'profound and devastating concept, what mischief you have done me!'. Elsewhere, in one of his letters, he calls Goethe and Shakespeare 'the interpreters of my life'. But this is a terrible idea when you think about it. Like the mystics who reached a point where they experienced in their own bodies the agonies of the Passion, Berlioz experienced the tortures of Faust, of Hamlet, of Manfred. He became himself the incarnation of these poetic creations, whose imagined sufferings were transformed for him into painful reality. Was it Camille and Harriet that he loved, or simply Ariel and Ophelia? At certain moments it is no longer he who lives, it is Shakespeare who lives in him. One watches a curious phenomenon, a poetic form of mysticism which leads, as the other does, to grave disorders of the nervous system and to a cruel and interminable torture that gnaws little by little at a man's existence and only ends with death.

And it is because he took himself for Faust or for Hamlet that he painted himself, in the *Mémoires*, in such false colours, making out that he hated his fellow men – he whom the least mark of sympathy would move to the point of tears. He hated only the vulgar herd, like Horace, like all artists and all poets.

In his heart of hearts he was not only sincere, he was naïve in the best sense of the word, naïve like the great Haydn, whose naïvety he was so fond of laughing at. Why should anyone deceive him, he who never deceived anyone? And so he let himself be taken in by applause, by compliments, by the flattery of some, the promises of others.

[Saint-Saëns 1885: 251–3]

I knew Berlioz well and I loved him very much, and I don't recognise him in the portait he has painted of himself. Certainly, when we are young, these rapturous emotions, these wild exaggerations, have nothing astonishing about them. But throughout our lives – always furies, always tears, always delirious enthusiasms, praise and blame driven to their ultimate extremities . . . is all this really true, isn't there a good deal of literature mixed up with it? He speaks of that little rehearsal for *Armide*, when I was playing the piano; he says 'we were suffocating!'* I remember the occasion very well: we were gripped by Gluck's music, very moved certainly, but it didn't go as far as suffocation.

I saw him frequently, because I admired and loved him a great deal, but I wouldn't have seen nearly so much of him if he had really been what he himself describes. I am a very highly strung person myself, and I couldn't have borne this continual assault on the nerves. His judgments were bizarre: it was impossible to foresee if something would please him or not . . . he judged everything unconditionally . . . he took account of nothing but his immediate impression.

He suffered a lot physically because of the impossibility of persuading him to follow any regime, as a result of which he developed an excruciating stomach condition which eventually led to his death.

[Letter to Adolphe Boschot, 19 January 1920, in Saint-Saëns 1990: 17–18]

> It was during the later 1850s that the gastric disorder, diagnosed by doctors as 'intestinal neuralgia' and apparently a form of acute inflammation caused, or at least encouraged, by the emotional and physical tensions to which he was so constantly subjected, began to intensify its grip.

During the last years of his life, when by virtue of its simplicity and sweetness *L'enfance du Christ* had triumphed over the prejudice that would only see him as a noise-maker and an organizer of pandemonium, public opinion began to move in Berlioz's favour. It was not the injustice of men that hastened his death, as has been said, but a gastric condition brought about by his obstinate refusal to follow in any way the advice of his doctors or the requirements of a well regulated diet. I saw this clearly, without being able to do anything about it, during an artistic tour on which I had the honour of accompanying him. 'Something extraordinary has happened to me,' he said one morning, 'I'm not in pain.' And he told me about his sufferings, his continual stomach cramps, and how he

* In a letter to Humbert Ferrand, 17 January 1866, in *Lettres intimes* (Paris 1882), p. 292.

was forbidden to take any stimulant or deviate from a prescribed regime on pain of terrible agonies, which would always go on getting worse.

Now, in fact he followed no regime, and he ate and drank anything that took his fancy without worrying about the next day. On the evening of the day of which I speak, we attended a banquet. Sitting close to him, I did everything I could to prevent him having coffee, or champagne, or Havana cigars, but it was no good – and the next day the poor man was writhing in his usual agonies.

[Saint-Saëns 1899: 11–12]

> The relationship with Gounod, who was seventeen years older than Saint-Saëns and therefore only fourteen years younger than Berlioz himself, was more that of colleague than friend, and certainly nothing like as close. The characters involved were too different.

'What an elegant man is Berlioz!' said Gounod to me one day. The remark was a profound one. Berlioz's elegance is not apparent at first sight from his clumsy and awkward-looking handwriting;* it is instinct in the texture, one might say the very flesh of his work and exists, latent, within that prodigious nature, which cannot be compared to the disadvantage of another since no other can be compared with it. With Gounod, the reverse is the case: his writing, of an impeccable elegance, can sometimes conceal a certain vein of vulgarity; from time to time, he is 'of the people', and for that very reason addresses himself easily to the people – so that he became popular long before Berlioz, whose *Damnation de Faust* only achieved popularity after the death of its composer.

[Saint-Saëns 1899: 85]

CHARLES GOUNOD

There are two men, two beings in Berlioz. First, there is the child (both boy and girl) adorable in its charm, gentleness, tenderness,

---

* This opinion of Berlioz's handwriting will come as a surprise to many who have had the opportunity to study it, but the words '*gauche et maladroite*' do not seem susceptible of any other interpretation.

simple unconstraint – second, there is the grown character (man and woman), ardent, passionate, deep, a thinker and a dreamer, often carried away to the point of dizziness and just as often arguing to the point of splitting hairs. It is, I think, in this duality of make-up (if one may say so) that we must seek explanation of Berlioz's lack of success, *in general*, with what is called the *Public*. The Public doesn't *want* to be asked to work: it doesn't *seek* to understand: it wants to *feel*, and to *feel immediately* . . . Now in Berlioz's [music] there is often a texture which the public finds difficult to grasp; it always wants to get back to *what it knows*: Berlioz has forgotten, or rather disdained, to check up on his music; it is gold which hasn't been coined and therefore is not in general circulation . . .

[Letter to Mme Charles Rhoné, 10 August 1862, in Harding 1973: 73]

> It was a view which Gounod tailored a little for public
> consumption twenty years later.

Berlioz was a man all of a piece, without concessions or compromises. He belonged to the race of [Molière's] Alceste: naturally he had the race of Oronte ranged against him – and God knows, the Orontes are thick on the ground! People found him capricious, grumpy, ill-tempered and I don't know what else. But along with a sensitivity so excessive as to border on irascibility, one had to take into account the irritants, the personal afflictions, the thousand rebuffs suffered by this proud spirit, incapable of smug complacency or weak bowing and scraping. And the fact remains, if his judgments seemed harsh to those at whom they were aimed, never for a moment could they be attributed to the shameful promptings of a jealousy that would have been utterly foreign to the high ideals of this noble, loyal and generous nature . . .

With Berlioz, all impressions, all feelings went to the extreme. He knew joy and sadness only as states of wild passion; as he said himself, he was a 'volcano'. For intensity of feeling can carry us as far in pain as it can in pleasure: Tabor and Golgotha are one. Happiness is not in the absence of suffering, any more than genius consists in the absence of flaws.

The great geniuses suffer, and must suffer, but they are not to be pitied; they have experienced states of intoxication unknown to the rest of men, and if they have wept from grief, they have shed tears of ineffable joy. That alone is a heaven beyond price.

[Gounod 1882: pp. iv–v, vii]

> In the summer of 1854, when Berlioz was encouraged by many of his friends to apply for the vacancy that had occured at the Academy of Fine Arts (the Institut), there was no lack of help in the arduous task of campaigning for votes from the 'Immortals' already installed there.

DANIEL BERNARD

One of Berlioz's intimate friends, the shrewd organ-builder M. Édouard Alexandre, took an active part in supporting Berlioz's candidature. There was the question of gaining Adam's vote. Now, the composer of *Le Chalet* had practically nothing in common with the composer of the *Symphonie fantastique* and bringing the two of them together was difficult. 'Come on now,' said M. Alexandre to Berlioz, who could not bring himself to do any canvassing, 'Make your peace with Adam. Hang it all! he's a musician – you can't deny that?' 'Certainly – I don't deny it at all. But why does Adam, who is a great musician, persist in dirtying his hands in the world of *opéra-comique*? For heaven's sake, if he wanted to, he could write music like I do!'

M. Alexandre wasn't discouraged and went to see Adolphe Adam: 'My dear friend,' he said, 'You will give Berlioz your vote, won't you? There's no point in refusing to get on with him – you know as well as I do that he is a musician . . .' 'A great musician certainly' (and little Adam readjusted his glasses on his nose) 'a very great – a very great one . . . Only, he writes tedious music; if he wanted to, he could write very differently . . . He could write quite as well as me!' It was a scene worthy of Molière.

'But seriously,' said Adam, 'Berlioz is a man of great talent. I give you my word that, after Clapisson, to whom we have all promised our votes already, Berlioz shall have the first available place'.

[Bernard 1879: 51–2]

Offenbach, whose brilliant career as a composer of operetta had yet to take off, later remembered another story in this connection.

JACQUES OFFENBACH
(1819–80)

A friend of Hector Berlioz had gone to solicit a vote from one of the Immortals. He enumerated all the serious qualities of his friend, as a symphonist and a great composer. 'That's all very fine', said the Immortal, 'but tell me the names of a few of these famous works'. The other replied: '*Roméo et Juliette*, *La Damnation de Faust*, etc., etc.' 'Upon my word, I don't know any of these. In any case we have already promised our votes to the celebrated composer of *Le postillon de Madame Ablou,* who is known in every quarter of the globe'.* 'And in the *cafés* too', replied the Berliozian as he went out. And so M. Clapisson was elected on the same ticket as M. Adam – that is to say, on the strength of a *postillon* – which proves that the Académie is right on the ball in matters of art.

[Article in *L'Artiste*, in Tiersot: Berlioziana V, 1911: 276]

Berlioz made new friends too, among them his exact contemporary, the historian and political philosopher Edgar Quinet, now exiled and living in Brussels.

EDGAR QUINET
(1803–75)

The other day I had the great joy of a visit from Berlioz, whom I didn't know but have always admired in the teeth of the ungodly. I like and admire this artist who follows his own muse without bothering to ingratiate himself with the public. I love this disinterested conflict, with no holds barred and no thought for easy success.

* *Le Postillon de Lonjumeau* was the title of one of Adam's most popular *opéras-comiques*, but no Postillon – let alone any Madame Ablou – appears in the list of Clapisson's operas.

Berlioz himself interests me as much as his music: his determination, his energy, his proud demeanour – for my taste, these are the most beautiful symphonies of all. He always had my admiration, he has left with my friendship.

[Letter to Bernard Lavergne, 5 April 1855, in Quinet 1885: i, 217–8]

> The visit to Brussels (for a performance of the now completed *L'enfance du Christ*) gave him the opportunity to go a little way in repairing bridges with an old enemy.

FRANÇOIS-JOSEPH FÉTIS

I have had Berlioz here; his *L'enfance du Christ* was a success. It is simple and naïve, but there is feeling in it. It certainly marks a change from the crudity of his earlier style. I found him much altered and aged. He did me the pleasure of dining with me, with his wife; he's a man of great intelligence, musically as well as in other ways; sadly, the richness of his imagination is not up to the level of the technical skills he has acquired.

[Letter to Liszt, 1 April 1855 in Prod'homme 1913: 248]

> And there is one other glimpse of the Brussels visit. George Eliot (still in those days Miss Mary Ann Evans) was on her way home from Weimar.

GEORGE ELIOT
(1819–80)

At Brussels, as we took our supper, we had the pleasure of looking at Berlioz's fine head and face, he being employed in the same way on the other side of the table. The next morning to Calais . . .

[Eliot 1885: i, 373]

> In Paris social life claimed a good deal of his time, if only because it enabled him to get away from Marie, with whom life was becoming more and more difficult.

Among his friends for some years had been the celebrated mezzo-soprano Pauline Viardot, daughter of the
Spanish tenor Manuel García and sister of the legendary
Maria Malibran. Mme Viardot's salon was a centre for
the intellectuals of Paris, and Berlioz, with whom she
shared many tastes and enthusiasms, was a frequent
visitor – particularly after he and Marie moved into
their last apartment at 4, rue de Calais, just round the
corner, in October 1856.

Pauline's daughter Louise, at this time a precocious
fifteen year old, later left her memories of these occasions.

LOUISE HÉRITTE-VIARDOT
(1841–1918)

Every Thursday there was a musical evening at our house, and
whoever had made himself a name in literature or art came to it.
Ary Scheffer, Delaroche, Corot, Berlioz, Stockhausen, Saint-Saëns,
Godard, Wieniawsky, Vieuxtemps, Léonard, Ernst, de Bériot,
Gounod, Ambroise Thomas, Massenet, César Franck, Damcke,
Lalo, Gustave Doré, Frederick Leighton, Renan, Rudolph Lindau,
Flaubert, Turgenieff, Ponsard, Bonnat, Carolus-Duran, Dickens,
Jules Simon, Henri Martin, George Sand, the Countess d'Agoult,
the old Prince Czartorysky, whom the Poles looked on as their
legitimate king, and addressed as 'Your Majesty', and many others
whose names have escaped me.

There were some very eccentric people in this motley crowd,
who caused us a good deal of amusement. One was the old and
very amusing Countess d'H—, who was simply furious if her
favourite seat by the fire was taken. She maintained that she was
very fond of music, but she regularly fell asleep at the sound of the
first note. She always wore white gloves, the fingers of which were
much too long, and she stuffed them into her mouth. As soon as
she fell asleep, the gloves slipped out of her mouth, she woke up, and
immediately began to clap violently, whether there was occasion or
no. And this performance was repeated over and over again.

Her intimate friend, Countess de Ch—, was still more ridiculous. She considered herself a muse; her hair, in which lilac was
entwined, hung down over her shoulders in long ringlets; she was

scraggy, but she arrayed herself in girlish white frocks. Every word she uttered was worthy of one of Molière's *Précieuses ridicules*. She never travelled without a doctor; she was so nervous in railway tunnels, that she had herself chloroformed . . .

Whenever George Sand could make up her mind to leave her beloved Nohant and come to Paris, she very soon called on us. This small woman, with her beautiful, observant eyes, spoke little and sat quietly smoking her cigarette. If anyone came whom she did not know, she never opened her mouth. We were often asked: 'Who was that quiet little lady we saw at your house?' 'Madame Sand.' 'What! And you let me chatter!' She corresponded regularly with my mother to the day of her death.

Berlioz, who suffered much from ill-health, lived quite near to us and came to see us daily, in order to give vent to his feelings and to obtain a little rest from his quarrelsome wife.

I often saw him. He was always in extremes, either up in the clouds or in the depth of depression. He had his diabolical moods too, when he fumed with rage and fury against artists, composers, the public, life, and the world in general. At those times no one could manage him. The only instruments he could play were the guitar and flageolet, but he was able to tell every member of the orchestra how he must play his instrument. As he could not play the piano, he used to come to us whenever he had composed something for the orchestra, and my mother and I had to play it as a duet. One took the strings, the other the wind instruments. Many a wrong bass was discovered by me, pert thing that I was. This story about the wrong bass has been told elsewhere, but incorrectly.

The first time I was bold enough to draw his attention to the matter, he looked at me utterly astonished. 'And pray, what would be the correct bass?' I played it to him, and suddenly he exclaimed: 'Why, she's right!'

[Héritte-Viardot 1913: 43–5, 49–50]

> The anyhow probably mythical story about 'correcting' Berlioz's basses has usually been told of Pauline Viardot (who had after all been a pupil of Berlioz's old teacher, Reicha, and is known to have given Berlioz occasional advice) rather than her daughter, whose memoirs can be unreliable. In any case, one or two of the people on

Louise's guest list can hardly have made an appearance at this stage – Massenet, for example, who was a year younger than Louise herself, or Benjamin Godard, who was only born in 1849 – and one whom she does not mention has left his own memory of Berlioz *chez* Viardot.

EUGÈNE DELACROIX

At Mme Viardot's. She again sang Armida's aria *'Sauvez-moi de l'amour!'**

Berlioz was unbearable. He kept on and on about the trills and ornamentation in Italian music, which he regards as barbarism and in the most detestable taste. He won't even accept them in the older writers, like Handel, and he gets wild with anger at the *fioriture* in the great aria of D[onna] Anna.

[17 January 1856, in Delacroix 1895: iii, 127]

Pauline herself took a perhaps more realistic view of Berlioz's state of mind.

PAULINE VIARDOT-GARCIA
(1821–1910)

Berlioz came to see me today – he is very sick – body and soul are diseased. His wife is really too disagreeable! How could such a man marry such a woman! better to eat raw lemons all day and drink vinegar all night! dreadful!

[Letter to Julius Rietz, 3 January 1859, in Viardot-Garcia 1/3, 1915: 372]

Berlioz's old friend Legouvé was another whose soirées were famous for the talent they attracted. François Guizot was a writer and historian of immense distinction and an elder statesman who had served as a government minister and, briefly, as prime minister before the revolution of 1848.

* In Act 3 of Gluck's opera: the aria actually begins *'Venez, venez, haine implacable'*.

FRANÇOIS GUIZOT
(1787–1874)

I am writing to you today after returning last night at midnight from a soirée at M. Legouvé's. I don't like these contrasts in life. I like a single, prolonged impression; in Paris there is no way to avoid contrasts. I spent yesterday evening passing from one introduction to another. First the musician, M. Gounod, with whom I had dined there before, and who made me promise to go to the first performance of his *Reine de Saba*. I told him that I hadn't been to the Opéra for twenty-nine years. He only became more insistent that I should go, and in the end I gave way. After M. Gounod, Legouvé brought me M. Ritter, the great pianist of the day – and of the evening – lively, straightforward and not in the least full of himself. Then Théophile Gautier, whom I had never seen before; the head of Vitellius, a *gourmand* sunk deep in his fat and the recesses of his beard, the model of the portly epicure, mocking and witty . . . I sat down again. A young man sat down beside me. Another introduction: M. Gustave Doré, the artist of the *Contes de Perrault*. I told him of the pleasure his pictures gave to my grandchildren. He didn't appear to think much of the compliment. So I talked to him about his illustrations of Dante, which he liked better . . .

M. Doré moved away. A moment later I see standing beside me a lean gentleman with a dishevelled head of hair, a piercing eye and a lively, rather noble look. M. Legouvé came up. 'My dear Berlioz!' he said, and we were introduced. There's a man who is a true enthusiast, not at all loquacious until the moment when his enthusiasm grips him – when he becomes eloquent and bursting with ideas. A striking contrast to Théophile Gautier, the sensual sceptic. The music put an end to the introductions and conversations, and I got home at midnight.

[Letter, February 1862, in Guizot 1884: 384–5]

ERNEST LEGOUVÉ

M. Guizot, who was a good judge of men, said to me one day: 'I've met a good many famous artists at your house, but the one who impressed me the most was M. Berlioz. There's a really original creature!'

M. Guizot had picked the right word. Everything about Berlioz was original: the extraordinary mixture of enthusiasm and mockery; the ideas that you could never predict; the way of talking that kept you always on the alert by its constant changes of direction. Sometimes there would be long silences, accompanied by a sombre, downward gaze that seemed to plumb the depths of God knows what abyss – and then a sudden radiant awakening with a flood of brilliant observations, now comic, now touching, explosions of Homeric laughter and moments of childish delight.

[Legouvé 1886: 327]

> And there were evenings of a quieter kind, when Berlioz could relax in more intimate surroundings. It was in January 1855 that he first heard the fourteen-year-old pianist prodigy, Théodore Ritter, for whom he (wrongly) predicted a great future; during the next few years he took Ritter under his wing and gave him the task of completing the piano arrangement *of L'enfance du Christ*, and later arranging the whole of *Roméo et Juliette*. The composer Ernest Reyer was another young protegé who had recently attracted Berlioz's friendly critical attention.

ERNEST REYER
(1823–1909)

Berlioz had recognized in the young Théodore a remarkable precocity and exceptional talents, and had taken great interest in him. He gave him the scores of the masters to read, and pointed out their beauties. Berlioz and I often met at the rooms of Toussaint Benet [Ritter's father] . . . After dinner, young Ritter would sit down at the piano and play his favourite works, 'Romeo and Juliet' and

'The Damnation of Faust' in turn. This was long before the appearance of the 'Trojans.' Berlioz, seated before the fire with his back toward us and his head bowed, would listen. From time to time a sigh would escape him: a sigh – perhaps a sob. One evening, I remember, after the sublime adagio of the 'scène d'amour', he suddenly rose, and, throwing himself into the arms of Théodore, exclaimed in an ecstacy, 'Ah, that is finer than the orchestra!' No, it was not finer; but it gave the impression, produced the illusion, of orchestra, so exquisite were the nuances in the playing of this most skilful virtuoso, so various were the qualities of tone . . .

No stranger, no friend even, – if we except a young relative of the family, – assisted at these reunions. Berlioz and I would withdraw together; he would accompany me to my house, I would see him to his, and we would walk the distance over two or three times, he smoking ever so many cigars, which he never finished, sitting down on the deserted sidewalks, giving himself up to the exuberance of his spirits, and I laughing immoderately at his jokes and puns. Ah, how few have seen him thus! The moment came to separate. Usually I accompanied him to his door, covetous of the last word. As we approached his house in the Rue Calais . . . his enthusiasm vanished; his face, lighted up by the flickering gas-jet, settled into its habitually sad, careworn expression. He hesitated a moment as his hand touched the bell-pull, then murmured a cold, chilly adieu in a suppressed voice, as if I were never to see him again. He entered his house; and I – I went away with my heart torn, knowing well what a painful reaction would succeed the few hours of unbending delight and childish glee I had just witnessed.

[Reyer 1893: 306]

> Clearly, there was little solace to be found, these days,
> in the rue de Calais.

After the disastrous première of *Faust* in 1846, no significant new work by Berlioz had been heard in Paris for
eight years, and when the long silence was broken by the
first performance of *L'enfance du Christ* in December
1854, Berlioz was ill-prepared for its immediate success;
it had to be repeated twice, and was quickly taken up in
Weimar and Brussels (the occasion of the rapprochement with Fétis). Berlioz's pleasure was tempered with
irritation that this deliberately simple work should have
had such an easy passage compared with its more ambitious predecessors – and perhaps particularly because
the huge *Te Deum*, which he had composed in 1849,
was still waiting for performance. As early as 1851, at
the time of his visit to England for the Great Exhibition,
Prince Albert had accepted the dedication, but the
opportunity for a performance in London had never
materialized, and subsequent hopes for its incorporation
in the Emperor's coronation ceremony in 1852, or his
wedding in 1853, had come to nothing. It was eventually given at Saint-Eustache at the end of April 1855
and, encouraged no doubt by the wave of popularity set
up by *L'enfance du Christ*, achieved a good, if not brilliant, success. But the scale of the performance created
a sensation.

LÉON ESCUDIER
(1815–81)

Let one imagine nine hundred musicians, players and singers, the
ones grouped in the midst of the nave in serried ranks, the others
on benches rising in tiers above the altar, and Berlioz at the centre,
plunging his eagle glance into the army of performers whom he

seemed to hold at the end of his marshal's baton – it was a spectacle that defies description.

[Review in *La France Musicale*, 6 May 1855, in Barzun 1950: ii, 64]

JEAN-HIPPOLYTE VILLEMESSANT
(1812–79)

Berlioz conducts the orchestra and performers of his music with his arms, with his hands, with his shoulders, his head, his hips – with his whole being in short; he has the air of a man completely at home, making sense to himself, following his own tracks through a shindy of his own creation. At the next concert to which he invites us, it is to be hoped that the performance will take place in the Champs-Elysées: each musician will be hoisted into a tree (I reserve a numbered branch), the rumble of the omnibuses will provide an orchestral pedal, the canon at the Invalides will be the tam-tam, and Berlioz will beat time sitting astride a swing – ringmaster of his own circus.

[Article in *Le Figaro*, 6 May 1855 in Prod'homme 1913: 252]

> A month later, Berlioz set off for what was to be his last visit to London, to conduct two concerts of the New Philharmonic Society. These repeated his earlier successes with the same orchestra, in sharp contrast to the fortunes of the old Philharmonic which was being guided through one of the most controversial seasons of its history under the baton of Richard Wagner. Inevitably the two men saw a good deal of each other, and what appears to have been the first meeting took place in the presence of the young Karl Klindworth, a pupil of Liszt's who had recently moved to London.

KARL KLINDWORTH
(1830–1916)

On one of the occasions when I visited [Wagner] at Portland Terrace, Berlioz, then in London, was expected. There had been an estrangement between the two composers, but the reconciliation took place in London. Wagner said to me, 'When Berlioz comes into the room play something from his *Romeo and Juliet*', which I did.

[Klindworth 1898: 515]

RICHARD WAGNER

I had a visit from Berlioz yesterday. He is struggling for his daily bread and is really hard pushed; in France he can't earn a sou, so he has to scrape a meagre living by giving concerts in England and Germany (which – as I know myself – can only bring him in very little). He has been invited here for two concerts with the *new* Philharmonic. He has already come to an agreement with the local press, after being horribly mauled by them to start with. As well as his own Romeo and Juliet symphony he conducted a symphony of Mozart, which he let them rattle through so hideously that it nearly did for me altogether. But that's quite English; they like it like that, and Berlioz, who is now only after the money, knows what is required of him. There is no *depth* in him, by the way.

[Letter to his wife Minna, 15 June 1855, in Wagner 1988: 225–6]

> Wagner's comments about Berlioz's conducting style ('another time-beater of the most ordinary kind', he called him in *Mein Leben*) are indicative of the gulf that was gradually growing between the German view of musical expression and Berlioz's much less indulgent approach. Klindworth, who played Henselt's new piano concerto at Berlioz's second concert, was of the new German persuasion, and Berlioz's description of the rehearsal, at which Klindworth's *'style libre'* kept him 'dancing on a slack tightrope', makes a curious contrast to Klindworth's own.

[KARL KLINDWORTH]

Professor Klindworth relates an amusing anecdote relating to the absent-mindedness of Berlioz as a conductor. At the concert . . .

Professor Klindworth played Henselt's Pianoforte Concerto in F minor. During the progress of the slow movement at the rehearsal, Berlioz fell into a deep reverie, and, apparently forgetting all about the concerto, he stopped conducting. But the soloist and the orchestra went steadily on. At the end of the movement Berlioz was still entranced, and was only aroused when, at a sign from Klindworth, the orchestra began the last movement with an energetic attack of the opening passage!

[Klindworth 1898: 517]

> Entranced? Absent-minded? Or simply exasperated? This is surely the way that legends grow. In any case, Wagner had left London by the time of this concert, after having had several further opportunities to meet Berlioz.

RICHARD WAGNER

The Prägers, Sainton, Lüders, Klindworth and – *Berlioz* with his wife, drove back home with me and we sat over a bowl of champagne punch together until three o'clock in the morning. I have at last got to know Berlioz really well, and I am delighted to be able to say that we are now the best of friends. He is after all an amiable, but very unhappy, man.

Today I have an appropriate headache . . .

[Letter to his wife Minna, 26 June 1855, in Wagner 1988: 233]

> Fifteen or so years later, with characteristic modifications, Wagner expanded on this meeting.

Suddenly I was brought face to face with this man who had endured so much torment, whose fine edge was by then already blunted in some respects, and who yet possessed such singular gifts. Having come to London myself more from a desire for distraction and stimulation, I was entitled to consider myself completely happy and floating on the clouds by contrast with him, a man considerably my senior, who had come to London merely in the attempt to earn a few guineas. His whole being expressed weariness and despair, and I was suddenly seized by deep sympathy for the man, whose gifts obviously, to me, far surpassed those of all his rivals. Berlioz seemed to like the merry spontaneity with which I responded to him; his customarily short and almost frosty manner thawed considerably during the hours we spent together . . .

. . . It was less easy to communicate with him on more serious artistic concerns, for on such matters he always showed himself to be the glib Frenchman, expressing himself with well-honed arguments, and in his own certainty never entertaining any suspicion that he might not have understood his interlocutor properly. Once, when I had warmed to the subject, and to my astonishment suddenly found myself a master of the French language, I tried to express myself to him on the mystery of 'artistic conception'. I sought by this term to designate the strength of the impressions life makes on our inner self, which hold us captive in their way until we disburden ourselves of them by the unique development of forms out of the innermost soul, which those external impressions have by no means summoned up but merely stirred from their deep slumber, so that the artistic form takes shape not as the effect of the impressions received from life but rather as a liberation from them. Hereupon Berlioz smiled in an understanding and condescending way and said: 'Nous appelons cela: digérer'.

[Wagner 1983: 520–1]

> For the time being, however, Wagner seemed happy with the turn of events.

There is one real gain that I bring back from England: the close and cordial friendship that Berlioz and I have formed. I was at a concert of the New Philharmonic under his direction, at which, certainly, I was little edified by his performance of the Mozart G minor symphony, though I had to feel sorry for him about the execution of his own Romeo and Juliet symphony, which was very inadequate. But at dinner at the Saintons . . . he appeared to me in a totally different light to what he had previously. We suddenly saw ourselves to be companions in misfortune, and I found myself thinking that I was luckier than Berlioz.

After my last concert, he called on me with my few other London friends – his wife was there too; we sat together until three in the morning and this time took leave of one another with a warm embrace. I told him that you wanted to come and see me [in Zürich] in September, and asked him to arrange a meeting with you at my house. The money difficulty seemed to be his chief worry, but he would certainly love to come.

[Letter to Liszt, 5 July 1855, in Wagner 1988: 240]

> The financial problem, at least, obtained some relief on his return to Paris, where he had been officially appointed to organize and direct a series of immense concerts at the Palais de l'Industrie to mark the closing ceremonies of the Exposition universelle of 1855. For once, all expenses were paid, he received a substantial fee and was applauded by musicians and public alike.

FERDINAND HILLER

Berlioz was brilliant at organizing the enormous forces that he needed for his performances – I don't believe anybody in Paris possessed a more detailed knowledge of the people involved in music, and their individual abilities, from the leading first violinist to the last triangle player. He knew their engagements, their circumstances, where to look for them and how to treat them; like Egmont, he could say: 'I do not easily forget anybody with whom I have once spoken' – though in his case it would have to be 'whom I have once engaged'. For it must be admitted that it was only the musicians who were in a position to draw his attention to their abilities who really took root in his memory; those he couldn't make use of in his symphonies he forgot easily enough, even if he saw and spoke to them often.

In his musical undertakings he spared no pains, and no detail was too small to receive his personal attention. One day he explained to me, in the hall itself, the arrangements he had made for a *concert-monstre* in the Palace of Industry, where it was a question of assembling and conducting more than a thousand performers in a thoroughly unsuitable building. Electricity and magnetism had to be brought into play – not in the usual sense, by electrifying the musicians through words and looks, and through them electrifying the public – no, but by using the electro-magnetic telegraph to bring the sub-conductors into the closest possible contact with the general music director (in this case no empty title!). The experiment was entirely successful, and similar arrangements have since been widely used, notably in the French operatic theatre.

[Hiller 1880: 99–100]

> It was no doubt the growing recognition of his success at public occasions like this that facilitated his election to the Institut in the following year. Ironically, the chair to which he succeeded had been Adolphe Adam's.

At the end of the first draft of the *Memoirs*, dated October 1854, Berlioz had written of the idea for a vast opera which had been 'tormenting' him for the last three years, but it was not until the Berlioz week at Weimar, in 1855, that the first hint of any practical possibility reached other ears. That these were the ears of Liszt and Carolyne Sayn-Wittgenstein was a stroke of good fortune; both his friends, particularly the Princess, gave him urgent encouragement which, at his visit in the following year, turned to a refusal by the Princess to see him again if he did not set to work at once on his great Virgilian epic. And so on his return to Paris in April 1856 he began the composition *of Les Troyens*: the libretto was completed in less than two months, and the whole immense score in less than two years.

Among his closest friends at this period was Pauline Viardot, and it was to her that he eventually entrusted the first public performance of any part of the roles of his beloved Cassandra and Dido. This was during the fourth of his summer visits to Baden-Baden in 1859, when he rehearsed her in the scene with Coroebus in Act I and the love duet for Dido and Aeneas in Act IV with unforeseen results.

PAULINE VIARDOT

Yes, the orchestra was splendid – we had four full rehearsals . . . The scenes from *Les Troyens*, particularly the one between Cassandra and Coroebus, are very much in the Gluck style, very melodic and dramatic. Frankly, if the other parts of the five acts are as fine as these two scenes, Berlioz has written a masterpiece.

He is going to show me the whole opera. Poor man, he makes me really sad. He is so very ill, so embittered, so unhappy. I am very fond of him, and he loves me very much I know – only he loves me too much! But that would be a long story to tell – and it's still too new – I am still far too shaken to be able to write about it. Perhaps I have already said too much – a word to the wise . . .! Who could have foreseen such a thing! Just think of it, after a long, cordial friendship, Berlioz has had the misfortune to fall in love with me all of a sudden!

Sunday. Good-morning, dear excellent friend. I was interrupted yesterday in the middle of a sentence, and re-reading it unintentionally I think I probably shouldn't have written it. It seems so strange to say things like that – you will make fun of your friend – you will think it indiscreet of me to tell even you a secret that is not mine to tell – but I hope that this kind of bout of brain-fever on the part of my poor friend Berlioz will pass without unhappiness or violent scenes. He is in such a frail condition that any emotion kills him. He feels himself that he has very little time to live and the idea of death horrifies him and fills him with rebellion – alas, what good is rebellion! And I can assure you that I find myself in a very painful position, because I feel clearly that I, and only I, can be of any help to this poor bleeding heart. It's a hard task, very delicate and at the same time extremely difficult to carry out, because I know the pain a sick heart can bring.

[Letter to Julius Rietz, 2 September 1859 in Viardot-Garcia 2/1, 1916: 41 and 43]

> Berlioz was now convinced that Pauline Viardot would be the ideal Cassandra, or Dido, or possibly both, when his opera finally came to performance. That, alas, was still a distant prospect, but a more immediate collaboration with her was offered by the invitation to prepare a new version of Gluck's *Orphée* for revival at the Théâtre-Lyrique. Soon after his return from Baden-Baden, he was at the Viardots's château in the country to work on the project.

I have been plunged in sadness for several days, my dearest friend, without quite knowing the reason why . . . You will understand everything when you hear that Berlioz has been to stay with us for a couple of days. What I have had to suffer is beyond any description. The sight of this man in so much mental and physical pain, so unhappy within himself, so touched by the warm welcome that we gave him, a prey to horrible torments of the heart and yet violent in his efforts to hide them – this passionate soul which breaks its sheath, this life which you might say only hangs by a thread, the great tenderness which flows from his looks, from his least words – all this, I say, has left me shattered. We went for a long walk together, in the course of which he relieved his feelings a little and became calmer. 'My whole life', he said 'has been one long and ardent pursuit of an ideal that I created for myself. Wherever I found a single one of the qualities, of the graces that define this ideal, my heart, avid for love, fixed on it – and, alas, disillusionment soon followed to show me how mistaken I had been. All my life has passed like that, and now at the moment when I feel it to be near its end this same ideal, which I had given up as the fantastic creation of a deranged imagination, appears suddenly before my dying heart! How can you expect me not to adore it! Let me pass the days that remain to me in blessing you, and thanking you for coming to prove to me that I wasn't mad.' Then he begged me fervently, his eyes hot with tears, to grant him a favour; it was that I would not refuse, if he called for me, to go and see him in the event of a serious illness, and to go into his room in spite of all obstacles. I promised to do it, and I will.

He brought with him the first two acts of his opera *Le Troyens*, of which I sang two superb scenes at Baden. Well, my friend, I can assure you that I am enthusiastic about most of it, with the exception of a few passages that are flagrantly bizarre and out of place. I have pointed these out to him and they are to be changed. There has been a veritable transformation in his style – it is melodious, singable, limpid, restrained in the orchestral accompaniment – and grandiose. There are pages of a really incredible *élan*. I can honestly say that I shall be happy the day that this work is performed, and I can tell you there is even vague talk about it for next year. *Qui vivra verra* . . . But alas, I fear that Berlioz will not be present at the performance of his work. In short, you must understand that I find myself at the moment in a really difficult situation, because I have the greatest affection for him, and the pain that I inflict on him (quite involuntarily) distresses me greatly. When he finally succeeds in taming the violence of this emotional excitement (and God grant that it be soon!) I hope I may be able to bring a little calm back into his life. But until then . . .!

[Letter to Julius Rietz, 22 September 1859, in ibid: 43 and 45]

> Pauline Viardot's interest in *Les Troyens* was not limited to criticism, as Saint-Saëns later told the journalist Armand Gouzien.

ARMAND GOUZIEN
(?–?)

As is well known, Berlioz was no pianist, but he didn't trust arrangers and courageously set about reducing the score for piano himself; he aimed above all at avoiding technical difficulties, but didn't realize that he was too often replacing them by clumsy transcriptions which were very much more difficult to play, and in any case mutilated his work more than any arranger would have done. When he arrived at the *Royal Hunt and Storm* he found it impossible to get to the end. A celebrated pianist to whom he turned for help had no better luck. Matters were at this stage when Berlioz recounted his troubles to Mme. Viardot. The great singer asked if she could try her hand at this impossible task, and succeeded in it where the composer and the celebrated pianist had failed. 'With my own eyes,' M. Saint-Saëns has told us, 'I have seen Mme. Viardot, pen in hand, her eyes aglow, the manuscript of *Les Troyens* on her piano, writing the arrangement of the *Chasse royale*'.

[Gouzien 1876]

> In October, a short visit to Paris by Carolyne Sayn-Wittgenstein was the occasion for a performance of several scenes from the opera at the Viardots's salon, accompanied by Théodore Ritter at the piano. The Princess was horrified by the deterioration in Berlioz's condition since she had last seen him in Weimar.

CAROLYNE SAYN-WITTGENSTEIN

I have never seen such thinness, he is no longer a body, he is scarcely anything like a human being . . . I no longer know how much longer he has to live . . . [And Berlioz cried out] 'It's absurd, it's terrible to die, horrible, horrible!'

[Letter to Liszt, 20 October 1859, in Walker 1989: 518]

FRANZ LISZT

I envy you the opportunity of hearing the duet from *Les Troyens* – though I think it is charming of Berlioz to offer you such a lovely surprise. Poor great friend, he is making a sad departure from this unhappy world, 'bleeding from every pore' as you tell me. If at least one could do something to ease his misery – but it's difficult to see how.

[Letter to Carolyne Sayn-Wittgenstein, 24 October 1859, in Liszt 1893–1905: iv, 495]

> *Orphée* in November was an outstanding success, and attracted audiences from every quarter of Parisian artistic and intellectual society. Among them was the young Juliette Lamber, later (as Juliette Adam) to be a considerable figure in the intellectual world of the Third Republic, but now still a bluestocking of twenty-three.

JULIETTE LAMBER [ADAM]
(1836–1936)

Madame Viardot was simply sublime. We seemed to hear the voice of the divine Orpheus himself. All her gestures, her expressions, magnificently and adequately rendered the poignant and distracted grief of antiquity . . .

At the point where Orpheus sings, 'I have lost my Euridice,' and the whole audience, with enthusiastic applause, cried for a repetition, and Madame Viardot, with yet more pathos, divinely sang 'I have lost . . .' I who have never known hysteria fairly broke down and fainted. On recovering I found that Ménard was holding my hand . . .

Berlioz and Saint-Victor, leaning over our box, said a few words to us as the people were leaving the theatre. Ménard told them of the fright I had given him. Berlioz pressed my hand, and kept it within his.

'Yes,' he remarked, 'it is beautiful enough, it is true enough, the torture of misfortune has been sufficiently endured, Orpheus is Orpheus enough, that the expression, rendered as it has been, should annihilate all the senses.' And he left us repeating: 'I am going to tell Orpheus.'

[Adam 1904: 246–8]

23   WAGNER IN PARIS

It was while Berlioz was busy with the preparations for *Orphée*, in September 1859, that Wagner arrived in Paris once more, this time with the intention of organizing a series of concerts of his own music and, if possible, a production of one or more of his operas.

He had in fact made a fleeting visit in the previous year, during which it had already become evident that the amicable understanding reached in London did not necessarily extend to Berlioz's latest artistic ambitions.

RICHARD WAGNER

I now looked up my newly won friend of London days, Berlioz, and found him on the whole disposed to be amiable. I let him know that I was in Paris just for a short excursion and for my own amusement. At that time he was busy working on the composition of a big opera, *Les Troyens;* to obtain some impression of this work I wanted above all to become acquainted with its text, which he had written himself. He devoted an evening to reading it aloud for me alone.

[Wagner 1983: 559]

The admiration that one owes to a great artist is something I lack almost entirely, for I myself lack sharply defined, exceptional gifts. I have only the ability to concentrate more ordinary talents into forceful action, so that, in the process, things can be achieved that would be technically impossible to the individual talent by itself . . . This was made very clear to me in the case of Berlioz, my opposite in this respect. Here is a man who undoubtedly has all the attributes of genius without its controlling spirit – the binding power, in fact. He only ever sees the detail of the subject he is considering, and what makes him important is his ability to seize and expand these details with such liveliness. He read me the libretto of his opera, and in doing so increased my anxiety for him to such an extent that I really found myself wishing that I might never see him again since, in the end, to be so utterly unable to help a friend can only become unbearably painful. This text is clearly the pinnacle of his misfortune, which nothing can now surpass. To see this wretched concoction, which nobody could take for anything else, held up as the last and highest achievement of his artistic career, for which he is sacrificing everything (for he means to write nothing more), fills me with something more than sadness. The manner in which he delivered the text was significant: he read with strong emphasis, much expenditure of effort and every indication of enthusiasm, yet without ever revealing the least sign of genuine enthusiasm, so that his outbursts reminded me of a bad actor who has been given the wrong role to play. The only thing that carried conviction was his own obstinate view of his own meaning – and even that didn't ever seem really sure of itself. I had great difficulty in making him understand, by limiting myself to doubts and misgivings about specific details, my painful bewilderment at the improbable nature of the whole thing; naturally, when humane considerations require that the work as a whole be left uncriticized, it is not possible to make yourself properly understood. I left in great distress, but at any rate he spared me the painful necessity of speaking about his probable failure, since for his part he never displays any real sympathy or interest in others. There is no love in him: that is the key to the stifling riddle of his personality. It is hard, now, for his friends to satisfy him. He puts us in the embarrassing position of having to delude ourselves, and ultimately everybody else as well, simply to preserve his own delusions about us and himself. You can see in a moment that any attempt to disillusion him would immediately result in rupture and the loss of his friendship, for there has never been anybody in the world for whom he might be prepared to sacrifice himself or his point of view.

[Letter to Princess Marie Wittgenstein, 8 February 1858, in Wagner 1912: 216–7]

On Wagner's return in 1859, Berlioz seems to have done
his best to be friendly, though without making any
particular effort to seek Wagner out. Wagner made no
secret of his reasons for being in Paris and, with *Les
Troyens* now completed and awaiting performance
under increasingly discouraging circumstances, Berlioz
must have seen him as a potential rival – as well as
wanting to maintain the distance proper to a professional critic. Nevertheless, Wagner's memories of this
period some thirteen years later were clearly influenced
by later developments; there seems little reason, for
example, to draw such personal conclusions from a
'twinge of pain' that was just as likely to have been an
after-effect of the shock treatment from which Berlioz
was returning.

RICHARD WAGNER

Still under the spell of the favorable impression my London meetings with Berlioz in 1855 had left with me, and which had been
strengthened by the friendly correspondence we had kept up for a
time, I had gone straight to his apartment after my arrival on this
occasion; as I did not find him at home, I had gone back down to
the street, where I met Berlioz on his way home and could not help
observing that the sight of me caused him a twinge of pain horrify-
ingly evident in his countenance and whole physical bearing. I saw
at a glance how matters stood between us but concealed my own
uneasiness under an expression of natural concern for his condition, as to which he immediately assured me that he was suffering
severely, and that he could only bear up against vehement attacks
of neuralgia by electric shock treatment, from a session of which he
was just returning. In order not to make his pain any worse I
offered to take my leave at once, but this made him feel so ashamed
that he implored me to come up with him to his apartment once
again. Here I succeeded in making him somewhat amicably disposed by describing my true intentions in coming to Paris: even the
concerts I proposed to give, I told him, were merely designed to
attract the attention of the public to the extent that a German opera
company could be established that would enable me to perform
works of my own I had not yet heard; as to a French production of

my *Tannhäuser* . . . I was entirely willing to do without it. As a result of these disclosures my relations with Berlioz remained good for a time and were even seemingly very friendly. I consequently thought that, with respect to the recruitment of the necessary orchestral musicians, I would do well to refer my agents in this matter to my experienced friend, whose advice would surely prove invaluable. They told me that Berlioz had shown himself to be very obliging at first, but that all this had changed completely when one day Mme Berlioz had entered the room during their discussions and had exclaimed in irritated astonishment: '*Comment, je crois que vous donnez des conseils pour les concerts de M. Wagner?*'

[Wagner 1983: 597–8]

> Marie, as so often, was making trouble, but Berlioz's own doubts were real enough. Juliette Lamber was at a *soirée* given for Wagner and Hans von Bülow (now Liszt's son-in-law).

JULIETTE LAMBER [ADAM]

[Wagner] began to talk of Parisians with much wit, and of their way of treating all things with banter. He expressed his disappointment at not being understood in France, and of his feelings at having such a powerful rival in Berlioz.

Madame d'Agoult, who liked Berlioz in spite of his embittered character, and who knew the state of his relations with Wagner, replied: 'You are neither of you made ever to live at peace with each other.' . . .

A few days afterwards I met Berlioz in the Court of the Louvre, and spoke to him of Wagner.

'He has a satanic soul,' he said. 'His pride is limitless. He fancies himself the overtopping tree in the musical forest. But that is not so. He belongs to the *Mandragora* species. Woe to him who sleeps under its shade! It means death. Poor Bülow! Wagner bitterly hates every one who has humiliated him by rendering him a service. I know something about it myself.'

[Adam 1904: 256, 253–4]

The three concerts given by Wagner in January and
February 1860 were the event of the season. Berlioz was
at the first of them, and so was the twenty-year-old
composition student Victorin de Joncières.

VICTORIN DE JONCIÈRES
(1839–1903)

The whole of Paris is there: the art world, the literary world, the
aristocracy and the bankers, the whole crowd of the critics. In
the great stage-box on the right sits the Princess Metternich, the
declared protectress of the avant-garde musician, hiding under a
commanding smile her anxiety at the approach of the impending
battle.

In the boxes of the first tier there is Auber, with an air of bored
indifference, escorted by his two female *aides de camp* . . . Berlioz,
buttoned up in his frock coat, his neck imprisoned in a tall cravat
of black silk, style 1830, above which rises that proud head like a
bird of prey, with its huge forehead under an abundant mass of
grey hair, its piercing gaze, its air of sardonic amusement; further
along, Fiorentino, the influential critic of the *Constitutionnel*,
caressing with his fat prelate's hand the opulent beard that spreads
over his white waistcoat.

In the orchestra stalls, Gounod, the young composer recently
brought to prominence by the performance of *Faust* at the Théâtre-
Lyrique, chats with Carvalho who pulls at his chestnut side-
whiskers; the blond Reyer . . . is deep in conversation with his
friend and collaborator Théophile Gautier, with his leonine mane
and flowing beard. Azévédo, the intractable critic of *l'Opinion
nationale*, less unwashed than usual, cleans his nails and picks his
teeth alternatively with the point of a penknife.

At the back of a ground-floor box lurks Hans von Bülow, the
fervent apostle of the new messiah who has been rehearsing the
chorus for the last month in the Salle Beethoven, and his young
wife, the blonde Cosima, Liszt's daughter . . . And, more or less
everywhere, Germans who have come to support the cause of their
compatriot, and professors from the Conservatoire – Ambroise
Thomas, Reber, Carafa, Leborne, Elwart, etc . . .

All of a sudden the conversation stops and there is a great silence. A man, nearing fifty, short but with an enormous head covered by long hair thrown arrogantly backwards, a bulging forehead above two eyes of flame, thin lips and a prominent chin framed by dark side-whiskers, walks with a quick and nervous step through the ranks of the musicians. He is followed by a servant dressed in the formal livery from the second act of *La Traviata*, who carries, with an air of comic gravity, an ebony baton on a silver dish. Wagner clambers feverishly onto the conductor's rostrum, unfastens his white gloves, throws them with a superb gesture onto the dish, and picks up the conductor's baton – while the attendant bows profoundly before withdrawing. This little pantomime, which would no doubt impress a naïve German audience, produces a mild ripple of amusement which is quickly suppressed by the sharp taps on the music desk as the conductor gives his signal to the orchestra.

And the astonishing tempest of *The Flying Dutchman* unleashes its strident squalls at an audience literally dumbfounded by this unlooked-for hurricane . . .

[Joncières 1898]

> After the concert, Marie could not resist putting her oar in.

ERNEST REYER

The first concert given by Richard Wagner at the Théâtre Italien . . . had just come to an end. Madame Berlioz, passing by leaning on the arm of her husband, said to me in her sarcastic tone, 'Oh Reyer, what a triumph for Hector!' And why? Because a certain air of kinship seemed to be discoverable between this or that passage [and certain passages in the *Roméo et Juliette* Symphony] . . . And the flatterers, happy to be able to point out those supposed coincidences to Berlioz, who perhaps had already perceived them, did not fail to exaggerate them. No, no; Hector would not have triumphed for so small a thing.

[Reyer 1893: 309]

And he did not. His review of the concert in the *Journal des débats* was a serious piece of critical writing, conservative but not unfair. If there were things, like the *Tristan* prelude, that he simply couldn't stomach, there were others about which he was lavish in his praise. But Berlioz had by now become deeply suspicious of the 'Music of the Future', and at the end of his article felt bound to dissociate himself from its apparent ideals. It must have been with mixed feelings that he attended an evening at the Viardots', organized as a tribute of thanks to Liszt's friend Marie Kalergis, who had helped Wagner cover the loss resulting from his concerts.

RICHARD WAGNER

Especially for her I improvised a hearing of the second act of *Tristan*, at which Mme Viardot, whom I got to know better on this occasion, shared the vocal parts with me, while for the piano I had Klindworth come over from London at my expense. This highly unusual and intimate performance took place at the home of Mme Viardot; apart from Mme Kalergis, for whom alone it was being given, Berlioz was the only other listener. His inclusion had been instigated by Mme Viardot, seemingly in the determination of easing the strained relations between Berlioz and myself. I really don't know what effect was produced on the participants and the listeners by the performance of this extraordinary fragment in such peculiar circumstances; Mme Kalergis said nothing, while Berlioz merely expressed himself favorably as to the *chaleur* of my delivery, which may very well have afforded a strong contrast with that of my partner, who rendered most of the part with half voice. This situation seemed to anger Klindworth particularly; he had in fact done his part superbly but told me he had been consumed with fury when he observed Viardot's lukewarm delivery, which was probably determined by the presence of Berlioz.

[Wagner 1983: 618]

CAMILLE SAINT-SAËNS

May I be permitted to recall a few personal memories in connection with *Tristan und Isolde*?

Berlioz detested this score . . . As I always spoke to him quite frankly, I made no bones about disagreeing with him; I told him of the admiration I felt for the whole conception, and a great part of the works, of *le grand Richard*, and I was then able to see for myself just how deep was his antipathy for [Wagner's] dissonances and enharmonic modulations. Certainly there are harshnesses in his own works, but they arise from an altogether different harmonic approach, and one would have to disregard the facts entirely to force the same hat on to two heads about as dissimilar as it would be possible to find.

[*Le Ménestrel*, 5 October 1884, in Tiersot 1904: 371]

> For his part, Wagner seems to have overlooked this curious episode when he wrote to Liszt a few days later.

RICHARD WAGNER

I haven't seen Berlioz again since my concert: I had noticed before that it was always I who had to invite him round or go in search of him – he never bothered himself about me. It made me very sad: I have no ill feelings towards him, but I do ask myself whether the good Lord would not have done better to leave women out of His creation altogether. They very rarely serve any useful purpose; as a rule they are harmful to us, without in the end gaining anything out of it for themselves. With Berlioz, I have once again been able to observe, with a positively anatomical precision, how an ill-natured wife can wantonly ruin an altogether exceptional man and even reduce him to appearing ridiculous . . .

But . . . I have come to realize that conspicuously talented men can only find truly understanding friends among those who are equally talented, and this leads me to the belief that, today, only we three really belong together, because only we three are of the same species – you, him, and me! But we must on no account tell him

this: he would see red at the very idea. A god who suffers such torments is only a poor devil like anyone else!

[Letter to Liszt, 22 May 1860 in Wagner 1910: 281–2]

> The changes in Berlioz produced by emotional pressures
> and deteriorating health made a forcible impression on
> Eduard Hanslick after an interval of fifteen years.

EDUARD HANSLICK

I visited Berlioz in Paris . . . in the summer of 1860. That vigorous
upright figure, that regal head with its eagle eyes – I found them
very much altered. Had I met him again anywhere else than in his
remote apartment at 4, rue de Calais, I would have had difficulty
in recognizing him. True, the pallor of his sunken face and the now
completely whitened hair threw the cut of his features into even
bolder relief, but the power and vitality of earlier days had faded.
His eyes were clouded and sickly, with only rare flashes to remind
one of the old fire.

[Hanslick 1894: i, 60–1]

[He] is in such pain that writing down a few pages can often cost
him a whole day's effort. Sleepless nights vie with nerve-racking
days for the master's peace of mind. And hand in hand with his
physical suffering goes a deep depression of spirit, an ever growing
sense of bitterness and isolation. To what extent his physical pain
is made worse by this darkening mood, and how much the other
way round, is something that Berlioz alone can tell.

For a musician of Berlioz's tendencies and aspirations, Paris is a
hopeless theatre of activity. He has always been misunderstood by
his own countrymen, and always will be. The respect that his name
commands in Paris is due exclusively to his brilliant work as a critic;
the composer Berlioz is still invariably ignored, indeed would
probably be openly derided if his fame and influence as a journalist
didn't keep the small fry in check. Only seldom and with the greatest
difficulty can he bring himself to go into town for a performance of
one of his own works; the orchestras are afraid of his symphonies,

the theatres of his operas. The colossal score that I found lying open in front of Berlioz is his last great work – his most important, as he believes – the opera *Les Troyens*. Finished more than two years ago, this work had already been more or less accepted by the Opéra, but was turned down in favour of other novelties. Now Berlioz hopes it will be taken up in the new lyric theatre that is being built in the vicinity of Boulevard Sebastopol . . .

The hopes of earlier days seem to have forsaken him, he will not take consolation from the idea of any coming refinement and deepening of French music. *'J'ai pri mon parti'* – this whispered sigh of agonized renunciation cast a long shadow over the patriotic and artistic glory of the French . . .

That the latest movement in the world of music has received its most significant stimulus from Berlioz, and has him to thank for its most brilliant effects, is unquestionable. But when the 'musicians of the future' refer to Berlioz with easy familiarity as one of 'theirs', and deck out their dubious products with his colours, they take a liberty they are not entitled to. I can attest that it causes Berlioz deep pain to be associated with the standard bearers of the *'Zukunftsmusik'* and to see himself held responsible for their experiments. His opinion of the most notorious of these composers I do not allow myself to repeat, as Berlioz may perhaps be in friendly personal relations with him, but in comparison with his diplomatically smoothed out judgments in the *Journal des débats* the verbal comments he made to me certainly sounded very drastic. Berlioz's bitterness over his artistic impotence in Paris makes it understandable that he also cultivates no personal relations with the celebrated composers of the metropolis. With Rossini he had never spoken.

[Hanslick 1897: 546–9]

> 'He's a shadow, this Berlioz! – is he dead?' * wrote Jules Janin after meeting him during an interval at the theatre. The constant dashing of his hopes for a performance of *Les Troyens* was telling on his nerves – a condition not improved by having to watch the preparations for Wagner's début at the Opéra by command of the Emperor. 'In Paris they are waiting for *Tannhäuser* with a

* Janin iii, 1979: 243.

mixture of impatience and irony', wrote Pauline Viardot; 'Berlioz is fuming . . .' *

The first night of *Tannhäuser* in Paris was one of the great scandals of operatic history. Judith Gautier, Théophile Gautier's daughter, left what may be a somewhat inaccurate account of Berlioz's reaction to it: she was only eleven at the time, and her later involvement with the Wagnerian cause probably coloured her memory. To begin with, what she refers to as the dress rehearsal was more likely to have been the first night.

JUDITH GAUTIER
(1845–1917)

The dress rehearsal of *Tannhäuser* was marked for me by a curious incident. I was then at boarding-school, but we had a day out, and my father took my sister and me to Paris to meet M. Victor Hugo, who was making a short visit to France and had invited us to dinner.

At this period Théophile Gautier was not working as a music critic so he had no *entrée* to the Opéra. But my mother had managed a meeting with the composer, who had received her very courteously and given her a seat for the dress rehearsal. It had been agreed that after our dinner we would pick her up at the door of the theatre so that we could travel back to Neuilly together. Towards midnight, then, we were strolling to and fro as we waited for her in the *passage de l'Opéra*, when the rehearsal came to an end and the street was suddenly flooded with a crowd of people who seemed to be in an extraordinary state of excitement and unrest.

I didn't know anything about the great battle that was being waged around the composer of the new work, and I didn't understand the reason for this agitation.

A man with a very unusual, striking face stopped to greet my father. He was small and lean, with bony cheeks and a nose like an eagle's beak, piercing eyes under a broad forehead and a ravaged, impassioned look. He had been to the rehearsal, which had provoked an indescribable furore and had been roundly booed, and this caused him savage pleasure; he spoke about it with violence

* Viardot-Garcia 2/1, 1916: 57.

filled with hate. I looked at him with that fixed, wide open-eyed stare that was always my reaction when something astonished me, and I don't know what feeling it was that impelled me to break suddenly out of the silence and reserve proper to my years and exclaim, with unbelievable impertinence: 'Anyone could see that you're talking about a colleague! . . . and no doubt about a masterpiece too!'

My father, astounded, scolded me out loud – though he was laughing under his breath.

'Who was that?' I asked, when the gentleman had left us.

'Hector Berlioz.'

[Judith Gautier 1903: 172–3]

> Berlioz refused to write a review of *Tannhäuser* for the *Débats*, and maintained in public a diplomatic silence on the subject – though not always in private.

JULIETTE LAMBER [ADAM]

In the early part of [April 1861] I went with the Vilborts to a first performance of *La Statue* at the Lyric Theatre. The composer was Reyer, a young man who, as Madame Vilbort said, 'had a future in spite of his being a Frenchman.' Can one conceive the impudence of these Wagnerians? . . . Gautier sat between his two lovely daughters, Judith, a wonder of beauty, and the other charming. Berlioz, who condescended to come and pay his respects to me, was more tragic than ever. He was so unlucky as to say to me, in the presence of Madame Vilbort: 'Do you feel proud now [that] you placed so many tickets for the concert of the *Tannhäuser* gentleman?'

Madame Vilbort was on the point of making a reply, but with my eyes I begged her to refrain. When Berlioz left the box she said to me:

'You were wrong in not letting me tell such a partial musician that I am a devoted lover of Weimar, and that I can with the same breath admire the great Berlioz and the great Wagner . . .'

'With Berlioz's character, my dear friend, I can easily anticipate the reply and the sneer; and for my part I would prefer not to be either cause or witness of such unpleasantness.'

[Adam 1904: 361–3]

FRANZ LISZT

Our poor Berlioz is very down-hearted and embittered. His domestic life weighs on him like a nightmare and in the outside world he encounters nothing but opposition and disappointment. I dined at his house with d'Ortigue, Mme Berlioz and Mme Berlioz's mother. It was sad, gloomy, desolate! The tone of Berlioz's voice has become feebler – he speaks habitually in a low voice – and his whole being seems inclined towards the tomb! I don't know how he has managed to isolate himself in this way. In effect he has no friends, no supporters, neither the bright sunlight of public approval nor the sweet shade of intimate friendship. The editorial staff of the *Débats* still supports him and offers him protection. That's how he got the commission for a little opera in one act to be given at Baden-Baden next year; Bénazet, a contributor to the *Journal des Débats*, is giving him 4,000 francs for it. As for *Les Troyens*, it has little chance of being put on at the Opéra. In the autumn they are doing Gounod's *Reine de Saba*, then Meyerbeer's *L'Africaine*, and after that new works by Félicien David and Gevaërt. This last is a protégé of the director of the Opéra, M. Royer, with whom Berlioz has more or less fallen out over some alterations that Royer wanted made in the libretto of *Les Troyens*. Berlioz said to me: 'That's the grain of sand on which I must run aground. All the press are on my side, any number of friends encourage me and support me, Count Walewski asks me to dinner, I have the honour of dining with His Majesty the Emperor – but none of it is any use. M. Royer doesn't want it, and nothing will be done!' His article on the Wagner concerts has harmed Berlioz at least as much as it has Wagner. And he hardly did any better by abstaining altogether in the case of *Tannhäuser*, and getting d'Ortigue to write his notice in the *Débats* that day. Those he had hoped to win over by doing this gave him no credit for it, attributing it partly to jealousy, partly to fear of compromising himself; others saw it as a clumsy trick – if not something worse!

[Letter to Carolyne Sayn-Wittgenstein, 16 May 1861, in Liszt 1893–1905: v, 171–2]

> Wagner finally left Paris in August 1861. In spite of its
> unhappy fate, the fact that *Tannhäuser* had actually

reached the stage by the Emperor's specific command still rankled with Berlioz. He continued to have hopes of finding imperial favour for himself, but Napoleon III was only interested in music at a social level, and the people who produced it not even at that.

EDMOND & JULES DE GONCOURT
(1822–96 and 1830–70)

At Compiègne, from time to time, a writer or an artist gets included at the tail end of the queue: tradition must be respected, after all! Here is an example of the gracious reception that awaits them. It comes from one of their number who has had the good fortune to attract the Emperor's favour.

The Emperor was complaining that his sight was getting weaker. 'It's odd, but I can no longer tell the difference between blue and black. Who is that over there?' 'Sire, it's M. Berlioz.'

He raises his voice: 'M. Berlioz, is your tail-coat blue or black?'

'Sire,' Berlioz hastens to reply, 'I would never permit myself the liberty of appearing before Your Majesty in a blue tail-coat. It is black.'

'Good,' said the Emperor.

And that is all the Emperor said to him in four days.

[15 November 1862 in Goncourt 1956: i, 1164–5]

A performance of *Les Troyens* seemed as far away as ever.

24   AFTER MARIE'S DEATH

Marie died, of a sudden heart attack, in June 1862. Berlioz's life with her had not been happy for a good many years, but she had been company, she had always supported him (not always wisely) and she had looked after him meticulously. The last function was now taken over by her mother, Madame Martin, who was to care for her son-in-law devotedly to the end of his life. But the apartment in the rue de Calais must have seemed empty without so energetic a presence.

After Berlioz's own death seven years later, two inventories were made of the contents of the apartment, the first on the day after he died, the second a couple of months later. These have been the subject of two articles by Hugh Macdonald and Peter Bloom published in 1991 and 1996 respectively.

The rooms of the fourth-floor apartment consisted of an ante-chamber (which looked on the main courtyard of the building as well as on to a small interior court), a large salon (which looked onto the rue de Calais . . .), and a dining room, bedroom and kitchen (which looked on the interior courtyard) . . . As well as the fifth-floor room occupied by Berlioz's servants . . .[there was] a *cave* in the basement, and, next to the salon, a study (the *cabinet de travail*), which also looked onto the rue de Calais. Adjoining the bedroom was a dressing room (the *cabinet de toilette*). All these rooms, as well as the connecting corridor, were crowded with various belongings. In the *cave* were thirty litres of claret . . . along with 150 empty bottles, wood for the fire, and coal – this last for the cast-iron stove that operated from the corridor of an apartment that as a whole reveals its occupant not as the disheveled romantic of the *Symphonie fantastique* but as an orderly and by no means impoverished member of the Second Empire middle class.

[Bloom 1995: 8]

The salon, for example, lit by three windows, contained

... a moquette carpet covering the whole floor, a fur rug, a bronze bust, a carved oak sideboard, a similar small sideboard, a rosewood music cabinet, a rosewood card table, a gilt brass chandelier, a clock and two gilt brass candelabra, a pair of copper fire-dogs, a bevelled mirror in a carved oak frame, pictures, drawings, paintings and lithographs in gilt frames, an armchair and a sofa of carved oak upholstered in green velvet with loose white linen covers, four similar chairs, four dark cherrywood chairs upholstered with tapestry, an easy chair upholstered in green damask, six casement curtains in green damask with red cabinet curtains in embroidered muslin, a rosewood piano stool, two candlesticks in brass and porcelain, a fire-iron stand with copper tongs and accessories ...

[Macdonald 1991: 16]

to which the second inventory adds 'a grand piano by Érard in rosewood ... two large engraved portraits of the Emperor and Empress ... a panel painting of a woman having herself dressed ...' and a cabinet containing Berlioz's decorations, his sword as a member of the Institut, and three conductors' batons.

A glimpse of Berlioz in his apartment at about this time has been left by a young English girl, a pupil of Henselt, who had come to Paris with the intention of giving a piano recital.

ALICE MANGOLD [A. M. DIEHL]
(1844–1912)

With a certain trepidation, we set out upon our first visit to the great critic, for some among our French acquaintances had shrugged their shoulders, raised their eyebrows, and smiled when Berlioz was mentioned. He was nothing if not exclusive. We might expect – anything. He seldom saw strangers. We might spare ourselves the trouble of a journey which would most likely be fruitless.

It was not in the most fashionable quarter of Paris that we found the composer's abode – a huge, desolate-looking house in a long, narrow street. There was a *boulangerie* opposite, also a *charcuterie*.

Entering by the big *porte-cochère*, we sought the *concierge*. But the small, untidy lodge was close shut. He – or she – was out. Wandering into the courtyard to find someone who might give information, there was a desolate appearance about the square of cobbles strewn with straw, cabbage-leaves, and what not, where a few sickly-looking fowls were seeking food, and a woman was slowly and laboriously hanging out clothes – how they were to dry instead of freezing that bleak winter morning would be proved by-and-by. A bitter wind met us round the corner as we interrogated the woman. 'Monsieur Berlioz? Yes, he lived there. But the ladies would have to mount high – very high; it was the topmost *étage*.'

We mounted a dark wooden staircase, story after story, meeting no one. At the top of the flight there was a small three-cornered landing – and a window through which, peeping down, we saw the fluttering clothes, the woman, and the fowls. Berlioz, the author of the *feuilletons*, the musical autocrat of the *Journal des débats*, here, with this *entourage*! We glanced at each other; then one of us pulled the red woollen cord by the door. A bell clanged noisily, but there was silence within. Presently we heard slow footsteps – the door opened – we saw a stolid wench in a soiled blue cotton gown who gave us an astonished stare.

'Monsieur Berlioz *chez lui*? Oh yes; he was *chez lui*.' She took our cards in a protesting manner and shuffled off within, and, returning almost immediately – astonished, and still mutely protesting, as it were – ushered us into a room, placed chairs, and left us.

A small, untidy apartment, with dust everywhere, with book-shelves not neatly arranged, with tables and chairs strewn or laden with books, papers, manuscripts. Over the crowded mantelpiece was the oil-painting of a lady, a good-looking woman, with dark eyes and bunches of ringlets on either side of her oval face.

We were wondering whether this was the Henrietta Smithson of his earlier days, and, as the minutes passed, wondering also whether the sturdy handmaiden had erred in ushering us into her master's sanctum – when the door opened and a slight, middle-aged man entered. The portraits of Hector Berlioz are good. They give a fair idea of him as he was then – with sharp, pronounced features, flowing iron-gray hair, small but brilliant dark eyes, and a pensive, somewhat enigmatical expression.

He bowed, murmured a few words of welcome, and with a

courtly air insisted on our resuming the seats we had risen from as he came in. Then, seating himself behind the writing-table, he looked from one to the other, and gave a melancholy little smile.

'You are musical, you come from London, you must know my great friend Davison,' he said; and they were his first words. 'What a critic! what a man!' Then with intense feeling he spoke of Mr. Davison and of others, suddenly pausing, a trick of his, and abruptly changing the conversation.

'You are to make your *début* here?' he asked. 'And you are a pupil of Henselt? His *études* are known and liked here.' Then he gave us practical advice, and, unbending, was so kindly and encouraging that it was almost impossible to realize that we were talking to the unapproachable, inaccessible being of whose absolute exclusiveness we had been warned. Most valuable were his hints, practically priceless was his advice; and on our rising to end the interview he promised to shortly visit us at our hotel, and escorted us to the door . . .

Monsieur Berlioz kept his word. One evening we were dressing for a dinner-party at the Galignanis', when there was a tap at the door communicating with our little *salon*, and a card was presented by the rough-and-ready *garçon* – 'Hector Berlioz'.

Hurrying on the first frocks which came to hand, we hastened to receive our distinguished guest. He was standing with his back to the wood fire, and to the lighted candles in the bronze branches on the mantelpiece. He looked stiffly grave, his black coat tightly buttoned almost to the throat, his hand inserted under the lapel after the manner of old-fashioned portraits. At first he was politely abrupt, and presently requested that I would play to him.

For a neophyte, a mere tyro and aspirant, to be called on suddenly to be tested by a great critic is a severe trial. But Berlioz, listening silently as he leant against the mantelpiece, seemed to cast a protecting mental shadow upon the trembling player, even as his material shadow was cast upon the keyboard. He was anything but chilly or severe. He was, indeed, both compassionate and sympathetic, and afterwards gave his views of what a young artist's life should be. He condemned the practice of many consecutive hours at the piano, and of the use of nerve stimulants, such as tea and coffee. '*Surtout*,' he insisted, '*point de café noir.*'

[Diehl 1897: 64–70]

Whatever Liszt may have thought Berlioz was not without friends, among them the many younger colleagues
in whom he was interested. If Alice Mangold's memory
tends to romanticize around the Grand Old Man image,
others were more inclined to be impressed by the vitality
that still inhabited that fragile body – like Louis Bourgault-
Ducoudray, later to be a distinguished musicologist and
teacher, but at this period only twenty-two years old.

LOUIS BOURGAULT-DUCOUDRAY
(1840–1910)

'Well, who got the prize then?'
  'I did.'
  'Excellent! I'm delighted. What are you doing this evening?'
  'Nothing.'
  'Let's go for a walk.'
The conversation took place on the corner of the Chaussée-
d'Antin and the boulevard in June 1862, the day after I had been
awarded the Prix de Rome by the Académie des Beaux Arts.

The man I was talking to was Hector Berlioz, who had been prevented by a recent bereavement from attending the voting session
at the Institut the night before. He was fifty-nine years old and still
at the height of his powers, his imagination as lively as ever.

The composer of the *Symphonie fantastique* had the physical
attributes to match his genius. A mane of grey, almost white hair,
attractively curly; a nose like the beak of an eagle; a straight ledge
of powerful eyebrows, and beneath them the glitter of two penetrating eyes; a tragic forehead, broader than it was high; a thin-
lipped mouth, proud and mocking at the same time; a finely sculpted
chin – everything contributed to give his face an incomparable
expression of poetry and fearlessness. His body, though frail in
appearance, revealed nerves of steel, capable of multiplying its
muscular energy tenfold and enabling him to bear the most
gruelling fatigue. The strange timbre of his voice with its abrupt,
mordant delivery, the fire of his glance and the sense of electrical
energy behind the restraint of his movements, completed the outward projection of an extraordinary personality, as attractive and
engaging as it was formidable and aggressive.

He was an incorrigible idealist, an inveterate dreamer, with all the appearance of a *revenant* from the fantastic realm of ghosts and spirits, and the contrast between the higher plane where his thoughts habitually soared and the world of reality nagged continually at his susceptibilities. It was these constant aggravations, inflamed by a natural irritability of temperament, that inspired his caustic, biting intelligence to the flights of pleasantry and sarcasm in which he would indulge, on a good day, with naïve enjoyment and devilish glee.

I was twenty-two years old and loved Berlioz with passion, unable to escape the fascination of that penetrating gaze. At the preliminary test, which comes before the confinement of the candidates for the main competition of the Prix de Rome, I had my first opportunity to study that extraordinary physiognomy at close quarters, and I did so with profound emotion. During the dictation of the text to which the competitors must apply their talents, Berlioz several times abandoned the dignity proper to a member of the Immortals in order to fire off some malicious quip or startle us with an off-the-cuff pun.

The glamour of his personality wielded a powerful influence on the whole of my generation. I can still see him, when we came out of the examination, walking back across the Pont des Arts escorted by a mob of students dogging his footsteps and hanging on his words. Though his music was more or less proscribed and his best works had no success with the general public his influence as musician and poet on the young of those days was no less potent for that; indeed, reinforced by the impressiveness of his external appearance, it had about it something of the mysterious, almost the occult. We felt in Berlioz a force whose work had begun, but whose outcome was still not entirely understood. The fragments of his compositions that we heard performed at rare intervals revealed a power and audacity of conception of a superior order – and yet on the great majority of people his music had no effect. The unjust ostracism which Berlioz suffered at the hands of the general public only increased his stature in our eyes: to the aura of the great composer was added the halo of the persecuted artist, of the warrior hero, you could almost say of the martyr.

To meet Berlioz on the very day after I had emerged from the schoolroom, walk with him arm in arm and chat with him on familiar terms like an old friend – this was an unexpected piece of luck, an unheard-of godsend. And I think I may say I made the most of it. He was in terrific form that evening – you could almost say in a state of eruption, for there was something positively volcanic about his high spirits and the brilliance that poured out as if from a crater. His mind didn't sparkle, it exploded. What a walk we had! If I lived to be a thousand I should never forget it. His dazzling improvisations touched every subject, sounded every key: memories of his childhood, intimate outpourings, theories of art, great musical confrontations, works composed or dreamed of, favourite books, historical figures exalted or cut down to size . . . we pushed our way through the passers-by, abruptly retracing our steps or threading our way down narrow alleys as if the wild ferment of his ideas had set up a swirling current that swept us in its wake.

All the great names of history were conjured up and judged, from Cleopatra (that 'prostitute' as he called her) to Savonarola (whose sublime aspirations intoxicated him), and in this flood of characters and ideas it could not be long before Shakespeare made an appearance – Shakespeare, his favourite poet, whom he worshipped with a passion amounting to fanaticism, whose plays were the Bible that nourished this votary of poetry and art. Berlioz admired all Shakespeare, but I think he had a special feeling for *Hamlet*. He had written out long passages in translation and dreamed of translating it all. 'Have you never thought of making an opera out of *Hamlet*?' I asked. 'I would never dare', he replied. 'I composed three entr'actes for the play* that I called *Tristia*, 'sad things', but I have never had them performed. When I am overcome by melancholy I play the music through in my head and listen to it there . . .'

We spoke about the best conditions for writing music. 'Everything I have composed', he told me, 'I have begun spontaneously, almost by accident. Even for those works that I have carried around in my head for a long time there had to be some lucky circumstance that decided me to write them down. It was my extreme dislike of card games in general, and of whist in particular, that started me composing *L'enfance du Christ*.' 'How was that? I don't see the connection'. 'It's very simple. I was with some friends

---

* In fact only Nos 2 and 3 of *Tristia* ('La mort d'Ophélie' and the 'Marche funèbre') relate to *Hamlet*; No 1 is the 'Méditation religieuse', a setting of words adapted from Thomas Moore.

one day. They were playing cards. As usual I turned my back on the players and amused myself by prodding at the flame that flickered in the grate. While I was handling the poker, I heard a melody forming itself in my head . . . It was a soft and graceful air, primitive and pastoral in character, rather like an old Christmas carol. There were flutes and oboes harmonizing with it. That evening, I was far from bored, and by the time the game of whist was over I had finished the chorus, which I called "The shepherd's farewell to the Holy Family". A few days later I added two more pieces to it, making the fragment of an oratorio. Later still I added two more movements to my 'hand of whist' – and the result was *L'enfance du Christ*.' 'And this didn't reconcile you to whist?' 'I hate it more than ever! I just don't understand this passion for cards.

'Another time – it was in St Petersburg – I was with some rather grand people and the conversation turned to Virgil. "What a beautiful opera one could make out of the *Aeneid*," I exclaimed; "I have it in my head already. I haven't written a single line of the verses or a note of the music, but I have the feeling that it could be a masterpiece . . ."

> [Bourgault-Ducoudray seems to have confused two incidents here. It is true that Berlioz met Carolyne Sayn-Wittgenstein at St Petersburg in 1847, and perfectly possible that the idea of Virgil as a subject for opera was mentioned on that occasion, but it was not until Weimar in 1856 that the matter was seriously discussed and the Princess issued her ultimatum.]

'Among those present was a great lady, who liked my music and supported it; she looked me straight in the eye and said: "Berlioz, I *desire* that you write this opera that you have in your head. If, within a month from now, you do not bring me the finished libretto, I shall have no more to do with you." Three weeks later, I sent her the libretto of the *Troyens*. But once I had done the text, there was no way I could avoid writing the music too, for I was utterly obsessed by the need to compose'. 'When are you going to have the opera performed? I can't wait to hear it and applaud. You won't have a more ardent champion or a more determined supporter on the first night.' 'For that, I need a singer who is a great tragic actress as well; I am looking for one . . . but it's a seed that doesn't flourish readily in the streets of Paris.'

As we emerged on to the boulevard, born along by the inexhaustible flow of words, we bumped into a tall, rather stooping figure, walking with a pensive air. His melancholy appearance was in such strong contrast to our own high spirits that I stopped short, and I uttered a cry as I recognised this solitary pedestrian: it was Berlioz's friend and colleague, my revered teacher Ambroise Thomas!

We greeted one another. At once, by one of those sudden transformations that were peculiar to him, the grave features of Ambroise Thomas relaxed and lit up with a smile. Like an instrument tuned in a moment by a practised hand, he picked up the lively mood of our conversation and he too, the great melancholic, was kindled by the volcanic energy of Berlioz and took fire as he recalled old memories and the impressions of far-off days. The two of them vied with one another in remembering their first great musical experiences, above all the emotions provoked by Spontini's *Vestale*.

What youthful energy! I cannot give any idea of the flood of enthusiasm that poured from these two great artists during this hour of intimate confidences. All I can say is that there came a moment when Berlioz could not restrain himself any longer and, spurred by the double demon of artistic inspiration and youth restored, began to sing a passage from *La vestale* at the top of his voice in the middle of the boulevard . . . The passers-by were thunderstruck, all turning round and whispering to one another . . . 'Be quiet, Berlioz,' said Ambroise Thomas, taking him by the arm. 'If you go on like that they'll arrest us.'

Just how long our walk continued I don't remember. But during the hour or two that it lasted I lived ten years. I left the two masters in an indescribable state of emotion. I felt myself transfigured, made bigger, as if I had gained from my contact with their glory. That night my sleep was one long, golden dream. The memory of that blessed encounter has left a trail of light throughout my life.

A long time has passed since then. Every time that I think of Berlioz, and I think of him often, I like to remember him as he was on that day, gay, brilliant, youthful . . . as no one is nowadays.

[Bourgault-Ducoudray 1886: 276–8]

> During the six years before Marie's death, she and Berlioz had paid a visit each summer to Baden-Baden, where Berlioz conducted an annual gala concert. He

continued the habit after her death, and during the long, frustrating wait for a performance of *Les Troyens* it gave him his one regular chance of an appreciative audience. It also provided him with the occasion for his last major composition, the opera *Béatrice et Bénédict*, performed there in August 1862. Though he arrived in Baden-Baden for the final rehearsals only six weeks after Marie's death, the stimulus of bringing a new work to life clearly did him good. Richard Pohl, who was later to make the German translation of the libretto, came from Weimar for the occasion.

RICHARD POHL

On the afternoon of the 8th I arrived in Baden-Baden at the *Darmstädter Hof,* the hotel at which Berlioz, like most French artists, was staying.

The master wasn't there. I found him in the *Salle de la Conversation* where he was dining in good French style with his leading tenor. Berlioz was in the best of spirits; the dress rehearsal that morning (which sadly I had missed) had gone splendidly – although that was hardly a surprise, because he had held half a dozen orchestral rehearsals in Baden and more than thirty piano rehearsals in Paris: the opera was, as they say, 'a dead cert'. He was full of praise for his singers, who had followed his every indication with a devotion, intelligence and attention to detail that left nothing to be desired, and mastered their anything but easy roles to perfection.

The leading tenor had not once been hoarse or difficult to deal with; the prima donna had not demanded either cuts or cadenzas in her part; the smallest subsidiary roles had been taken by first-rate singers who had never complained about not having solos or effective exits: absolutely magnificent, yes, almost unbelievably auspicious omens, that gave grounds to hope for the best.

[Richard Pohl, iii 1884: 176–7]

> Several of Berlioz's friends and colleagues were in Baden for the first performance: Reyer, Gounod, Pauline Viardot – and Legouvé, as always the recipient of his latest confidences, particularly in matters of the heart.

ERNEST LEGOUVÉ

Berlioz's predominant characteristic was his capacity for suffering. All his feelings tended in the direction of grief. Even pleasure, for him, bordered on pain. When he fell in love for the first time, what was his first feeling? He has described it himself: 'I felt in my heart a deep pain' . . .

[In Baden] one morning, I met him in the woods that lead up to the old castle. He seemed to me older, changed and sad. We sat down on a bench, because the climb had tired him. He held in his hand a letter that he clutched convulsively.

'Another letter!' I said laughing, in an attempt to cheer him up.

'As always.'

'Ah! . . . Is she young?'

'Yes, alas.'

'Pretty?'

'Too pretty! And with a mind, and a soul!'

'And she loves you?'

'She says so . . . She writes that she does . . .'

'It seems to me that, if she gives you proof of it as well . . .'

'Oh yes, she gives me proof of it . . . but proof – what does that prove?'

'Oh for goodness' sake – here we are at the fifth act of *Othello*!'

'Here, take this letter. Don't be afraid of being indiscreet if you read it – there's no signature. Read it and judge for yourself.'

After I had read the letter I couldn't prevent myself from saying: 'But what do you find in that to distress you? This is the letter of a superior woman; more than that, it's filled with passion, with tenderness . . . What's wrong then?'

'What's wrong?' he cried, interrupting me in desperation, 'What's wrong is that I am sixty years old!'

'What does that matter, if she only sees you as thirty?'

'But look at me, for heavens' sake! Look at these sunken cheeks, these grey hairs, this wrinkled forehead!'

'Wrinkles don't count on a man of genius. Women are different from us. We men find it difficult to understand love without beauty. But they lose their hearts to a man for all sorts of reasons. It may be courage, it may be glory, it may be misfortune. Sometimes it is what we lack that they love in us.'

'That's what she says to me when she sees my moods of despair'.
'You talk to her about it then?'

'How can I hide it from her? Sometimes, suddenly, for no reason at all, I sit down and begin sobbing. It's this same, terrible thought that assails me – and she guesses it! And then, with an angelic tenderness, she says: "Wretched ungrateful man, what can I do to convince you? Look – do I have any other motive in saying that I love you? have I not forgotten everything for you? do I not expose myself to countless dangers for your sake?" And she takes my head in her hands, and I can feel her tears falling on my neck. And yet, in spite of it all, always this terrible thought re-echoes in the depths of my heart: "I am sixty! She can't love me! She doesn't love me!" Ah, my friend, what torture this is – to create oneself a hell out of paradise!'

I left him without having been able to console him, and much moved, I confess, not only by his unhappiness but by his humility. How far this is from the puerile vanity of Chateaubriand and Goethe, who so complacently believed that their genius had invested them with eternal youth that no amount of adoration could surprise them. How much more I love Berlioz! How much more human he is! And how touched I was to see this allegedly arrogant figure so readily forgetting that he was a great artist and remembering only that he was an old man.

[Legouvé 1886: 320–3]

> Her name was Amélie. He appears to have met her soon after Marie's death, at what must have been, even given his equivocal feelings about Marie, a vulnerable period. We know nothing more about her, and the affair, if there was one, didn't last for long. But his age continued to haunt him and his mood remained volatile – as Pohl's daughter Louise remembered when *Béatrice et Bénédict* was given at Weimar in the following April.

LOUISE POHL
(born 1855)

At this time, just when he was being heaped with honours and applause at Weimar, Berlioz – who was already suffering acutely –

was deeply melancholy, nearly always silent and turned in on him-self. The only creature that could occasionally coax a smile out of him was a large, beautiful Newfoundland dog, belonging to one of his friends whom he enjoyed visiting. The hound loved him too and liked to lay its handsome head on Berlioz's knee. Then Berlioz would stroke it and say that the dog had '*des yeux aimants*'. Often he suffered so much that he would lie motionless on his bed; in the doctor's opinion, his nerves, unlike other people's, had no protec-tion but lay too near the surface. His bearing was always refined and distinguished, in the best sense French. There was nothing at all affected about him, he was just infinitely sensitive; this over-highly-strung man was a martyr to his music, but not the poseur that he was only too often declared to be by his enemies.

[Louise Pohl 1900: 252]

> Yet a few days later when, at the express desire of the bedridden Prince of Hohenzollern-Hechingen, he had delayed his return home to conduct a concert in Löwenberg, Richard Pohl found Berlioz in a totally different mood.

RICHARD POHL

When Berlioz entered for the first rehearsal he was greeted by a triple fanfare from the Hofkapelle, after which Kapellmeister Seifriz, speaking in French, welcomed him cordially on behalf of everybody present. Berlioz made an appropriate reply, in which he remembered that he had already appeared once, twenty years before, at the head of this same Hofkapelle, when the Prince was still living in Hechingen . . . [He] was delighted with the result of the rehearsal, lavish in his praise after each piece, and confessed that he had never experienced such a first rehearsal before . . . At the final rehearsal [he] was so moved by the overall effect that he could scarcely hold back his tears. He embraced Seifriz and told him that in more than twenty years he had never been at a rehearsal of his works that had given him such unalloyed pleasure, and that here there was no sign even of those imperfections that as a rule inevitably cropped up here and there with other orchestras . . .

I have already described the brilliant reception given by the public to every piece: he was recalled after the *Lear* overture, after the Love Scene, after the Pilgrims' March, as well as at the end of the first and second halves of the concert . . .. The Love Scene and the Pilgrims' March were vigorously encored, but Berlioz did not comply, although the programme was fairly short (it lasted exactly two hours). When I asked him, after the concert, why he hadn't repeated at least one movement I realised at once that he hadn't understood what they were calling out at all! Instead of *'da capo'* he had simply heard *'bravo'* – whereas in France the call for an encore is *'bis'*. Lovable, archetypical Parisian, who had been coming to Germany for twenty years but had still not learned enough of German habits to understand what the public was calling for at his own concerts! The ill-disposed put this down to arrogance; but I know that it comes from genuine shyness on the one hand, and a disinclination to take the trouble on the other . . .

The following evening the Hofkapelle had arranged a banquet in Berlioz's honour, combining it with the closing celebration of the concert season. The attendance was as large as it was cheerful; there was no lack of enthusiastic toasts, and Berlioz replied with warmth and geniality – naturally in French. I acted as interpreter for him and translated phrase by phrase into German. I have seldom seen him so happy and talkative at a social occasion; you could see how much at ease he felt in this company of artists. And indeed with reason, because all the homage paid to him in Löwenberg, from the loftiest to the most humble, bore the unmistakable stamp of sincerity and enthusiasm. There was nothing formal, nothing artificial about it; it was all completely spontaneous, a genuine expression of innermost, personal conviction . . .

. . . On the evening before Berlioz's departure the Prince gathered another large and well-chosen audience in his salon, and Berlioz read the libretto of *Les Troyens* with the doors open, so that the Prince could take part from his room in this poetic epilogue to the visit. At the end my wife played a few pieces on the harp, but further musical performances had to be abandoned because the Prince was exhausted.

[Richard Pohl, iii 1884: 203–4, 208–10]

In November 1863, after five and a half years of pre-
varications, broken promises and official indifference,
Berlioz's last masterpiece finally reached the stage. But
not at the Opéra, as he had always hoped, nor even
complete: the exhausted composer had eventually closed
with the offer of a production at the newly built Théâtre-
Lyrique, only to discover later that the resources of the
theatre would not extend to a complete performance,
and that the first two acts would have to be cut. So
Berlioz was never to hear a performance *of La Prise de
Troie*, or see his heroic Cassandra on the stage. Instead,
the last three acts were given, under the title of *Les
Troyens à Carthage* – and even this truncated version
suffered more and more cuts as rehearsals progressed.

Nevertheless, he was at last hearing much of his
greatest music for the first time.

DANIEL BERNARD

When he came out of the dress rehearsal, he had gone to visit
Madame d'Ortigue, the estimable wife of one of his oldest friends.
He looked to her like a ghost, so pale, thin and emaciated had he
become. 'Whatever is the matter?' she cried in alarm; 'Did something go wrong at the rehearsal?' 'On the contrary,' he said, falling
back into a chair, 'It's beautiful, it's sublime!' And he started to cry.

[Bernard 1879: 55]

In accordance with the inflexible rule of French opera
houses, Berlioz was not permitted to conduct the opera
himself, though he had involved himself closely with
every aspect of its preparation during the five months of

rehearsal. On the first night his status and reputation ensured a full and expectant house; though Victor Hugo was in exile, and Vigny and Delacroix were dead, there were still many friends and supporters from his earliest days, and the Parisian musical world was there in strength: among the younger generation, Bizet and Delibes, both of whom had helped at rehearsals, and of course Saint-Saëns; among the older, Ambroise Thomas (but not Berlioz's old antagonist, Adolphe Adam, who had died seven years earlier). Spontini's widow was there – and though Meyerbeer missed the first night through illness, he came to twelve subsequent performances 'for my pleasure and my instruction'. There was applause for many of the numbers, particularly for the love music in the gardens of Dido, and the septet had to be repeated in response to vociferous acclamations in which even Berlioz's enemies were observed to be joining. '*Bien rugi Lion!*' wrote Auguste Barbier in a letter to Berlioz the next morning, and it was what many felt.

Nevertheless, in a Paris currently flocking to hear Offenbach's latest *opéras-bouffes*, the high seriousness of Berlioz's subject, and the return to a classical manner sometimes redolent of Gluck, did not find easy acceptance with the general public.

RICHARD POHL

People have often said to [Berlioz] that he has changed his style in recent years, and his latest works (*L'enfance du Christ* and to some extent *Béatrice et Bénédict)* provide strong justification for this view. When I spoke to him about this, he replied laughing: 'The style in which I write arises invariably out of the work – not the other way round. You could just as well reproach me for choosing different poetic subjects now to the ones that I chose before. Maybe – only first, just hear my *Troyens!*'

[Pohl, iii 1884: 208]

> Among the audience on the first night was the teacher and musical historian Félix Clément, who set down his memories some four years later.

FÉLIX CLÉMENT
(1822–85)

From the first hearing of *Les Troyens* three pieces were understood, admired and encored to the applause of the entire audience. The first was the duet between Dido and Anna, full of charm, originality and distinction, the second a septet . . . with rich and penetrating harmonies, and the last a duet between Dido and Aeneas which will take its place among the most beautiful love duets in opera. The rest seemed obscure and tortuous – and therefore long and boring – with here and there a few melodies surfacing like Virgil's shipwrecked sailors: *rari nantes in gurgite vasto*. Such was the first impression of the general public, and the press hastened to confirm it with 'flippant cruelty', to use the legitimate phrase of Joseph d'Ortigue. However, serious and impartial music lovers wanted to hear this important work more than once; by coming to a better understanding of the composer's style, probing more deeply into his thoughts, and having the forbearance to pass over one or two defects in view of his qualities, they discovered at each hearing beauties that they had not at first appreciated, and ended by considering *Les Troyens* one of the most remarkable works to have reached the stage in the last fifteen years. Which is not, after all, an exaggerated eulogy. This was my personal impression after having seen *Les Troyens* six times in succession.

[Clément 1873: 494–5]

> Others were less prepared to make an effort.

ARMAND FERRAND DE PONTMARTIN

I was there. It was a disaster. There had been too much talk about it, and I am astonished that Berlioz, who was himself so given to irony, seems from his letters* to have taken seriously the polite eulogies that greeted his libretto in this or that *salon*. At the first performance there was enthusiastic applause for a few delicious pieces, but the opera as a whole, music and words, gave us the

---

* The *Corréspondence inédite*, the first volume of Berlioz's letters to be published, had appeared in 1879, the year before this piece was written.

impression of something that simply didn't hold together, that was going to fail – and that in fact failed.

[Pontmartin 1880: 115–6]

> The impression given by the press was certainly not one of failure; reviews were serious and largely favourable – apart from the usual lunatic fringe (where Scudo was in characteristic form). But on the first night the less well-disposed members of the public had been offered a golden opportunity to create havoc when a scene-change after the 'Royal hunt and storm' caused a delay of three quarters of an hour, and Carvalho, the director of the theatre, took fright and started to make cuts. Juliette Lamber received the latest news from a friend in Paris.

JULIETTE LAMBER [ADAM]

'All the friends of Berlioz knew,' he wrote, 'that the *Troyens* was much too long . . . It was necessary to shorten it, and Berlioz had agreed to this. But every day since the first performance at the Lyric, Carvalho removes 'all that the public does not like.' Well, except a few unprejudiced musicians and ourselves, the friends of Berlioz, who are ever on the increase, there is no public that does like the *Troyens*. The performers are so bad that the performance drags, and we are unanimous in thinking it will not run three weeks . . . I write with my eyes full of tears. To see Berlioz thus tortured makes me miserable, and you two, who love our poor 'Lucifer', will both understand me' . . .

Madame de Pierreclos and I talked a whole evening of Berlioz . . . Ought we to write to him? We asked ourselves the question, but finally decided that as we could not congratulate him on a success, we had better keep silence. We decided, however, to send him a basket of flowers with these simple words:

'Madame de Pierreclos and Madame Juliette Lamber send some flowers from the Golfe Juan to Berlioz.'

He replied without thanks in a single line: 'Was it worth while? Berlioz.'

[Adam 1904: 505–6, 508–9]

In fact, it ran for seven weeks, at the rate of three performances a week, and though this could not be regarded as a failure, it was certainly not the climax to his creative life that Berlioz had hoped for.

ADOLPHE JULLIEN

At one of the twenty performances of *Les Troyens* . . . some friends who were with Berlioz, seeing the theatre practically full, said to him: 'But look – they are coming!' 'Yes', he replied, with a melancholy smile and a look of utter despondency, 'they are coming. But I – I am going.'

[Jullien 1882: 9–10]

One absolute satisfaction he had, however. Louis, who had been seeing more of Berlioz since Marie's death and become touchingly aware of his father's musical stature, was at every performance.

26 LIFE AFTER CARTHAGE

DANIEL BERNARD

Les Troyens had been Berlioz's last great hope; its failure precipitated his long, six-year death agony. From this moment onwards, his thoughts became more and more sombre, his physical sufferings left him less and less respite. He had counted so much on his opera! . . .

He lived in his apartment in the rue de Calais, withdrawn and disillusioned, besieged by cheeky sparrows who came to peck at the bread which he put out for them on his window-sill, near to his immense grand piano, his harp and the portrait of his first wife, Harriet Smithson. His mother-in-law, Madame Recio, looked after him with extraordinary care and devotion; his friends made every effort to make him forget the injustices of fate, and no one ever had more attentive, more faithful friends than he: Édouard Alexandre, Ernest Reyer, M. and Madame Massart, M. and Madame Damcke, the Ritter family and so many others that I can't name them all – the list would be too long. He had begun teaching French to a young Danish composer, M. Asger Hammerik (now director of the Conservatoire at Baltimore): 'I am much to be pitied,' he would sometimes say; 'here am I with a mother-in-law who speaks to me in Spanish, a maid in German – and now you, with your Danish, lacerating my eardrums!'

[Bernard 1879: 55–6]

> It was to the intimacy of this circle, which also included his old friends d'Ortigue and Stephen Heller and the composer Léon Kreutzer, that Berlioz turned more and more in the last years of his life. Adolphe Jullien, one of Berlioz's first biographers, later assembled the impressions and recollections of the surviving members of this group and incorporated them in a description which bears the stamp of authenticity.

ADOLPHE JULLIEN
(1845–1932)

Whenever he found himself in intimate company, his spirits would revive and sometimes overflow in a torrent of jokes. Even among friends, however, he was subject to violent swings of humour, and his mood would change from one moment to another; he would arrive frowning and morose, suddenly burst into infectious gaiety, and then for no apparent reason sink back into icy reserve – some happy chance remark had been enough to galvanize him into life, but it only needed an unlucky one to put him once again beyond reach. So that, if he was laughing, if he was in the vein for brilliant paradoxes or gay persiflage, you had to be careful not to interrupt or contradict him, and above all had to avoid mentioning the name of one of his *bêtes noires,* say Fétis or Scudo or Richard Wagner, which would make him flare up in anger . . . In the middle of even a serious conversation, he loved introducing one of his bad puns, especially one of the far-fetched ones for which he had an irrepressible passion. And this was actually no small matter in his eyes: 'Yes, that's an excellent pun,' he said proudly of one that he threw out one evening – 'but of course it took time to prepare. You can't knock a pun together like an *opéra-comique,* they don't happen by chance like any banal tune: you have to think about it a lot, and give it very serious consideration' . . . The weakest, the most pointless puns were a source of endless delight, and he brought them into his conversation, slipped them into his letters and wrote them in albums. This one, taken from the album of his little friend Adelina Patti, is not one of the worst:

> *Oportet Pati*
> The Latinists translate this as: *suffering is our lot,*
> The monks as: *serve the pâté,*
> The lovers of music: *we must have Patti.*

. . . There was something of the pedagogue about him, and in more than one place in his letters and articles he comes out with comments on purity and style in language, some of which are not very charitable and some not even justified . . . Was it very considerate to pull up Heller, in the course of a conversation, over one or two turns of phrase that were not quite accurate? – at which Heller laughed good-naturedly and excused himself as being a Hungarian, though not without gently reminding his critical friend that he himself, with all his connections and travels in Germany, had not picked up a word of the German language.

[Jullien 1888: 347–8]

It appears that Heller really did take it all in good part.

EDMOND HIPPEAU

M. Heller told me that, during the intimate *soirées* with his friends Damcke and Massart, [Berlioz] didn't hesitate to direct his witticisms and his epigrams at those who were present as well as at absent people. One day, the unfortunate man who was serving as the butt of some joke was so mortified by this tirade that Heller felt moved by pity to intervene on his behalf . . .

[*To which Hippeau appends a note*] M. Heller has written me a letter about this passage, of which the following is an extract: 'I said that Berlioz liked to tease his friends and sometimes, I admit, did so rather harshly. But this banter, these epigrams, didn't upset us, particularly as we were free to reply to them boldly, without risk of wounding the sensibilities of the man – in whom we admired a musician of genius doubled with an accomplished humorist.'

[Hippeau 1889: 142–3]

Berlioz's witticisms, which were notorious, had not always been so well received. Wagner remembered Berlioz's visit to Spontini when he was dying.

RICHARD WAGNER

I learned from Berlioz, who had not left his deathbed until the end, that the master had struggled most fiercely against his decease; he had cried repeatedly: *'Je ne veux pas mourir, je ne veux pas mourir!'* When Berlioz tried to console him with the words: *'Comment pouvez-vous penser mourir, vous, mon maître, qui êtes immortel!'*, Spontini had cut him off angrily: *'Ne faites pas de mauvaises plaisanteries!'*

[Wagner 1983: 290]

> (A scene which recalls Heine's reputed comment when Berlioz came to see him on his deathbed a few years later: 'Ah, Berlioz – original as ever!')

STEPHEN HELLER

At that time he was seized with a sort of passion for reading Shakespeare aloud to small groups of friends; we would assemble in his apartment at eight o'clock in the evening, and he would read anything up to seven or eight pieces by the great poet in a French translation.

He read well, but too often let himself be overcome by emotion; beautiful passages always drew tears from him. Nevertheless, he continued reading while dabbing rapidly at his eyes. The listeners were very few – M. and Mme Damcke and two or three other friends. One of these, an old and devoted comrade of Berlioz but not well versed in literature, had taken it upon himself to act as *claqueur*; he would listen with the deepest attention, trying to guess from the expressions on the faces of the reader and his audience the right moments to give vent to his enthusiasm. As he didn't dare actually to applaud, he had found an original way of expressing his admiration: every moving passage, as indicated by the tone of voice of the reader and its effect on the assembled company, was underlined by some oath of popular cast which he would let slip in a low voice, as if in spite of himself. At the most touching moments of a Shakespeare play one would hear our man exclaim, in an aside:

'Nom d'un nom! . . . Nom d'une pipe! . . . Sacré matin! . . .'

One evening, after dozens of these interjections, Berlioz couldn't stand it any longer and stopped reading:

'For God's sake!' he burst out, directing a withering glare at his unfortunate admirer, 'will you just go to hell with your *nom d'une pipe*! . . .'

The other left, terrified, and is still running . . . And Berlioz quietly took up again the balcony scene from *Romeo and Juliet*.

[Letter to Hanslick, 1 February 1879, in Heller 1981: 252–3]

> In particular, the Damckes and the Massarts, both of whom lived within easy walking distance, were liberal hosts and often included visiting musicians in their informal gatherings – like the young violinist Benoit Hollander.

BENOIT HOLLANDER
(1853–1942)

I met Berlioz in 1865. A boy of twelve, I had come to Paris to study the violin with M. Massart, the great virtuoso. At the end of one of my lessons, M. and Mme. Massart asked me to stay to dinner. Hector Berlioz and M. Taudou [another young violinist] were expected. As [Berlioz] entered the room he looked a striking figure. I can see him now, very aristocratic, like an old émigré. Of medium height, his body was very emaciated. Thin-lipped, with a Roman nose, his long hair was white. It had been a reddish blonde colour and he had the white skin of that type. If he had had his hair short he would have resembled a Roman Emperor. He wore a black satin tie well up the collar. His trousers were a white and black check. They told him who I was. He was very kind and gentle in his manner. I remember as he sat there he made me sit on a foot-stool and began plaiting my hair (I wore it long) at the back of my head, and talking about Shakespeare. Of course I did not know what it was all about. When he left, he put on a light grey overcoat with a fawn collar. This much impressed me and later on when I had the money I had one made of the same colours.

[Ganz 1950: 213]

> Other friends and acquaintances turned up periodically, like Liszt, now an *abbé* and living in Rome, who was in Paris for the performance of his Graner Mass at St Eustache. The reception of the Mass had been cool; neither Berlioz nor d'Ortigue had liked it and Damcke didn't even go.

FRANZ LISZT

My session at Léon Kreutzer's with d'Ortigue, Damcke and Berlioz
has had one good result: I am now perfectly at ease with two of my
old friends, d'Ortigue and Léon . . . As for Berlioz, I treated him
with all the respectful consideration that I owe him. I imagine that
this hour of friendly chat will not have diminished any good
opinion he may have of my slight musical *savoir faire*. We naturally
spoke of you, and on this subject we shall always be in agreement!
The same evening, Monday, I saw him again at dinner with Mme.
de Blocqueville . . . He brightened up towards the end of the meal,
on the subject of Shakespeare. The conversation kept going agree-
ably at a lively and interesting level.

[Letter to Carolyne Sayn-Wittgenstein, 21 April 1866, in Liszt
1893–1905: vi, 113–4]

> It was the last time the two old friends were to meet.
> The Liszt faction have always blamed Berlioz for not
> writing a notice of the Graner Mass in the *Journal des
> débats*, but as he had handed over his job to d'Ortigue
> two years earlier, and had not written a word of official
> journalism since, this is patently unfair. The true source
> of the change in his relations with Liszt lay elsewhere,
> as Liszt admitted later.

FRANZ LISZT

From 1829 [actually 1830] until '64 my relations with Berlioz
could hardly have been simpler. Total admiration on my side,
cordiality on his. That is how it was in Paris, Prague and Weimar –
where I count it an honour to have put on, and conducted, a performance of his *Benvenuto Cellini* . . . After '64, without any silly
personal estrangement, the then burning question of Wagner (now
much cooled) caused a certain coldness between Berlioz and myself.
He could not accept the idea of Wagner surpassing Beethoven and
Weber as the future of music drama in Germany.

[Letter to Edmond Hippeau, 15 May 1882, in Liszt 1893–1905: viii, 397]

Nevertheless, Liszt took the opportunity, during the same visit, of applauding what turned out to be one of his old friend's last public triumphs in Paris. Also among the audience was one of Berlioz's newest admirers, the young journalist Georges de Massougnes.

GEORGES DE MASSOUGNES
(1842–1919)

On [7th March 1866] M. Pasdeloup gave the septet from *Les Troyens* at a charity concert. The best seats were occupied by society people, but the elite of serious concert-goers were massed in the highest tiers of the arena. The programme was superb and the listeners of this last group, the ones who weren't there for charitable reasons or because it was fashionable but for love of what is great, seemed eager and excitable, easily carried away by this succession of master-pieces. I have some experience of the public's ingrained prejudices and lack of discrimination, and when Meyerbeer's detestable over-ture to *Le Prophète* threatened the harmonious effect of the whole and was hissed by a few young people from the Conservatoire I trembled for the fate of the septet that was to follow. My fears were signally unfounded: no sooner had the last chords sounded of this hymn of infinite love and peace than these same young people, together with the whole theatre, erupted into such a tempest of bravos as I have never heard in my life. Berlioz was there, hidden away in the last rows of the audience, and scarcely had he been spotted and recognised but the work was forgotten in favour of the man; his name flew from mouth to mouth and in a moment four thousand spectators were on their feet, excitedly stretching out their hands in the direction of the place where he had been pointed out. By chance I was sitting near to him, and I shall never forget the scene that day: the crowd, who had at first seemed not even to know his name, had picked it up in a minute and was now repeat-ing as if it were the name of a popular hero. And he – he seemed bent beneath the weight of one of the greatest emotions of his life: with his head bowed on his chest, he heard these voices calling him, crying '*Vive Berlioz!*', and when he lifted it up and saw the faces, the thousands of arms stretched out to him from all corners of the immense hall . . . he could bear the sight no longer, he trembled, wanted to smile, and burst out sobbing . . . He wasn't the only one; I saw men there with their eyes filled with tears, and to be honest I think we were none of us dry-eyed.

[Massougnes 1919: 99–101]

> But not all Pasdeloup's efforts on Berlioz's behalf met with equal success, and the attitude of the musical establishment remained as obdurate as ever. Even to a would-be admirer, like the young composer Henri Maréchal, Berlioz could appear perplexing as well as awe-inspiring.

HENRI MARÉCHAL
(1842–1924)

At this time most of the musicians of my generation were still students, and among the members of the examining board at the Conservatoire [Berlioz] cut a sombre figure that seemed to us melancholy and taciturn. While his colleagues grouped themselves round the green baize table cloth customary at these sessions, and took notes or consulted one another in low voices, Berlioz sat alone in a corner of the room with his elbow resting on the back of his chair and listened with a bored expression – his hand buried in his hair in that characteristic attitude of his, familiar from the likeness in one of his best portraits.

We had divided our examiners into two groups: those whose severity we already knew and feared, and those from whom we had hopes of indulgence. But Berlioz we couldn't make out at all; he seemed determined to remain neutral in this display of academic gymnastics – which he had had to go through himself, in 1830, in order to win his term at the Villa Medici in Rome, that cradle of so much of what is best in French art.

Mysterious and enigmatic, he seemed to us like the sphinx awaiting Oedipus. When we studied his scores, they were so utterly at variance with what we were being taught every day that even the boldest among us were nonplussed; when we went to our teachers for an explanation, they took refuge in the most scrupulous reserve and confined themselves to advising us not to read the Master's music. So that if we wanted to find out his true standing with the public we had to go to Pasdeloup's concerts. It was Pasdeloup . . . who, alone and against all the odds, dared from time to time to risk a few notes of Berlioz in his programmes. Between a Haydn symphony and the overture to *Freischütz* you might hear the *Carnaval romain* overture or some fragments from *Roméo et Juliette*. But hard upon the last chord would burst a storm of protests from the audience, and if the composer ventured into the fray he was quickly recognized and the boos directed at his music degenerated into the lowest personal abuse.

My friends and I, incensed, were on our feet in the gangway which led to the stalls; burning with the enthusiasm of the young, we wasted no time in staging a counter-demonstration, which as far as we were concerned amply repaid the jeers from the upper reaches of the Cirque Napoleon. And at least it was by making his way courteously through our ranks, and surrounded by our applause, that Berlioz was able to get away from the crush. His head bowed, holding back his tears, he mumbled a few words of thanks in our direction and made his escape for all the world like a criminal caught *in flagrante* . . .

[Maréchal 1907: 273–5]

> Berlioz's abnormal sensitivity to audience reaction had long been known to his friends, though it could still surprise and shock new admirers – as it had the young Bourgault-Ducoudray back in 1861.

LOUIS BOURGAULT-DUCOUDRAY

It was the day after a big concert at the Opéra, at which the programme had included among other things a movement from *Roméo et Juliette* – the 'Fête chez Capulet'. I was at the concert, and had rapturously applauded this wonderful piece which was entirely new to me. But I had been seized by a pang of angry indignation at hearing an insolent whistle mixed with the warm applause that came from the greater part of the public. I went straight to Berlioz's apartment, to let him have personal evidence of my admiration as well as my disgust.

I found the poor man downcast, shattered, destroyed! His face was even paler than usual, and in its lines of exhaustion one could see the cruel marks of insomnia. He received my offering of congratulations and youthful enthusiasm with a smile full of bitterness. 'That whistle', he said to me in a pitiful voice, 'was like the stab of a dagger in my chest!' Then, pulling himself up with an impetuous, almost menacing gesture, he waved his fist and added: 'And to think that this piece, which they dare to hiss in Paris, has been acclaimed and encored in all the capitals of Europe!' With that, he fell back into a state of prostration from which nothing could revive him. It was no good my protesting at the prejudice of the public and the iniquity of his enemies, or attempting to brighten his spirits with hopes of revenge or rehabilitation in the years to come. He looked at me with an air of utter disbelief, lying there like a wounded lion.

[Bourgault-Ducoudray 1886: 279]

27 ESTELLE – AND LOUIS

It was in September 1864, while on a visit to his family in the Dauphiné, that Berlioz took it into his head to revisit the memories of his childhood, and in particular to search out once again the love of his earliest days, the girl with the pink shoes. Not only his mother and father but both his sisters were dead, and Estelle Dubeuf, now Estelle Fornier, was the sole survivor of a period that had never left his heart. She agreed to see him and, after a moment of very natural astonishment, allowed him to write to her; she replied to his letters, and gradually a relationship between them grew up, passionate on his side, gently understanding on hers, which was to underpin the whole of the rest of his existence.

To begin with, only a few close confidants knew of this development; the Damckes certainly knew by the time of his next visit to Estelle in August of the following year, and friends who received advance copies of the *Memoirs* (privately printed in July 1865 for posthumous publication) would have read the whole story, and several of the letters, in its final chapter.

But even so close a friend as Legouvé was not told until the early summer of 1866 – unless he has got his dates wrong, which in Legouvé's case is always possible.

ERNEST LEGOUVÉ

With Berlioz, it is always necessary to come back to love: it was the alpha and omega of his existence. Chance had it that in this I was his last, as well as his first, confidant . . .

Gounod had just been elected a member of the Institut, and Berlioz had campaigned willingly and vigorously on his behalf (another reply to the charge of egotism). Gounod invited us all to dine with him to celebrate. The party broke up at midnight. Berlioz was tired and found walking painful; I gave him my arm to accompany him back to his house in rue de Calais – and there we were once again in those deserted streets, starting on one of those nocturnal rambles of which we had made so many in our youth. He said nothing, walked with a stoop, and from time to time emitted one of those deep sighs that I knew so well. I asked him the ever-recurring question: 'Well, what is it now?'

'It's a few lines that I received from her this morning'.

'"Her" – who? The lady from Baden or someone else?'

'Someone else', he replied. 'Oh, I'm going to seem very strange to you. Do you remember Estelle?'

'What Estelle?'

'The girl from Meylan?'

'The one you loved when you were twelve years old?'

'Yes. I saw her again some time ago, and now . . . Oh my friend, how right Virgil is! What a cry from the heart in that line: *Agnosco veteris vestigia flammae*. I recognize the signs of my ancient flame!'

'Your ancient flame? What's this?'

'Oh it's absurd, it's ridiculous . . . I know, I know . . . But what does it matter? "There are more things in heaven and earth, Horatio, than are dreamt of in your philosophy." The fact is that at the sight of her my whole childhood, the days of my youth, flooded back into my heart . . . The electric shock that I felt then, when I saw her first, again struck deep into my heart, as it did more than fifty years ago.'

'But how old is she then?'

'Six years older than me – and I am more than sixty!'

'But it's a miracle! Another Ninon!'

'I don't know about that. I don't think so. But what do her face or her age matter to me? There is nothing real in this world, my dear friend, but what goes on there, in that small corner of a human being that is called the heart. And so, you must understand that I, as an old man, a widower, more or less alone in the world – I have concentrated the whole of my life on this obscure little village of Meylan where she lives. I can only tolerate my existence by saying to myself: "This autumn I shall go and spend a month with her." I would die, in this hell that is Paris, if she hadn't given me permission to write to her, if from time to time she didn't write a few letters to me.'

'Have you told her that you love her?'

'Yes.'

'What did she say?'

'She was astonished, a bit alarmed at first, I seemed to her like a madman. But little by little I finished by touching her heart. I ask so little! My poor passion needs so little to keep it alive! To sit near her and watch her at her spinning wheel – for she spins . . . to pick up her glasses – for she wears glasses . . . to hear the sound of her voice . . . read her passages from Shakespeare . . . ask her advice on whatever affects me, listen to her scolding me . . . Oh my friend, my friend – first love! It has a power that nothing can equal!' And, suffocated by emotion, he sat down on a corner-stone at the end of rue Mansard. The gleam of a gas-lamp fell on his ashen face, giving it the pallor of a ghost, and I saw running down his cheeks those same young man's tears that had so often moved me in years gone by. A great wave of pity and tenderness swept over me at the sight of that great artist imprisoned by his own passion, and with suddenly intensified emotion I found myself recalling an ancient and glorious memory, the figure of the seventy-year-old Michelangelo kneeling in tears before the body of the woman he loved . . .

[Legouvé 1886: 317 & 324–6]

Heller was one of those who knew at an early stage.

EDUARD HANSLICK

Stephen Heller told me how one day Berlioz threw himself sobbing into his arms, overcome by this despairing late love. Heller rebuked him with gentle severity for this folly, which made him at the same time unhappy and an object of ridicule. 'What do you expect?' retorted Berlioz; 'it's a matter of common knowledge that the wounded bull, when it knows it's dying, always runs out of the bull-ring through the same gate it came in by.'

[Hanslick 1885: 92]

In spite of the emotional turmoil into which it threw him, the knowledge of Estelle's interest and sympathy

gave him new energy – even if it came fitfully and was
constantly interrupted by depression and pain. In any
case, after having only once ventured beyond Baden-
Baden in the last ten years, he now found it impossible
to resist two new invitations to travel: one from Vienna
to conduct a complete performance of *La Damnation
de Faust*, and the other from his old friend Hiller for a
concert in Cologne. He left Paris, with no companion
this time, in early December 1866.

ADOLPHE JULLIEN

He arrived in Vienna completely exhausted by the journey and fell
into the arms of his new friend, the conductor Herbeck, who had
been directing the preparatory work on the score with untiring
energy. From the very first rehearsal [Berlioz] realized that the
result was almost perfect, and he concerned himself only with
imparting his own personal stamp to the performance. But he was
in a state of extreme over-excitement, and was unable to control his
feelings: to judge from what we have been told by M. Oscar
Berggruen, who followed the rehearsals with passionate interest,
the least hitch put him in a fury. A cellist comes in too soon:
'*Taisez-vous donc!*' cries Berlioz, white with anger, at the unfortunate man – who in any case doesn't understand French. The cor
anglais makes a mistake in Marguerite's Romance: Berlioz gives a
terrible cry and flings his baton at the head of the culprit; Herbeck
picks it up and hands it back to the master. 'Oh, I am mortally ill',
cries Berlioz in a voice of unutterable pain.

[Jullien 1888: 301–2]

> In spite of difficult rehearsals the concert was a tri-
> umphant success.

FÉLIX CLÉMENT

A curious anecdote shows the level of musical fanaticism reached
by certain members of the German audience. At the end of the
concert . . . an over-enthusiastic music-lover leaps on to the

platform and snatches the conductor's baton which he hides away furtively under his overcoat. The composer observes the theft, stops our German friend and says to him: 'Ah no, monsieur! I am very willing to give it to you, but I am not willing to let you take it.' The music-lover was obliged to submit and give back the coveted object, at which Berlioz presented it to him saying: 'And now, monsieur, have the goodness to accept it'. Our friend went off triumphantly, doubly happy at possessing the magic wand and having received it from the hand of the master.

[Clément 1873: 494]

> Berlioz was fêted to the point of exhaustion, and much of the press was favourable. But Hanslick, by now settled into his lifelong role as arbiter of Viennese musical taste and perhaps a little sheepish about his youthful excesses, declared against the work and attributed its success to personality rather than musical worth.

EDUARD HANSLICK

Anyone who was present at Berlioz's concerts in 1846 and 47, and who supported and cheered them as I did in Prague and Vienna, can testify that no dazzling musical phenomenon was ever greeted with greater excitement and enthusiasm. And again in 1866, by this time half-forgotten and greying with age, he was lionized in exactly the same way when he came to conduct his *Damnation de Faust* in Vienna . . . But the rapturous reception had more to do with the notorious and extraordinary personality of the composer than with his compositions.

[Hanslick 1885: 93–4]

. . . I was at the banquet given in his honour [in Vienna], but didn't speak to him because I knew from Parisian friends that he had been wounded by my more recent, much less appreciative notices. In spite of all his pretended indifference, Berlioz was not unaffected by criticism, at least not invariably – any more than Richard Wagner, with whom I was later to find myself in a similar position. But Berlioz was a gentleman, to me a far more sympathetic character than Wagner. I still remember with pious gratitude the depth and purity of his artistic nature and, in spite of untold suffering and increasing bitterness, the truth and sincerity of his character.

[Hanslick 1894: i, 62]

> A more faithful supporter was the composer Peter Cornelius, who read a poem in Berlioz's honour at the same banquet; Cornelius had been an admirer of Berlioz ever since hearing *La fuite en Égypte* at Leipzig in 1853, and had made German translations of most of his works.

PETER CORNELIUS

I would always take on work of this kind for Berlioz, even if I were to become an acknowledged and well-regarded opera composer myself, because he is a figure of genuinely great importance whose friendship I value . . . At the same time, he is generous, as any true artist is; he had hardly arrived here when he settled the fee for my latest work with thirty shining thalers – and that with the added note *'avec mille amitiés reconnaissantes'* – whereas I only got my thirty thalers out of Rubinstein after waiting for ages in real need, almost as if I was begging some special favour.

[Letter to his mother, 23 February 1855, in Cornelius i, 1904: 195]

> A Liszt protegé, and by now a member of the Wagner circle in Munich, Cornelius had nevertheless crossed the ever-widening gap between Wagner and Berlioz and arrived in Vienna on the day of the last rehearsal.

PETER CORNELIUS

I have taken the plunge and come to Vienna. Hector is very close – he is in room number 49, I am in number 50. He has just spent an hour singing me parts of the *Troyens*, and told me a love story linking his earliest youth with his latest years in a way that is incredible . . .

[Letter to his fiancée, 14 December 1866, in Cornelius ii, 1905: 460]

[He] is going to give me the translation of his *Troyens* to do, which . . . will bring me in at least 1,000 francs; that's a dowry which could make you believe yourself rich for a month, and be happy! Dear, good Berlioz! He is so genuinely an artistic creature, so utterly innocent of worldliness or political guile, or of any special flirting with the Good Lord – he has remained such a pure artist and musician! I was staying in the next room to him, and before the concert he moaned and groaned and coughed and sighed the whole night through. After the concert, he slept like a log!

At the end of a storm-tossed life he has turned back again to a romantic young love, which is now flowering as a yet more romantic love in old age. Unbelievable! His *Memoirs* tell the story – he told it to me one evening. The man still has a heart like Paul and his Virginie – sixty-three and seventy, and it began at twelve and nineteen!

[Letter to Rosa von Milde, December 1866, ibid: 469]

> Back from Vienna just before Christmas, Berlioz only had a couple of months in Paris before keeping his engagement with Hiller in Cologne.

FERDINAND HILLER

For a long time I had wanted to invite Berlioz to Cologne for a performance of one of his works, so as to have the double pleasure of presenting the friend of my youth to our orchestra, and of introducing the orchestra to him. In the autumn of 1866 I was at last able to start making the necessary arrangements. There followed an exchange of letters about the how, what and when – and I confess it was not easy. Berlioz made objections about things that didn't exist, and had doubts where there was no cause for doubt, though when I succeeded in calming his fears, I at least had the satisfaction of receiving a letter saying that I was the best comrade that a man could find. He promised to come, and in February 1867 he spent a number of unforgettable days with us. But more abrupt changes of mood and condition in a man than those we experienced with him at that time can hardly be imagined. Often when I called to collect him at his hotel room, I would find him weary and miserable, usually in bed, no matter at what time of day; he would complain that he was unable to eat, that he could scarcely speak, yet half an hour later he would be eating a meal – half-reluctantly, I admit, but as heartily as any landlady could wish – and chatting away, telling stories or turning over opinions with the lively, impetuous eloquence that was peculiar to him. One morning, he dragged himself with agony to the orchestral rehearsal (he wouldn't take a carriage) – but no sooner was he standing at the conductor's desk than he was transformed: vigorous, energetic, bubbling with life. He made me think of the swan, which gets with difficulty to its feet, waddles laboriously to the water, but as soon as it lets itself down on the surface glides away across it in majestic calm. In Berlioz's case it was certainly not calm that characterized his demeanour – but then neither is an orchestra a lake, even if the heavens can sometimes be reflected in it. Happily the performance of his *Harold* symphony went splendidly . . . the composer was applauded with heartfelt warmth and departed satisfied and grateful.

[Hiller 1880: 94–5]

> Paris provided him with little such satisfaction, and though his younger colleagues continued to give him hope for the future of French music, he had moments of terrible doubt about his own career.

HENRI MARÉCHAL

[Not long] before his death, armed with a letter of introduction . . . I went to call on [Berlioz] in the rue de Calais. It was about some trivial matter, not worth recalling. My business didn't involve much discussion, and the visit was short, though it was long enough to send me away deeply shaken by the despondency, the profound sadness of the Master. His movements were slow, his voice weak, and one felt oneself in the presence of acute suffering.

But the evening of that same day was one that I shall never forget. I was at the Opéra-Comique; the first act was coming to an end, when Berlioz came in and sat down in the seat next to mine.

At first he didn't recognize his visitor of earlier in the day, but when we stood up in the interval he remembered and, holding out his hand, engaged me in a conversation which continued in the corridors of the theatre, out into the Place Boieldieu and along the Boulevard des Italiens.

It was spring, the evening was soft and calm and the conversation, which had begun at about nine o'clock, didn't finish until after one in the morning, at the door of the house in the rue de Calais to which I had returned with the Master. We walked slowly, he leaning on my arm.

From the ordinary small talk with which we started, we soon moved on to subjects closer to his heart. Aware, no doubt, of the polite deference felt by a mere recruit in the army of which he was one of the generals, this quiet and melancholy old man, in whom nothing remained of the pugnacious Berlioz of former days, slid imperceptibly into a sort of profession of faith, an examination of his conscience and a return to the past, of which no detail has escaped my memory.

In the course of our long conversation I listened to the great man with respect and fascination, and garnered a rich harvest of philosophy. And among all the things that he said, and all the memories that he recalled, I have always remembered this:

'I was wrong! It wasn't *that* that needed doing! Oh, if you piled up all my works in front of me, there on the boulevard, and set fire to them, I wouldn't rush for the fire brigade! I would have some regret for my *Requiem*, certainly – but it needs five orchestras to perform it, and you can't lay out money like that every day'.

These words, which I record faithfully, impressed me so forcibly at the time that ever since, whenever I think of Berlioz, they come back to my mind with the melancholy smile that accompanied them.

[Maréchal 1907: 277–80]

> It was still possible to rally him when he got into these moods of despair, and one of the people who could do it was Heller. The dating of the following account is not easy: Heller remembers it specifically as December, but it could hardly have been at any time in the winter of 1868, and in 1867 Berlioz was in Russia from mid-November to the following February. On the whole, a date around Christmas 1866 seems most probable.

STEPHEN HELLER

I don't think I ever knew anybody more lacking in resignation than Berlioz. For many years I played the Plutarch to him, telling him stories from the lives of the artists he loved – Weber, Mozart, Beethoven, Schubert, Schiller and many others.

When he moaned in his usual bitter way, and bewailed his lack of success in comparison with the achievements of the composers who ruled the Opéra, I said to him: 'My dear friend, you want too much, you want everything. You despise the general public, and yet you want it to admire you. You disdain the plaudits of the crowd – that's your right as an artist of lofty and original genius – and yet you have an inexhaustible appetite for it. You assume the role of an audacious innovator, of a musical pioneer, and at the same time you want to be understood and appreciated by everybody. You are only interested in pleasing idealists and men of spirit, and yet you get angry at the lack of response from ordinary people and the apathy of timid souls. Would you perhaps rather live lonely, inaccessible and poor like some Beethoven, and see yourself surrounded by the potentates and mediocrities of a world laden with titles and honours and all the blessings of fortune? You have obtained everything that the nature of your genius and your personality could give you. You don't have the crowd, but you do have an intelligent minority who make every effort to support and encourage you. You have made an entirely original place for yourself in the world of art, you have many friends who are enthusiastic and active on your behalf; you don't even lack, thank God, highly competent enemies to keep your friends on the alert. Your material existence has fortunately been secure for some years now, and you can at last count with certainty on something that men of spirit and feeling have always valued: the full measure of justice that posterity has in store for you'.

I very often succeeded in reviving his drooping spirits, and each time he thanked me in a voice touched with emotion.

Here is a memory of this kind that I recall with particular pleasure. It was one evening with M. and Mme Damcke . . . Berlioz had started off again on the favourite topic of his grievances, and I replied to him in the terms that I have just indicated. By the time I had finished my sermon it was after eleven o'clock and out of doors a cold December night had spread its thick and gloomy darkness.

Exhausted and a bit put out, I lit a cigar. At this, with a sprightliness that can only be described as youthful, Berlioz leapt from the sofa on which he used to stretch out in his mud-spattered boots (to the extreme – but silent – displeasure of Damcke, who loved order and cleanliness).

'Well!', he cried, 'Heller is right! What am I saying – Heller is always right! He is good, he is just, he is wise, he is prudent. I should like to embrace him' (here he kissed me on both cheeks) 'and make this wise man a foolish proposition.'

'I accept, whatever it is,' I replied.

'I should like to go and have supper with you at Bignon. I ate very little for dinner, and your sermon has given me a craving for immortality and a dozen oysters'.

'Perfect! We'll drink to Beethoven, and Lucullus too, and forget our sorrows by drowning them in the best of French wine, with the assistance of a few good slices of *pâté de foie gras*.'

'Our host can stay here', added Berlioz; 'he has a charming wife. We, who are not so well provided for, will make for the restaurant . . . No objections! The matter's settled!'

That old, enfeebled body had recovered all the ardour of earlier days. There we were, arm in arm, laughing and joking the length of rue Blanche and then of the Chaussée-d'Antin – which made quite a long walk in itself. When we arrived at the corner of the boulevard we went into the brilliantly lit salon of the restaurant. It was striking half past eleven, and there were hardly any customers left, which suited us very well. We ordered oysters, a *pâté de foie gras de Strasbourg*, a cold fowl, salad, fruit, the best champagne and the most reliable Bordeaux. We were both of us generally very moderate in our eating habits and simple in our tastes, but on an exceptional occasion like this we only felt the more inclined to do honour to this excellent menu. At one o'clock they turned down the gaslights; the doors were closed, candles were brought to our table and the waiters circled round yawning (there was no longer anyone else in the restaurant), as if entreating us to raise the siege.

'Waiter!' called Berlioz, 'all this pantomime of yours is obviously intended to make us believe that it is late. Will you now bring us, if you please, two cups of coffee and some decent havanas'.

And so we sat on till two o'clock.

'Now, let's go', said Berlioz, rising from his chair. 'This is the moment when my mother-in-law is most deeply asleep, and I have high hopes of waking her up.'

During our supper we had talked of our artistic heroes, Beethoven, Shakespeare, Lord Byron, Heine, Gluck, and the conversation continued on the same lines as we traversed, with slow steps, the long distance that separated us from his door, not far from my own.

It was the last gay, sociable, lively evening that I spent with him – in 1867 or 1868 if I am not mistaken . . .

[Letter to Hanslick, 1 February 1879, in Heller 1981: 250–2]

> It was just as he was about to set out on another such sociable evening that the blow fell which was to darken the last days of his life.
>
> Berlioz's relationship with his son had often been a difficult one, largely on account of Louis' extravagant habits. But recently they had become very close; Louis, now an officer in the merchant navy, made a point of coming to Paris as often as he could, and after the last visit, in August 1866, had bidden his father an affectionate farewell before taking command of a ship bound for Mexico.
>
> Among Berlioz's circle of acquaintances was a certain Marquis Arconati-Visconti, a wealthy collector and music-lover.

ADOLPHE JULLIEN

One day [late in June 1867] this passionate admirer, who had not missed a single performance of *Les Troyens*, conceived the idea of arranging a small, intimate party for Berlioz; he had put a portrait of the master, wreathed in garlands, in the place of honour, and decorated the studio with scrolls carrying the names of his works. Only a few friends were in the secret, and they had a lot of fun planning to surprise the master when he entered by playing and singing him some of his most loved pieces . . . A full hour passed, and Berlioz didn't arrive. So Ritter, becoming uneasy, hurried to Berlioz's house. He found him in tears: the unhappy man had just heard of the death of his son from yellow fever . . .

And in what circumstances had he heard of this disaster! At that time he was deeply involved in the preparations for a great concert, to be given in July at the Palais de l'Industrie during the Exposition universelle . . . His mother-in-law and his friends the Damckes knew already of the calamity that had come upon him, while he, in happy oblivion, didn't dream that there was any reason for anxiety about his son. When he found himself surrounded by long faces and asked the reason, his mother-in-law and his servant, fearful of dealing him such a lethal blow, explained their distress as due to bad news from their own country [Spain]. Thus deceived, the poor father set off to the Damckes . . . But what should happen [on his way there] but he meets a friend of his son's, a friend who doesn't realize what is going on and blurts out the news point-blank. At that Berlioz, mad with grief, rushes back home and flings himself on the floor crying: 'Wretched boy, couldn't you have waited for me then? It was for you to live, for me to die! . . .'

[Jullien 1888: 303–4]

> The huge concert at the Exposition universelle of 1867, which included a performance of Berlioz's *Hymne à la France*, was to have been conducted by Berlioz – but that was now out of the question. Nevertheless, he remained a member of the jury set up to judge the competition for a celebratory hymn and cantata; under the nominal chairmanship of Rossini, this included Auber as director of the Conservatoire, Berlioz himself, Verdi from Italy, and from Vienna the redoubtable Hanslick.

EDUARD HANSLICK

Rossini, Auber, Berlioz – I saw all three of them again, and found scarcely any perceptible change since my first visit in 1860. Only Berlioz seemed gloomier and even more resentful than before. The loss of his only son, Louis, who had died on an East India ship far from home, had pierced the composer to the heart, and . . . the daily round of obstacles in connection with the performance of *Les Troyens* had plunged him into the blackest of ill humours. He had become so misanthropic that people were unwilling to disturb him with a visit. But the meetings of the jury for the [prize compositions], of which we were both members, brought us into close proximity. Filled with indignation at even the 'best' of these compositions, he shook his grey leonine head, banged his fist on the table and barked: 'We're not here to give prizes to street songs!'

Berlioz lived in absolute seclusion. He alleged that he had never spoken to Rossini, 'an old man who laughs at everything and makes fun of everybody'. Auber he called 'the greatest egoist – not an artist', and as to Wagner . . . he declared: 'He's mad, totally mad!'

[Hanslick 1894: ii, 63–4]

> Yet even if he was unable to conduct the concert for the Exposition universelle, his presence at the rehearsal did not go unnoticed.

GEORGES DE MASSOUGNES

Berlioz's triumphs may have been rare, but whose have ever been more brilliant? Even leaving aside his achievements abroad . . . who could mistake the character and the significance of those extraordinary ovations which from time to time greeted his name in our unpredictable city of Paris? There was an occasion [in July 1867] at the Palais de l'Industrie, during the general rehearsal of a big concert that included one of his works, when the twelve hundred musicians of the orchestra spotted him in the audience and, singling him out from the other composers being applauded by the public, bombarded him for ten minutes with cheers and cries of 'Bravo'.

[Massougnes 1919: 99]

> But such successes now counted for little: the death of Louis was a blow from which Berlioz was never to recover. His world was collapsing.

FERDINAND HILLER

I had the opportunity to see him, for the last time, when I was in Paris for a few days late the following summer. I had arranged to dine with him, and afterwards we went for a long stroll during which he poured out his heart to me; the mild, subdued lament that flowed out of him, so unlike his usual manner, cut me to the heart and moved me deeply. He had just lost his son, his only child, a young officer in the merchant navy for whose future the highest hopes were entertained, who had been killed by a malignant fever in a far-distant land. Berlioz's father, to whom he had for many years been bound once again in ties of warmest friendship, was dead, his beloved sister had followed her father, and the failure of *Les Troyens* had made him fearful of all further musical undertakings. Not another line, not another note would he write he declared; he had bequeathed his scores to the library of the Conservatoire and had already deposited them there himself – there would be nothing new to add to them. He thought sadly of former days, and had been deeply hurt by some comments in Mendelssohn's early letters* which had been translated to him in exaggerated terms – 'and yet he was always so agreeable and friendly to me,' he added. His *Memoirs*, too, had already been printed so that they could be published immediately after his death. But most of all he spoke to me, just as he might have done forty years earlier, about an affair of the heart: although it brought a melancholy smile to his lips, it provided him with the material for a deeply moving story . . . and he did not tire of describing this extraordinary situation, this retrospective passion, with the utmost animation.

[Hiller 1880: 95–6]

> Even if, to some, the romantic story of Estelle inevitably seemed rather ridiculous, to Berlioz it remained of deep and crucial importance; in any case, it had by now become common knowledge, and in October 1867 received the imprimatur of inclusion in the Goncourt diaries.

* Mendelssohn's *Reisebriefe aus den Jahren 1830 bis 1832* had been published at Leipzig in 1861. (See above, pp. 44–6.)

EDMOND & JULES DE GONCOURT

Dinner with [Ernst] Hébert . . .

He is a compatriot of Berlioz's. They lived in two houses in the mountains, one above the other. He saw him this morning, and Berlioz told him how, in the country, at the age of twelve, he had been in love with a young girl of twenty. Since then, he had been through many love affairs, wild, harrowing, romantic, but always with the secret memory of this first love in his innermost heart – until it came back to him in all its force when he found, at Lyon, the young girl now sixty-four years old. And since then, writing to her and talking to her of the memories of his twelve-year-old heart, he lives only by virtue of this ancient flame.

[16 October 1867, in Goncourt 1956: ii, 383–4]

> But by now Estelle was only a memory. Though she was
> to outlive him by seven years, Berlioz had seen her for
> the last time on 9 September, 1867.

28 THE FINAL JOURNEY

It seems incredible that, in his enfeebled state, and after the exhausting experiences of Vienna and Cologne, Berlioz should still have been prepared to contemplate, in the depths of winter, the 2,000 mile journey to St Petersburg. But in the August of 1867 he had received a visit from the Russian composer César Cui, who published an account of the meeting on his return home.

CÉSAR CUI
(1835–1918)

He is now sixty-three. He is extremely nervous and sensitive; his imagination is vivid to the point of morbidity. He speaks a most elegant French. He is handsome and impressive in appearance . . . There is an elegance about his figure and all his movements . . .

Naturally we talked mostly about musical matters. 'Mozart's operas are all alike. His imperturbable composure (*beau sang-froid*) irritates and exasperates,' said Berlioz. He remarked that Meyerbeer had not only the good luck to have talent but a great talent to have luck. In Rossini's music, Berlioz finds melodic cynicism, a perpetual, puerile crescendo, a coarse bass drum . . . [Among conductors he] thinks highly of Meyerbeer, Wagner and Litolff. But he dislikes Wagner's affected retards, when the orchestra reaches a climax and there is no change in either the tempo or expression. 'Liszt conducts and plays on the inspiration of the moment,' said Berlioz. 'He doesn't convey the composer's thought, but his own feeling at the time. He takes liberties with other people's works, and each time they sound different . . .'

Berlioz was very pleased to learn that parts of his *Lélio, Faust, Roméo* and other works are often performed in Russia, but he regretted that they are not played in their entirety.

[S.-Peterburgskiye Vedomosti, 1867 in Stasov 1968: 163]

> Cui told Berlioz about the new group of young com-
> posers in Russia who were excited about his music, and
> when the grand Duchess Elena Pavlovna, in Paris on a
> visit to the Exposition universelle, issued her personal
> invitation, the combination of a much-needed boost to
> his financial resources and, above all, the opportunity
> to conduct and make music where he knew he would
> be appreciated proved irresistible: in November 1867, he
> set off for Russia and his last journey outside French soil.
> The French musicologist Gustave Bertrand was on
> an official visit to Russia at the time.

GUSTAVE BERTRAND
(1834–80)

I met him again [in St Petersburg] and saw him first in his apartment at the Palais Michel, where he had been provided with hos-
pitality fit for a prince of art. He was practically always in pain, his
great profile, like a wounded eagle, sunk more dolefully than ever
on his chest. But when the moment came for a rehearsal, or a public
appearance, the call of duty and the love of art rallied his spirits.

He was always the most beautiful conductor that one could
imagine. His beat was broad, clean, magisterial; he combined solid
authority with infinite subtlety – as one might imagine a metro-
nome guided by the most unerring intelligence and the liveliest
sensibility. He understood, as no one does today, the secrets of
Beethoven, of Weber, of Gluck. As for his own works, they were
received with enthusiasm: I saw him called back four or five times
after a movement of the *Symphonie fantastique*, and I heard several
things of his that I had never had the chance to hear in France.

[Bertrand 1872: 263]

The six St Petersburg concerts included four of the Beethoven symphonies (the Third, Fourth, Fifth and Sixth – a projected performance of the Ninth had to be abandoned for lack of suitable singers and was replaced by the 'Emperor' Concerto) as well as excerpts from three Gluck operas. For the first time for years, works by other composers easily outnumbered Berlioz's own, and the challenge worked on him like a shot of adrenalin.

CÉSAR CUI

There is not another conductor whose performances are truer to the composer's intentions, who has a greater understanding of the spirit of a work, who preserves so completely all of its nuances . . . What a grasp he has of Beethoven; how meticulous, how thoughtful his performances are; how effective yet free of the slightest concession to false, tawdry brilliance. As an interpreter of Beethoven, I prefer Berlioz to Wagner who, despite excellent qualities, is sometimes affected and here and there inclined towards sentimentality. For us Gluck became utterly new, alive, unrecognizable . . . As for Berlioz's own works, the magnificent performances under his direction have revealed many wonders that we had not suspected were there, even after the most careful study of his enormous, complex scores. And how simple, how restrained Berlioz is on the podium; yet how amazingly *precise* his gestures are! And how modest he is! When the audience called for him after the first piece, he came out, and with a charming wave of the hand, indicated that it was the orchestra, not he, who deserved the honours. Of all the conductors we have heard in Petersburg, Berlioz is certainly the greatest; as an artist wholly dedicated to music, he deserves our admiration, respect and unbounded affection . . .

[S.-Peterburgskiye Vedomosti, 6 December 1867, in Stasov 1968: 166]

The only dissentient note in the glowing accounts of Berlioz's Russian concerts comes from Nicolay Rimsky-Korsakov, then only twenty-three years old and the youngest recruit to the group of nationalist composers known as 'The Five'. His description, written many years later, is curiously at odds with the contemporary evidence.

NICOLAY RIMSKY-KORSAKOV
(1844–1908)

The execution was excellent; the spell of a famous personality did it all. Berlioz's beat was simple, clear, beautiful. No vagaries at all in shading. And yet (I repeat from Balakirev's account) at a rehearsal of his own piece Berlioz would lose himself and beat three instead of two or vice versa. The orchestra tried not to look at him and kept on playing, and all would go well. Berlioz, the great conductor of his time, came to us when his faculties were already on the decline, owing to old age, illness and fatigue. The public did not notice it, the orchestra forgave him. Conducting is a thing shrouded in mystery.

[Rimsky-Korsakov 1935: 75]

> And clouded, perhaps, by memory. By the time his memoirs were written, Rimsky-Korsakov's enthusiasm for Berlioz had given way to positive distaste: 'his music is uncommonly ugly,' he said in conversation with Yastrebtsev. 'I don't know another composer who appeals to me less.'* And for one reason or another, his memories of Berlioz's personal behaviour seem to have suffered in much the same way.

Berlioz came to us already an old man; though alert at rehearsal, he was bowed down with illness and therefore was utterly indifferent to Russian music and Russian musicians. Most of his leisure time he spent stretched out on his back complaining of illness and seeing only Balakirev and the Directors . . . I imagine that it was not ill-health alone, but the self-conceit of genius as well as the aloofness becoming a genius that were responsible for Berlioz's complete indifference to the musical life of Russia and St Petersburg . . . There was no talk even of Musorgsky, Borodin and myself meeting Berlioz . . .

[Ibid: 74–5]

* V. V. Yastrebtsev: *Reminiscences of Rimsky-Korsakov* (Columbia University Press, 1985), p. 319.

Yet, at just about the period when he was writing this account, Rimsky-Korsakov gave his most famous pupil an entirely different version of the situation, and one that accords better with the known facts of Berlioz's visit.

IGOR STRAVINSKY
(1882–1971)

I remember a description of Berlioz by Rimsky-Korsakov who had met the French master after one of the famous Berlioz concerts in St Petersburg in the late sixties. Rimsky-Korsakov, who was then twenty-three or twenty-four, had attended the concert with other young composers of the group. They saw Berlioz – in a tail-coat cut very short in the back, Rimsky said – conduct his own music and Beethoven's. Then they were shepherded backstage by Stasov, the patriarch of St Petersburg musical life. They found a small man, Rimsky's words were 'a little white bird with pince-nez', shivering in a fur coat and huddled under a hot pipe which crossed the room just over his head. He addressed Rimsky very kindly: 'And you compose music too?', but kept his hands in his coat sleeves as in a muffler.

[Stravinsky 1959: 29n]

VLADIMIR STASOV

During his stay in Petersburg, Berlioz was in frequent contact with all the musicians of the new Russian school. The one he saw most often was Balakirev, who was assigned to rehearse the choruses and soloists for him and assist him at concerts. Berlioz thought very highly of Balakirev. He saw all of our other young composers frequently, too; they called on him when he was well, when he was ill, whenever he was not at rehearsals or visiting the Grand Duchess Elena Pavlovna, to whom he read his beloved *Aeneid*, Byron and Shakespeare in French. His young admirers would speak to him about the great new works they expected of him, but he would only sigh and answer sadly that this was no longer possible, he was too old, sick, and broken. Once he attended a performance of *A Life for the Tsar* in Kologrivov's box with Balakirev and me. But we heard none of the fresh, profound remarks we expected from one who had been so enthusiastic about this opera twenty-two years before. By now it was too much of a strain for Berlioz to sit in a theatre an entire evening (he was accustomed to retiring at nine o'clock). He praised Glinka's opera as a whole but made only one specific comment, concerning the orchestration: 'How pleasant it is to come upon such restrained, beautiful, sensible orchestration after all the excesses of today's orchestras!' Of course, at this moment Berlioz was thinking of Wagner, whose music and orchestration he strongly disapproved of . . . By now he did not even like Liszt. He no longer cared for the brilliant innovations in Liszt's latest works, his orchestration, piano transcriptions (which had so captivated and delighted him before) or even his conducting. He now found Liszt's conducting too arbitrary, subjective, capricious and arrogant. Berlioz was getting old and, like Glinka in his last years, he was beginning to love only the great composers of earlier days, particularly Gluck and Beethoven, the main idols of his youth.

[Stasov 1968: 166–7]

> By the middle of February, he had been away from Paris for three months and, in spite of the warmth of his welcome, he could bear the Russian winter no longer. After a final celebratory dinner party, he bade farewell to the scene of his last great triumph and headed for home.

29 THE LAST YEAR

DANIEL BERNARD

On his return from the banks of the Neva, Berlioz was in a state of total exhaustion; his nervous condition was becoming worse. He went to see the famous doctor Nélaton who, after having questioned him, listened to his heart and examined him thoroughly, said to him: 'Are you a philosopher?' 'Yes,' replied the patient. 'Well, draw courage from your philosophy, because you are never going to recover.'

[Bernard 1879: 58]

> His first need after returning to France was to get the snow and ice of Russia out of his bones with a visit to the south of France.

ERNEST REYER

In Monaco, where he had gone in search of the sun and a view of the sea which he loved so much, he had a serious fall and was obliged to return to Nice. Another fall, more serious still, forced him to take to his bed for several days; two young people who were passing by picked him up unconscious and took him back to his hotel. He had suffered a stroke while he gazed out to sea – that sea deep and restless as his own soul, whose immensity, monotonous roar and ever-changing reflections fascinated him always.

The musician had shattered his lyre, but the poet dreamed on. [In] August the town of Grenoble, which was almost his native town, invited him to attend a musical competition as its honorary president. The welcome he received from his compatriots must have touched him profoundly, but by then he was so exhausted and had fallen into such a state of prostration that he could no longer find it in himself to enjoy these belated ovations.

[Reyer 1875: 266–7]

> The actual occasion was described by an eye-witness, the journalist Mathieu de Monter.

ÉMILE MATHIEU DE MONTER
(born 1835)

On the 14th August 1868 . . . a group of Parisian composers and artists, who had been the judges of the competition, were gathered with a number of local worthies in the main gallery of the Hôtel-de-Ville.

The guest whom they were awaiting to take his place at the banqueting table soon entered, supported by two friends, and at the sight of him a shock of horror, of profound pity, ran through that convivial assembly. This man, with his sickly appearance, faltering steps, vacant expression and hair falling across his temples in great white folds; this sculpted head, so finely modelled but now defaced by the ravages of ill health and spiritual anguish, this battered brain whose intelligence had been almost extinguished by a cruel accident – this was Hector Berlioz.

They sat him down. I can see him still. The look on his face was that of a man who wants to remember, who wants to bring together the scattered threads of his memory. Was he trying to revive an echo of his enthusiastic reception in Russia? Or, weeping over his favourite work, the martyred *Troyens*, did he repeat like Dido: 'I have lived my life, I have fulfilled the career that destiny prescribed for me'? Where were his thoughts? Did they exist at all? From time to time his lips trembled, and with an uncertain movement he carried to them the glass in which he seemed, instinctively, to search for memory and strength . . .

The time arrived for toasts, and in the name of the townsfolk, of his admirers, of the two hundred musical societies gathered in Grenoble from all parts of France, and of a Dauphiné proud of its glorious son, the chief magistrate of the town laid on Berlioz's forehead a crown of gold. Unaware of what was happening he showed no reaction, and stood up ... At this moment the storm, which had been threatening for several hours, broke with appalling violence, and a sudden squall burst in through the open windows, tearing at the curtains, scattering the flowers, and blowing out the chandeliers. The thunder growled, lightning flashed over the Alps from valley to peak, and in the half-dark, by the light of a candelabra spared by the wind, there appeared to us, standing as if transfigured in his marmoreal pallor, his eyes deep set, his features inspired with that particular air of nobility that approaching death imprints upon them, the author of the *Symphonie fantastique.*

A few moments later Berlioz, plunged once again into his torpor, left the room as he had entered it. A solemn, religious silence followed his departure. Clearly this was a stricken man, one whom we should not see again.

[Monter, 13 June 1869: 193–4]

> Alas, the crown which the mayor had placed on the composer's brow was never intended for so exalted a purpose. It had already been awarded as a prize to one of the choral groups taking part in the competition and was lying on a nearby table when the mayor, sensing something missing in this scene of high drama, seized it and placed it on Berlioz's head as a symbolic gesture. Unfortunately, Berlioz, in taking his leave, did so with the crown under his arm. Panic ensued – there could be no question of asking Berlioz to give it back – and after much wrangling a new crown was made and presented to the deprived winners of the choral contest.
>
> Even if Monter's description is a touch melodramatic, Berlioz's health was now in a terminal state of decline, and he knew it. On 21 November, Louis Engel, returning from Rossini's funeral, remembered meeting him on the boulevard – ready, as usual, with an apt quotation from *Hamlet* * – and another encounter was recorded by the critic Henri Blaze de Bury.

* Engel 1886: ii, 84–5.

HENRI BLAZE DE BURY
(1813–88)

One autumn evening I met him on the *quai*; he was on his way
back from the Institut. Pale, emaciated, bent, shaking and dejected,
you could have mistaken him for a ghost. Even his eyes, those
great, fierce eyes, had lost their fire. For a moment he held my hand
in his thin, nerveless grasp, then disappeared into the mist after
quoting these lines of Aeschylus in a scarcely audible voice: 'Oh,
the life of man! Happy, and the merest shadow can trouble it;
unhappy, and a damp sponge effaces the image and all is forgotten.'

[Blaze de Bury 1880: 351]

ERNEST LEGOUVÉ

Yes, undoubtedly he was very much occupied with himself, but he
found the time . . . to occupy himself passionately with others as
well, to take an interest in everything that interested his friends, to
be affected by their sorrows, to share in their happinesses. He was
the most grateful of men, and if he sometimes remembered injuries
that had been done to him, he never forgot kindnesses . . . On
one occasion his gratitude amounted almost to heroism. In 1848
M. Ch[arles] Blanc, then Director of Fine Arts, managed, through
his department, to favour Berlioz with a mark of sympathy and
esteem. Twenty years later, twenty years in which protector and
protected had scarcely met again, M. Charles Blanc, independent
candidate for the Institut, paid his call on Berlioz. He found him
dying.

'I know why you have come,' said Berlioz.

'Don't let's talk about it,' answered the candidate quickly; 'I had
absolutely no idea of your sad condition. Don't let's talk about it,
I'll leave you in peace'.

'No stay, and let's talk. I will go to the Academy and vote for you.'

'Ill as you are . . . My dear Berlioz . . . permit me to say that I
forbid you!'

'Ill? yes I am, very seriously. My days are numbered, my doctor
has told me so. He has even told me the number', he added with a

half smile, 'but the election is on the 16th*. So I still have time . . . and would even have a few days left to prepare myself . . .'

[Legouvé 1886: 313–4]

> He still spent evenings with his friends nearby, and could show flashes of the old spirit.

STEPHEN HELLER

One more little story. Close to the house where Damcke lived, in rue Mansart, there was a conspicuous white flagstone on the pavement. Every evening, when we left our friend's house, Berlioz would stand on this stone to bid me good night. It happened on one occasion (this was a few months before his last illness) that we took leave of one another hurriedly, because it was cold and there was a thick yellow fog in the streets. I had hardly gone ten paces when I heard Berlioz's voice: 'Heller! Heller! Where are you? Come back! I haven't said good night to you on the white stone!' We made our way back towards one another and there we were, the two of us, in the pitch dark, searching for this indispensable podium – which had an unusual shape as well. I pulled out my box of matches, but the air was so damp that the matches wouldn't light. We bent right down towards the pavement, we practically went on our hands and knees to search, and at last the worn surface of the white stone appeared. Berlioz put his foot on it, and said to me with an expression of supreme gravity: 'God be praised! Here we are! Now – good night!'

[Letter to Hanslick, 1 February 1879, in Heller 1981: 254–5]

> But in the end, even the humour faded. Reyer describes what was probably one of the last occasions on which Berlioz left his apartment.

* Legouvé's memory again – it was actually 25 November.

ERNEST REYER

A short time before the death of his master [Berlioz's servant] had accompanied Berlioz to my house. Painfully did the poor musician mount up the four flights of stairs to come and sit at my table. After the meal I begged him to write his name on the score of *Benvenuto Cellini*. He seized a pen, wrote with a trembling hand '*A mon ami*', and then, looking at me with a wistful glance, said: 'I have forgotten your name'. It was a cruel blow, which went to my very heart. I was to see him no more till I gazed on his face as he lay upon his death-bed . . .

[Reyer 1893: 305]

> Some time in January or early February he suffered partial paralysis and in March he went into a semi-coma.

CAMILLE SAINT-SAËNS

My last interview with him was cruel.

I heard suddenly that he was dying and rushed to his house. It was cold, and my hands were frozen. 'Give me your hand,' he said to me. Knowing how impressionable he was, and how easily affected by his imagination, I refused to do what he wanted; this icy hand, I thought, will feel to him like the hand of death. 'I wish it,' he said. I obeyed. I hadn't been wrong: he gave a heart-rending cry, turned his face to the wall and didn't speak to me again.

[Saint-Saëns 1903: 175]

> Reyer sat with him during the last days.

ERNEST REYER

As I watched at his bedside, a copy of the *Memoirs* was handed to me, at his request, by the faithful servant who had not left him for a single moment during his long and painful illness, who had lavished upon him the most touching, the most reverent, most devoted attentions, who loved him, wept for him, and wrapped him in his final shroud. And as I read those pages so full of enthusiasm and disappointment, of passion and despair, those poetic descriptions and dreams of youth, the story of struggles and triumphs, the satires stamped with bitter irony, my eyes would turn now and again to the gaunt, motionless body which had housed so valiant a soul, a spirit so brilliant and full of vigour. What a sombre tableau this was, and what a tragic contrast as I sat there reading with the sound of the death-rattle at my side.

[Reyer 1875: 265]

> If Reyer is to be believed, his last words were: '*On va donc jouer ma musique!*'
> He died on 8 March, at half past midday.

> At his funeral three days later, the obligatory address on behalf of the Institute was given by its President, the sculptor Eugène Guillaume. It is unexpectedly perceptive.

EUGÈNE GUILLAUME
(1822–1905)

Messieurs, Berlioz will remain one of the great symbols of our century. Few artists are predestined, as he was, to epitomize the period in which they have lived. By the elevation of his aspirations, by his love for the most unfettered and pure wellsprings of art, by his veritable cult of a consummate ideal founded upon truth, he was one of the most vigorous representatives of the new spirit of the age. He was also modern by the notion he contrived of the artist himself, and by the particular character of his own originality. And he was modern as well by dint of a sensibility that took delight in its own sufferings, and that found ingenious ways of rendering them more colourful and more profound.

[Guillaume, 11 March 1869, in Bloom 1998: 174]

Older and closer friends struck a more personal note.

THÉOPHILE GAUTIER
(1811–72)

Hector Berlioz is no more. One could well write on his grave the epitaph of Marshal Trivulce: *Hic tandem quiescit qui nunquam quievit.* * This was a destiny as harsh, as tormented and as adverse as his . . . The ship of [Berlioz's] life was tossed by waves and wind, assaulted by lightning, driven out of port and flung back into the open sea at the very moment of touching land: but firm at the helm was an inflexible will, a will that the fall of the universe itself would not have shaken, and which, undeterred by tattered sails, broken masts and a hull that leaked at every seam, followed its imperturbable path towards the ideal.

Nobody had a more absolute devotion to art, nor sacrificed his life to it so completely. In these days of uncertainty, of scepticism, of compromise, of the abandonment of belief and the pursuit of success by any available means, Hector Berlioz did not, for a single instant, listen to the faint-hearted seducer who leans over the artist's chair in his weaker moments and whispers prudent counsels in his ear. His faith was never dented, and even at times of deepest misery, in spite of indifference, in spite of ridicule, in spite of poverty, it never occurred to him to purchase popularity with a commonplace tune or a popular ditty with some catchy rhythm. In defiance of everything, he remained faithful to his conception of beauty.

[16 March 1869, in Gautier 1911: 166–7]

CAMILLE SAINT-SAENS

He was a good, affectionate, highly original creature, certainly sarcastic from time to time, but arousing an irresistible sympathy in anyone capable of appreciating him . . .

---

* 'Here at last rests one who never rested'. Jean-Jacques Trivulce, of Italian origin, was an officer in the French army under Charles VIII and Louis XII whose chequered career ended in his rejection by François I.

I have always retained my devotion to his memory, and I would be entirely satisfied with the tributes being paid to him if I didn't sometimes hear him being described as a 'precursor'. He is nobody's 'precursor'. He is Himself, and he was the incomparable originator of the whole generation to which I belong. He opened the golden door that let loose into the world the swarm of dazzling, magical enchantments that constitute modern instrumentation, and he has left us the admirable example of a life consecrated entirely to pure art. Glory to him, glory for ever!

[Saint-Saëns 1903: 175]

And a last echo, 65 years after his death.

AN OLD INHABITANT OF LA CÔTE-SAINT-ANDRÉ

M. Berlioz? Ah yes – my grandfather often spoke of him. They used to say in the town that the Doctor's son had gone to the bad, given himself up to music, playhouses, Paris, and the Lord knows what else. It was rumoured his mother never got over it. He'd come back once in a while. There was a lot of whispering when he passed by; no one dared speak to him any more – he looked so out of humour with the place. But he didn't do too badly after all, did he?

[*Le Nouvelliste*, 2 September 1934, quoted in Berlioz 1969: 519]

LIST OF SOURCES

In order to simplify source references at the end of individual excerpts the date only of the relevant publication is given after the author's name. Such dates are printed in **bold** type in the following list.

Adam, Adolphe, 'Lettres sur la musique française, 1836–1850', in *Revue de Paris*, vol. 4, 1 and 15 August, and vol. 5, 1 and 15 September and 1 October **1903**, reproduced by Minkoff (Geneva, 1994)

Adam, Mme Edmond (Juliette Lamber), *My Literary Life* (New York, **1904**)

Avins, Styra & Eisinger, Josef, *Johannes Brahms, Life and Letters* (Oxford, **1997**)

Barbier, Henri-Auguste, 'Benvenuto Cellini: Avant-propos', in *Études dramatiques* (Nouvelle édition, Paris, **1874**)

– 'Hector Berlioz' in *Souvenirs personnels et silhouettes contemporaines* (Paris, **1883**)

Barzun, Jacques, *Berlioz and the Romantic Century* (2 vols, Boston, **1950**)

Berlioz, Hector, *Memoirs*, trans. David Cairns (London, **1969**, revised edn, 1990)

Bernard, Daniel, 'Notice biographique', in *Correspondance inédite de Hector Berlioz* (Paris, **1879**, pp. 1–61)

Bertrand, Gustave, *Les nationalités musicales* (Paris, **1872**)

Blaze de Bury, Henri, *Musiciens du passé, du présent et de l'avenir* (Paris, **1880**)

Bloom, Peter, 'Berlioz's furniture: a closer look', in *Berlioz Society Bulletin* No. 153, **1995**, pp. 7–11

– *The life of Berlioz* (Cambridge, **1998**)

Bourgault-Ducoudray, Louis, *Les Musiciens Célèbres*: 'Berlioz (Souvenirs intimes)', in *Le Conseiller des Dames et des Demoiselles* (Paris, 1 February **1886**, pp. 276–80)

Brenet, Michel, *Deux pages de la vie de Berlioz . . .* (Paris, **1889**)

Bülow, Hans von, *Briefwechsel zwischen Franz Liszt und Hans von Bülow*, ed. La Mara (Leipzig, **1898**)

Cairns, David, *Berlioz* vol. 1: *The Making of an Artist 1803–1832* (London, 1989; 2nd edn, **1999**)

- *Berlioz* vol. 2: *Servitude and Greatness* (London, 1999)
CGB, *Correspondance générale d'Hector Berlioz*, vols I to VI, edited under the direction of Pierre Citron (Paris, 1972–95)
Chorley, H. F., *Music and Manners in France and Germany* (3 vols, London, 1841)
- *Thirty Years' Musical Recollections* (London, 1862)
Clément, Félix, 'Berlioz', in *Les musiciens célèbres* (2nd edn, Paris, 1873, pp. 489–98)
Cone, Edward T. (ed.), 'Franz Liszt: A Berlioz Concert', in *Berlioz Fantastic Symphony* (Norton Critical Scores, New York, 1971, pp. 282–4), trans. Cone
Cook, Dutton, 'Harriet Smithson', in *Gentleman's Magazine*, June 1879
Cornelius, Peter, 'Ausgewählte Briefe', in *Literarische Werke*, ed. C. M. Cornelius, E. Istel and A. Stern (3 vols, Leipzig, 1904–5)
de Courcy, G. I. C., *Paganini the Genoese* (2 vols, Oklahoma, 1957)
(Court Journal), 12 October 1833, quoted in Edwards, July 1903, p. 442
Cui, César, article in *S.-Peterburgskiye Vedomosti* (1867), see Stasov 1968, pp. 163, 166
Davison, J. W., *The Musical World*, 12 February 1848 and 4 June 1853
Delacroix, Eugène, *Journal 1823–1856*, ed. Paul Flat (3 vols, Paris, 1893–5)
- *Correspondance générale*, ed. André Joubin, vol. 1 (Paris, 1935)
Deschamps, Émile, 'Macbeth et Roméo et Juliette, Préface de l'édition de 1844', in *Oeuvres complètes*, vol. 5 (Paris, 1874)
Diehl, A. M. (Alice Mangold), *Musical Memories* (London, 1897)
Dumas, Alexandre, 'Comment je deviens auteur dramatique', in *Théâtre complet* (1ère série, Paris, 1863)
- *Mes mémoires* (4ème série, Paris, 1867)
Duprez, Gilbert, *Souvenirs d'un chanteur* (Paris, 1880)
E[dwards], F. G., 'Berlioz in England', in *The Musical Times*, July–August, October–November 1903
Eliot, George, *George Eliot's Life as related in her letters and journals*, ed. J. W. Cross (3 vols, Edinburgh & London, 1885)
Ella, John, 'Music in Paris in 1837' (Musical sketches, MS) in *Musical World*, 15 December 1837, quoted in Edwards, July 1903, p. 441
Engel, Louis, 'Berlioz', in *From Mozart to Mario* (2 vols, London, 1886), vol. 1, pp. 53–110, reprinted from *Temple Bar*, vol. 69 (October 1883)
Fétis, F.-J., 'Théatre des nouveautés', in *Revue musicale*, vol. II, 1828, pp. 326–7
- 'Grand concert donné par M. Berlioz, élève de l'École royale de musique, le lundi 26 mai', in *Revue musicale*, vol. III, 1828, pp. 422–4
- 'Analyse critique: Épisode de la vie d'un artiste, Grande Symphonie Fantastique de H. Berlioz' in *Revue musicale*, IX année, No. 5, 1 February, 1835, pp. 33–5

- Letter to Liszt, 1 April 1855 see Prod'homme 1913, p. 248

Fouqué, Octave, 'Berlioz en Russie', in *Les revolutionnaires de la musique* (Paris, 1882), pp. 185–256

Ganz, A. W., *Berlioz in London* (London, 1950)

Ganz, Wilhelm, *Memories of a musician* (London, 1913)

Gautier, Judith, *Le second rang du collier: souvenirs littéraires* (Paris, 1903)

Gautier, Théophile, notice on the death of Berlioz, in *Journal officiel*, 16 March 1869, reprinted in *Gautier: La musique* (Paris, 1911)

Gazette musicale, 2e année, No. 3, 18 January 1835, pp. 22–4, 'Premier bal de l'Opéra'

Glinka, Mikhail Ivanovich, *Memoirs*, trans. R. B. Mudge (University of Oklahoma, 1963)

Goncourt, Edmond & Jules de, *Journal*, texte intégral ed. Robert Ricatte (4 vols, Paris, 1956)

Gounod, Charles, Préface, in *Hector Berlioz: Lettres intimes* (Paris, 1882)

- *Memoires d'un artiste* (Paris, 1896)

Gouzien, Armand, article in *Journal de musique*, 25 November 1876: see Tiersot, Berlioziana, III, July 1905, p. 220

Guizot, François, *Lettres de M. Guizot à sa famille et à ses amis* (Paris, 1884)

Hallé, Charles, *Life and Letters of Sir Charles Hallé*, ed. C. E. Hallé and Marie Hallé (London, 1896)

Hanslick, Eduard, 'Hector Berlioz in seinen Briefen und Memoiren' (Deutsche Rundschau, v. 30, 1882) reprinted in *Suite, Aufsätze über Musik und Musiker* (Wien u. Teschen, 1885)

- *Aus meinem Leben* (2 vols, Berlin, 1894)

- 'Hector Berlioz', in *Aus dem Concert-Saal* (Vienna and Leipzig, 1897, originally published as *Geschichte der Concertwesens in Wien*, vol. 2, Vienna 1870) 'Anhang, Musikalische Reisebriefe: II Musikalische Erinnerungen aus Paris' (1860), No. 3

Harding, James, *Gounod* (London, 1973), quotes letter to Mme Charles Rhoné, 10 August 1862 (Bibliothèque de l'Opéra, Acq. 25209), trans Harding

Heine, Heinrich, *Gesammelte Werke*, ed. Gustav Karpeles (9 vols, Berlin, 1887) vol. 7: pp. 145–54, 'Über die französische Bühne', Zehnter Brief; pp. 215–25, 'Musikalische Saison von 1844' (Erste Bericht, Paris, 25 April 1844)

Heller, Stephen, 'A Robert Schumann à Leipzig' (open letter), in *Revue et gazette musicale de Paris*, vol. VI, 22 December 1839

- 'Une lettre de Stephen Heller sur Berlioz' (open letter to Eduard Hanslick), 1 February 1879, in *Revue et gazette musicale de Paris*, 2 March 1879, pp. 65–6, and 9 March 1879, pp. 73–4, reprinted in Stephen Heller, *Lettres d'un musicien romantique à Paris*, ed. J.-J. Eigeldinger (Paris, 1981), pp. 246–55

Hensel, Sebastian, *The Mendelssohn Family* (2 vols, London, 1881)

Héritte-Viardot, Louise, *Memories and Adventures*, trans. from the German MS by E. S. Buchheim (London, 1913)

Hiller, Ferdinand, 'Hector Berlioz', in *Künstlerleben* (Köln, 1880) pp. 63–143, reprinted from *Westermann's Monatshefte, 45. Band* (Braunschweig, 1879)

Hippeau, Edmond, *Berlioz intime* (Nouvelle edn, Paris, 1889)

Holmes, Edward, review in *Atlas*, 12 February 1848, quoted in Edwards, July 1903, p. 448

– Letter to Clara Novello see Novello 1910

Hueffer, Francis, *Half a century of music in England* (London, 1889)

Janin, Jules, *735 lettres à sa femme*, ed. Mergier-Bourdeix, vol. 2 (Paris, 1975); vol. 3 (Paris, 1979)

Joachim, Joseph, *Briefe von und an Joseph Joachim*, ed. Johannes Joachim and Andreas Moser, vol. 1 (Berlin, 1911)

Joncières, Victorin de, 'Notes sans portées', in *Revue internationale de musique*, 1 March 1898, quoted in *Wagner et la France* (Paris, 1983), p. 26

Journal du Commerce, 31 October 1830, quoted in CGB, vol. 1, p. 380

Jullien, Adolphe, *Hector Berlioz, la vie et le combat, les oeuvres* (Paris, 1882)

– *Hector Berlioz: Sa vie et ses oeuvres* (Paris, 1888)

Kemble, Frances Ann, *Record of a Girlhood* (2 vols, London, 1879)

Klindworth, Karl, Interview in *The Musical Times*, 1 August 1898

Laferrière, Adolphe, *Mémoires* (1ère série) (Paris, 1876)

Legouvé, Ernest, 'Hector Berlioz' in *Soixante ans de souvenirs* vol. 1 (Paris, 1886) pp. 278–330

Liszt, Franz, *Franz Liszts Briefe*, ed. La Mara (8 vols, Leipzig, 1893–1905)

– *Correspondance de Liszt et de la Comtesse d'Agoult*, ed. Daniel Ollivier, vol. 1 (Paris, 1933)

– Letter to Ferdinand Denis, September 1838, trans. and reprinted in Hans Gal, *The Musician's World* (London, 1965)

– Review in *Le Monde*, 11 December 1836: see Cone 1971

Macdonald, Hugh, 'Berlioz's Furniture', in *Berlioz Society Bulletin* No. 142, Summer 1991, pp. 15–19, but see also Bloom 1995

Mainzer, Joseph, *Chronique musicale de Paris*, 1re livraison, 'M.Berlioz' (Paris, 1838)

Maréchal, Henri, *Paris – Souvenirs d'un musicien* (Paris, 1907)

Maretzek, Max, *Sharps and Flats* (New York, 1890), reproduced in *Revelations of an Opera Manager in 19th-century America* (New York, 1968)

Massougnes, Georges de, *Hector Berlioz (1803–1869): Son oeuvre* (1870, 2nd edn, Paris 1919)

May, Florence, *The Life of Johannes Brahms* (2nd edn, 2 vols, London, 1948)

Mendelssohn, Felix, Letters 1 March and 29 March 1831, reprinted in Peter Sutermeister, *Briefe einer Reise durch Deutschland, Italien und die Schweiz, und Lebensbild* (Zürich, 1958)

Le Ménestrel, 13 December 1903, unsigned letter from Estelle Fornier's niece de Monter, Emile Mathieu, 'Hector Berlioz' (Premier article), in *Revue et Gazette musicale de Paris* (36e année no. 24, 13 June 1869)

Moscheles, Ignaz, *The Life of Moscheles by his wife*, adapted by A. D. Coleridge (2 vols, London, 1873)

Novello, Clara, *Clara Novello's Reminiscences*, ed. Valerie Gigliucci (London, 1910)

Offenbach, Jacques, Article in *L'Artiste*: see Tiersot, Berlioziana v, 1911

D'Ortigue, Joseph, *Le balcon de l'Opéra* (Paris, 1833): pp. 270–76, 'Concert de M. Ferdinand Hiller'; pp. 287–95, 'Concerts de John Field – Concert de M. Dietz, Janvier 1833'; pp. 295–324, 'Symphonie et biographie d'Hector Berlioz' (originally published as 'Galerie biographique des artistes français et étrangers, v: Hector Berlioz' in *Revue de Paris*, vol. 45, December 1832)

Osborne, George, in *Proceedings of the Musical Association*, 3 February 1879 (5th session, 1878/9, pp. 60–75)

Pohl, Louise, *Hector Berlioz' Leben und Werke* (Leipzig, 1900)

Pohl, Richard, *Gesammelte Schriften über Musik und Musiker vol. 3 'Hektor Berlioz, Studien und Erinnerungen'* (Leipzig, 1884): pp. 176–200, 'Beatrice und Benedikt (1862)'; pp. 201–11, 'Ein Berlioz-Konzert in Löwenberg (1863)'

Pontmartin, Armand Ferrard de, 'Hector Berlioz', in *Nouveaux samedis* (18ème série, Paris, 1880)

– 'Les acteurs anglais à l'Odéon', in *Souvenirs d'un vieux critique* (1ère série, Paris, 1881)

Prod'homme, Jacques-Gabriel, *Hector Berlioz* (2nd edn, Paris, 1913)

Quinet, Edgar, *Lettres d'exil* (2 vols, Paris, 1885)

Reyer, Ernest, *Notes de musique* (Paris, 1875)

– 'Hector Berlioz : Biographical Notes & Personal Reminiscences', in *The Century*, New York, vol. xlvii (New Series, vol. xxv), December 1893

Rimsky-Korsakov, Nikolay, *My Musical Life*, trans. J. A. Joffe (2nd edn, New York, 1935)

Roger, Gustave-Hippolyte, *Le carnet d'un ténor* (Paris, 1880)

St Leger, H. J., *Reminiscences of Balfe* (London, nd, c.1871)

Saint-Saëns, Camille, *Harmonie et mélodie* (Paris, 1885): pp. 249–55 'Berlioz: publication de ses Lettres Intimes'

– *Portraits et souvenirs* (Paris, 1899): pp. 3–14, 'Hector Berlioz'; pp. 35–97, 'Charles Gounod'

– 'Discours lu à l'inauguration du Musée Berlioz, à la Côte-Saint-André', in *Le Livre d'Or du Centenaire d'Hector Berlioz* (Paris/Grenoble, nd (1903))
– *École buissonière: notes et souvenirs* (Paris, 1913): pp. 209–16, 'Le Requiem de Berlioz'; pp. 251–9, 'Seghers'
– 'Lettres inédites de Saint-Saëns, presentées par Adolphe Boschot', in *Arts*, 4 May 1951, quoted in Yves Gérard, *Saint-Saëns – Regards sur mes contemporains* (Arles, 1990)

Salomon, Hedwig, Autograph journal entry, Leipzig, 2 December 1853 (Richard Macnutt)

Sauzay, Eugène, Memoirs, transcribed by Brigitte François-Sappey in 'La vie musicale à Paris à travers les Mémoires d'Eugène Sauzay', in *Revue de musicologie* (No. 60, 1974)

Schloesser, Adolph, 'Personal Recollections of . . . Hector Berlioz', in *Royal Academy of Music Club Magazine*, No. 32, February 1911

Schorn, Adelheid von, *Zwei Menschenalter: Erinnerungen und Briefe* (Berlin, 1901)

Schumann, Robert, 'Aus dem Leben eines Künstlers: Phantastische Symphonie . . . von Hector Berlioz', in *Neue Zeitschrift für Musik*, vol. III, no. 1, 3 and 31 July, 4, 7, 11 and 14 August 1835
– *Tagebücher*, ed. Georg Eismann, vol. 2 (Leipzig, 1971)
– *Robert und Clara Schumann, Briefwechsel*, ed. Eva Weissweiler, vol. 2 (Stroemfeld/Roter Stern, 1987)
– *Briefe und Dokumente im Schumannhaus Bonn-Endenich*, ed. Thomas Synofzik (Bonn, 1993)

Scudo, P., 'De l'influence du mouvement romantique sur l'art musical et du rôle qu'a voulu jouer M. H. Berlioz', in *Critique et littérature musicales* (Paris, 1850), pp. 15–74

Seidl, Anton, quoted in *Modern Music and Musicians*, part 2, vol. 1 (University Society of New York, 1912)

Stanford, Charles Villiers, *Pages from an Unwritten Diary* (London, 1914)

Stasov, Vladimir, *Selected Essays on Music*, trans. Florence Jonas (London, 1968): pp. 15–37, 'Review of the Musical Events of the Year 1847'; pp. 117–94, 'Liszt, Schumann and Berlioz in Russia'

Stravinsky, Igor and Craft, Robert, *Conversations with Igor Stravinsky* (London, 1959)

Le Temps, 26 December 1830, 'Concert de M. Berlioz' (anon), reprinted in the original French in Peter Bloom *Berlioz Studies* (Cambridge, 1992, pp. xii–xiv) with intriguing considerations on its possible authorship

Tiersot, Julien, 'Ophelia en 1827', in *Le Ménestrel*, 3 October 1886
– *Hector Berlioz et la société de son temps* (Paris, 1904)

- 'Berlioziana' I–V, in *Le Ménestrel* (Années 70 [**1904**] to 72 [1906], and 75 [1909] to 77 [**1911**]), a series of 122 articles at irregular intervals
- *Lettres de musiciens écrites en français (de 1831 à 1885)* (Paris, **1936**)

Viardot-Garcia, Pauline, 'Pauline Viardot-Garcia to Julius Rietz: Letters of friendship', in *Musical Quarterly*, vol. I, Nos 3 and 4, July and October **1915**, and vol. II, no. 1, January **1916**

Viardot, Louise, *see* Héritte-Viardot

Victoria, Queen, Diary entry, 25 June **1853** (Queen Victoria's Journal, Royal Archives, Windsor Castle), quoted in George Rowell, *Queen Victoria goes to the theatre* (London, **1978**)

Wagner, Richard, *Briefwechsel zwischen Wagner und Liszt*, 3rd edition, ed. Erich Kloss (Leipzig, **1910**)
- *Richard Wagner an Freunde und Zeitgenossen*, ed. Erich Kloss (Leipzig, **1912**)
- *Sämtliche Schriften und Dichtungen*, 5th edn, vol. 12, ed. Richard Sternfeld (Leipzig, **1914**): pp. 85–9, 'Pariser Berichte für die Dresdener Abendzeitung, III, 14–17 June 1841'
- *Sämtliche Briefe*, ed. Gertrud Strobel and Werner Wolf (vol. 1, Leipzig, **1967**; vol. 2, Leipzig, **1970**; vol 4, Leipzig, **1979**); ed. Hans-Joachim Bauer and Johannes Forner (vol 7, Leipzig, **1988**)
- *Mein Leben*, published privately 1870–81; in English as *My Life*, trans. Andrew Gray, ed. Mary Whittall (Cambridge, **1983**)

Walker, Alan, *Franz Liszt, vol. 2, The Weimar Years* (London, **1989**)

Wieck, Clara, *see* Schumann

Zelter, Carl Friedrich, *Der Briefwechsel zwischen Goethe und Zelter*, ed. Max Hecker, vol. 3 (Leipzig, **1918**)

ACKNOWLEDGEMENTS

For permission to reprint copyright material from the English edition of Wagner's *My Life*, edited by Mary Whittall and translated by Andrew Gray (1983) my thanks are due to Cambridge University Press and to Paul List Verlag, Munich. I am also very grateful to David Cairns for allowing me to include short excerpts from Nanci Berlioz's *Journal* and from two letters of Adèle Berlioz and Rosanne Goletty as translated in *Berlioz* vol. 1: *The Making of an Artist 1803–1832* (Allen Lane, The Penguin Press, 1999, copyright David Cairns 1989, 1999), and to David Cairns again for a passage out of Jules Janin's article on the death of Harriet from his translation of the *Memoirs* (Gollancz, 1969). He also kindly provided me with a transcription of the unpublished letter from Nanci Berlioz to Rosanne Goletty of 7 June 1830.

By its nature a book of this kind is heavily indebted to the work of others, particularly to those who have produced reprints or quotations that have pointed the way to early material which might otherwise have eluded research. Though much of it is necessarily posthumous, my gratitude goes to all of them - as well as to recent scholars like Ian Kemp, but for whom the Laferrière memoir might well have remained unremembered, and Peter Bloom, whose reprint of the anonymous article in *Le Temps* of 26 December 1830 brought to light a remarkable picture of the young Berlioz at work. Peter Bloom and Hugh Macdonald have also provided a fascinating glimpse of Berlioz's domestic world in their articles for the Berlioz Society Bulletin on Berlioz's apartment and its furniture.

The publishers and I believe that we have contacted all relevant copyright holders for permission to use protected material, but the publishers would be pleased to hear from any who have not been acknowledged here or in the List of Sources.

FURTHER READING

For those who would like to know how Berlioz remembered himself, the first choice must be the *Memoires*, either in the most recent French edition by Pierre Citron (Paris, 1991), or in the excellent English translation by David Cairns (London, 1969, revised edn. 1990). Cairns's two-volume *Berlioz: The Making of an Artist* and *Servitude and Greatness* (London, 1999) is now the definitive biography, though Peter Bloom's *The Life of Berlioz* (Cambridge, 1998) offers an admirably concise alternative for those who want something rather less detailed. Hugh Macdonald's *Berlioz* in the Master Musicians Series (London, 1982) keeps its place as an excellent short study of the life and works, and his selection of Berlioz's letters (translated by Roger Nichols; Faber, 1995) provides a good English introduction to the voluminous *Correspondence générale* published under the direction of Pierre Citron (Paris, 1972–95), which still awaits its seventh – and presumably final – volume. Lastly, anyone who wants to know more about Harriet Smithson should certainly read Peter Raby's *Fair Ophelia* (Cambridge, 1982).

INDEX